Advance Praise for *The Old Breed...*
The Complete Story Revealed

"When discussing one of the best memoirs ever written by a front line combat soldier it seems almost criminal that a publisher could tell the author to excise two-thirds of the material. But that's what happened before *With the Old Breed* was published. Finally, more than forty years after the original was released, we get the rest of the story...What comes through clearly, just as in the original classic, is the basic humanity of Eugene Sledge. And like the book the elder Sledge penned, his son's version is a stark reminder of the price those we send to war continue to pay long after the conflict they endured leaves the headlines."

—Dan Carlin, host of *Hardcore History Podcast*

"Henry Sledge has brilliantly enhanced his father's work about the deprivations and brutality of war. He expertly weaves personal memories about his father with previously unpublished portions of the elder Sledge's epic book. Using his father's own words, the author recounts the horrors of combat on Peleliu and Okinawa and draws on these experiences to explain how the fighting and the Marine Corps shaped Eugene Sledge for the rest of his life. The book is a valuable addition to the history of the 1st Marine Division in the Pacific during World War II. It is a must read for those who want to understand the horrors and savagery of war. It is also a tribute to those who survive the depravity of war and go on to lead productive lives."

—General Charles E. Wilhelm, USMC (Ret),
former Commanding General 1st Marine Division

"The grim odyssey of Marine Eugene Sledge has become a pillar of comprehending the brutality and brotherhood of World War II in the Pacific. In this gripping and revealing sequel, Henry Sledge picks up and passes on the torch of his late father by resurrecting long lost tales of horror, humor, and heroism. The Old Breed is a fitting and poignant legacy project that enriches one of the finest combat memoirs ever produced."

—Dr. Jared Frederick, author of *Dispatches of D-Day*, *Fierce Valor*, and *Into the Cold Blue*

"Eugene Sledge's With the Old Breed is without a doubt the greatest memoir of World War II, a gritty and at times horrific account of the Pacific struggle to seize Peleliu and Okinawa. Now his son Henry Sledge has painstakingly researched the original manuscript, extracting a wealth of stories, anecdotes, fresh details, and adding his own memories that help flesh out his father, framing him not only as the warrior we all know but as a husband and a Dad. Henry Sledge has done an amazing service to his father, his family, and history. This is a book not to be missed."

—James M. Scott, Pulitzer Prize finalist and author of *Black Snow*, *Rampage*, and *Target Tokyo*

THE OLD BREED

THE COMPLETE STORY REVEALED

A Father, A Son, and How WWII in the Pacific Shaped Their Lives

W. HENRY SLEDGE

A KNOX PRESS BOOK
An Imprint of Permuted Press
ISBN: 979-8-88845-848-8
ISBN (eBook): 979-8-88845-849-5

The Old Breed... The Complete Story Revealed:
A Father, A Son, and How WWII in the Pacific Shaped Their Lives

Cover art by Conroy Accord

This book, as well as any other Knox Press publications, may be purchased in bulk quantities at a special discounted rate. Contact orders@posthillpress.com for more information.

This is a work of nonfiction. All people, locations, events, and situations are portrayed to the best of the author's memory.

Permuted Press
New York • Nashville
permutedpress.com

Published in the United States of America
4 5 6 7 8 9 10

For my mother, who inspired.

Eugene "Sledgehammer" Sledge was my father. The heart of this book is the unpublished material from his manuscript for his World War II memoir *With the Old Breed At Peleliu and Okinawa*, interwoven with my memories of conversations he and I had about his war experiences while I was growing up.

TABLE OF CONTENTS

FOREWORD

Eugene Sledge's *With the Old Breed At Peleliu and Okinawa* first emerged from a then obscure biology professor at a small southern college who served as a Marine junior enlisted man in the Pacific during World War II. The memoir was the product of Eugene's resolve to record his experiences just for his family—and, in no small measure, to quiet the raging demons that haunted him from his combat experiences. His wife, the lovely Jeanne, encouraged him to write down his recollections, with the not so concealed hope that this would have a therapeutic effect. Eugene labored away for many long hours, then years, compiling a draft—famously drawing heavily from notes in the pages of the Bible he carried in combat. Eugene asked Jeanne to type his completed manuscript. She thus became the first reader among the now countless numbers to experience its immense—even shattering—emotional power. Jeanne recognized the gravitas of her husband's work and propelled Eugene to seek publication. Thus, as this work underscores, her role in bringing his work to life and fame was invaluable.

Prior to publication, fate seemed against Eugene. Almost immediately after the war, many memoirs appeared by top leaders like Winston Churchill and Army General Dwight D. Eisenhower, as well as some individuals in what might be viewed as the second or third tier from the top. In contrast, before the 1970s, only a relative handful of accounts by junior figures in the war, particularly those in direct combat, received any serious attention. Notable in this latter group was Robert Leckie's *Helmet for My Pillow*. Leckie, a skilled wordsmith, also served in the 1st Marine Division from Guadalcanal to Peleliu. From the 1970s onward, for more than three decades, both publishers and a substantial public favored the steady stream of memoirs by junior officers and enlisted men. *With the Old Breed* thus faced a host of competitors upon its initial printing in 1981.

Then fate proved just. Several historians, including the eminent John Keegan, Stephen Ambrose, and Paul Fussell, immediately trumpeted its soaring qualities. Within a decade it vaulted to the top ranks of all American memoirs of World War II. Many historians, while not denigrating the merit of the many other accounts, rank it first. I share that view. Still others assign it a place in the pantheon of the greatest of all accounts of all wars. We are, in my view, perhaps still too close in the comparatively immense sweep of time to certify that conclusion. But I have ventured the belief that, with the passage of decades, Sledge's account will become for Americans an honored text defining his generation and their nation's role in the war. He and his buddies will be remembered by name long after far more prominent figures are forgotten.

What accounts for this acclaim? There are a multitude of possible answers to that question, but I will only submit mine. The prose has been called simple, even plain. I detect that its deepest root stems from a fundamental lesson taught by combat, a crucible that elevates utility above almost all other values. Sledge discarded rhetorical flourishes as he did his gas mask on Peleliu. As he stated, his mission was not another entry in the genre of "stirring tales of dash and excitement" but a visceral documenting of the agonies of "filth, shock, blood, and maggots."

The lean prose imparts a tremendous narrative drive. But the arc of the story spirals ever downward. You are relentlessly pulled down into an abyss, and in the abyss with Eugene and his buddies you stay. Every time you think you have hit the nadir you turn the page and learn you have not—but you cannot stop reading. In those pages you discover a particularly remarkable feature among memoirs. Eugene Sledge duly records his personal experiences—his understatement striking and a comment on his character—unabashed about his encounters with terror and despair. You often must read between the lines to appreciate fully how tough and courageous he was. But he habitually separates from his personal experiences to adopt the role of the central observer, not the central character. He aspires above all to memorialize his comrades, not himself. He is not wholly unique in this, but I am at a loss to name another account that does this so devotedly and so well.

What does this work add to *With the Old Breed*? Eugene's insistence on keeping himself frequently off scene, or as just one of a cast of observers, while guiding readers through an unimaginable abyss has an effect that I doubt Eugene sought when he first began writing: He leaves readers seeking to learn how he coped with life after these experiences. This work in your hands does a superb job of answering that question. Along the way, it sheds light on what is in *With the Old Breed* and what is not.

As his brother John remarked, Henry Sledge, Eugene's younger son, possesses a preternatural memory for details of distant events. Through Henry we learn that the original manuscript was much longer than the published version. Henry shrewdly excerpts illuminating omitted passages that add effectively to the original published work. He further takes us through conversations with Eugene, or comments made by Eugene, over the years referencing events during the war, how he viewed them at the time, and how he used them as a lesson book for his sons. Henry's mission is to amplify faithfully Eugene's experiences, insights, and achievements, not to magnify his own status or role.

Perhaps the most important revelation in these pages is that Eugene identified science as his salvation from the trauma of combat. The influence of science also forms part and parcel of his narrative: a relentless concentration on the facts, which also heft, without comment, the emotional impact.

Henry sums up his childhood and young adulthood with his father:

> I never felt as though I was living in a house with a disturbed individual. As I have stated publicly many times, he was an all-American dad. He was, in my own view, a paragon of self-control. He drank moderately, but never to excess. He swore frequently but never needlessly, and he absolutely eschewed the so-called four-letter

words. Like any man, he appreciated beautiful women, but there was only one who mattered—my mother. He treated her with absolute respect and devotion and demanded the same of my brother and me, not that that was a hard thing to do. He always called her Shug, Chief, and sometimes simply Mrs. Sledge.

Now, turn the page.
Richard B. Frank

PREFACE

I first read *With the Old Breed*, Eugene B. Sledge's classic account of combat in the Pacific with the 1st Marine Division, while I was researching my book on the Battle of Okinawa, *Crucible of Hell*. I was stunned by the power and unflinching honesty of Sledge's writing as he charts his unit's descent into what he calls the "depths of the abyss, the ultimate horror of war." On Peleliu a fellow marine who cut off and kept as a souvenir a shriveled and blackened Japanese hand had "lost (briefly I hoped) all his sensitivity," notes Sledge, and was a "twentieth-century savage now, mild mannered though he still was. I shuddered to think that I might do the same thing if the war went on and on."

Arguably the finest war memoir of the twentieth century, and among the best of all time—made all the more memorable because it was written from the perspective of a junior enlisted man—*With the Old Breed* convinced me to choose Sledge's company, K/3/5, as the focus of my second book on the Pacific war, *Devil Dogs*. Sledge's son Henry was kind enough to write the foreword, and when we met in person, in New Orleans in 2022, he told me he was working on a book of his own that would combine memories of his father with extracts from the eight hundred pages of the original unedited manuscript of *With the Old Breed*—an incredible 70 percent of the total—that were never published.

This was stupendous news. I knew that the original publisher, Presidio, had insisted on cuts, but not how many. Now they would see the light of day. What a treat for the legions of *With the Old Breed* fans around the world who would be given the opportunity to read more of Sledge's superlative prose. Even better, the unpublished extracts would be interwoven with Henry's "recollections, as his son, of watching that classic book come to life." I knew from a joint event I had done with Henry at the 15th International Conference on World War II in New Orleans just how powerful that combination was likely to be. "Henry Sledge gave a wonderful child's perspective on his father's later life," wrote an attendee, "his writing of *With the Old Breed* ("I'd see him up late at night, writing on a yellow legal pad, and ask 'What are you doing, Dad?' 'Nothing! Go to bed.' He was nicer than that, but..."), and the special place that memoir has in the lives of veterans, veterans' families, and the public's understanding of what it was like to serve in World War II."

The Old Breed...The Complete Story Revealed does not disappoint. Henry charts his father's journey from the moment he heard on the car radio of the Japanese attack on Pearl Harbor as he was returning from a hunting trip on December 7, 1941, to his funeral almost sixty years later, attended by a US Marine honor guard. "He was laid to rest in Mobile," writes Henry, "on a warm, sunny Alabama spring morning—the kind of morning he would have been out with the dogs bird-watching—the smell of flowers in the air, the Spanish moss hanging from those majestic oak trees and swaying gently in the breeze."

From Henry's assured pen—a skill he undoubtedly inherited from his father—and his canny choice of extracts from the unpublished manuscript (clearly marked in bold) we hear about Eugene's decision to flunk out of the V-12 officer's training program at Georgia Tech so that he could join the Marines as an enlisted man and get into a "shooting war" sooner rather than later, his rigorous training in the use of the 60mm M2 mortar, and hand-to-hand combat with the Ka-Bar knife ("**Practice shifting the Ka-Bar from one hand to the other**," Sledge was told. "**Learn to toss it from one hand to the other but keep your eyes on your opponent at all times because he is gonna move in fast.**")

The most powerful sections of the book are, of course, the ones that give us even more heartbreaking insight into Eugene's experience of combat: "**There we were, a patrol of about forty US Marines out in a pitch dark, rain-soaked mangrove swamp on a dangerous mission trying**

to keep our position secret from God only knew how many hundreds of Japanese, and this man was out of his mind and screaming like a maniac." In *With the Old Breed*, the deranged Marine is described as a "dog handler." Henry reveals that he was, in fact, a member of Company K, making his tragic death at the hands of his colleagues even harder to process.

There are many lighter moments, particularly Sledge's descriptions of life out of the line: "**If a man received a letter written on scented stationary, he might allow his buddies to inhale a whiff if their comments were not obscene. The unlucky ones at mail call always had sad expressions and stooped shoulders as they headed to their tents.**"

But, for me—as for the attendee at the conference—the particular charm of this brilliant book is that it allows us a ringside seat at those intimate conversations between father and son that reveal a deeper truth about Eugene's war, and maybe war in general. "One day I walked into his study while he was at his desk writing ," writes Henry. "I don't remember exactly how old I was- at least a teenager, I think- but I sat down in the rocking chair near the desk and asked him how many Japanese soldiers he killed during the war. He stopped writing, looked out the window thoughtfully, took a sip from the ever-present glass of iced tea, and answered the question like the scientist that he was—giving an articulate and analytically worded exposition on the effectiveness of the 60mm mortar when properly employed.

"Like the NCO had said back on Pavuvu all those years ago, 'it'll tear their asses up.'

"When he finished, I didn't say anything, just sat looking at him expectantly. A slight pause—he knew what I was looking for. Then he looked me in the eye and simply said, "_______, maybe-________

"It wasn't a large number, but some things must only be between father and son."

Saul David

INTRODUCTION

It was in the early years of my life that I began to form a long-lasting love and appreciation of WWII history. I think it began when we took family trips to Mobile to visit my grandmother. She still lived in Georgia Cottage, the beautiful old home at the end of a long oak tree lined driveway off Spring Hill Avenue that she and my grandfather purchased in 1935. It was the home where my father and his brother, my Uncle Edward, grew up. I still remember the sound of our tires on that pea gravel when we turned onto the driveway after the long trip down from Montevallo. I would pop up from the backseat and look through the windshield, captivated by the sight of that elegant old home sitting back amid the Spanish moss draped oak trees. Frequently my grandmother, Mary Frank (or Gran as we called her) would be standing on the verandah waiting for us. We'd tumble out of the car into the warm humidity as she would call out in her distinctive Mobile accent, "Halloo, how is everything?"

I'll never forget the smell in the air that greeted me, it was a combination of magnolia blossoms and the sulfurous odor from the paper mills upriver from Mobile. Amid the hullabaloo of Mary Frank greeting us and the raucous Blue Jays up in the trees, my brother and I would run into the house, and be taken back in time to the world that our father grew up in. Even though it was usually warm, my grandmother frequently had a small fire going in the gas fireplace in her front bedroom, and the soft hissing and sputtering sound it made added to the ambience.

"Come on," my brother would say, "let's go look at Uncle Edward's medals!" Whereupon we would run into the central hallway and go to the large bookcase with cabinet doors at the bottom. My brother would open those doors, and we would pull out the leather medal cases that held Edward's medals. Our uncle had been a tank platoon commander in the 741st Tank Battalion, landing at Vierville in Normandy on D Day, June 6, 1944. He fought across Europe and served with valor and distinction, and he had the medals to prove it—a Bronze Star, a Silver Star, and three Purple Hearts. To my young eyes, those venerable leather cases with the medals were history itself. I can still hear the creaking sound each case made when we would open it, still smell the musty aroma of the velvet that each medal rested on, still hear the crinkle of the aged, yellowed, sharply creased typed written citations that detailed his actions that each medal represented. After gazing at them for several minutes and imagining our uncle in the turret of his Sherman at Normandy, or running ahead of his tanks, hurrying, shouting orders, through snowy, fire swept roads trying to hook up with the 2nd Infantry Division on that hellish night in the Ardennes, John would say, "let's go look at his jacket that he wore at The Battle of the Bulge, it's in the back bedroom!" So we would run to the back of the house and pull Edward's tanker jacket out of the closet. I'd put it on—it was huge on me—and get lost in the scent of mothballs, and history. Then we'd put the jacket back in the closet and walk back toward the front of the house and the sounds of a lively family gathering. "Uncle Edward was in the Army and fought the Germans," my brother would say, "but Dad was a Marine, he was in the Pacific."

One pleasant spring afternoon my parents were driving down Spring Hill Avenue in Mobile, Alabama, when my mother saw something in the middle of the road. It was a squirrel that had been run over by another car when it had tried to dart across the street. It was eviscerated, bloody, and barely recognizable.

As they drove past it, she remarked, "Oh, that poor squirrel!" My father, preoccupied with the typical things that would be on the mind of a young, recently married husband, barely acknowledged it. This surprised her, and she glanced at him..

He shrugged. "I had friends that looked worse than that."

***

In the years after the war, my father often had nightmares. He would wake in a cold sweat, pulse racing. My mother may have found this somewhat unsettling at first, but she knew that he had been a Marine in the Pacific, had seen heavy combat, and had somehow survived against an enemy renowned for creeping around at night trying to slip into a man's foxhole and cut his throat. She talked to friends of his who were veterans themselves. One of these was Sid Phillips, also from Mobile. He told her that he had nightmares, too, because they had dealt with enemy infiltrators every night on the 'Canal. Sid advised her not to touch him when he was asleep. My mother asked, "What do I do if I need him in the middle of the night?" Sid answered, "I'll tell you what you do. Lean over and whisper in his ear, 'Sledgehammer!'"

The ways combat veterans dealt with their trauma varied from individual to individual. Some tried to suppress it, some turned to alcohol, some probably took it out on their families, and my father started to write. He would get up in the middle of the night and go sit by the fireplace in the living room. He had carried a small New Testament Bible through the entire war in the pocket of his dungaree jacket, and in it he made notes about locations, dates, and weather conditions. He also kept notes on pieces of paper that he tucked into this Bible. Not long after he got home, he had written a detailed outline with all this information. Armed with this, a pencil as sharp as his memory, and a yellow legal pad, he started writing what was to become his classic memoir, *With the Old Breed.*

My parents lived in Winter Haven, Florida, from 1956 to 1960. My brother John was born in 1957, the same year that the Russians put a satellite named Sputnik into earth orbit and scared the hell out of the United States. So, while the boys at NASA were trying to figure out how to get something of their own into earth orbit without it blowing up on the launchpad, my father pursued his PhD in biology from the University of Florida, which he received in 1960.

In 1962 my parents moved to Montevallo for my father to accept a position as assistant professor of biology at Alabama College, which is now the University of Montevallo. On her first visit to the tiny town south of Birmingham, my mother was less than impressed. It was surrounded by lime plants, rock quarries, and cow pastures. But she resolved to support her husband's career choice, and soon enough the day came when my parents couldn't imagine living anywhere else.

Their first home in Montevallo was in a converted barn apartment out by the college lake. Eventually, they moved into town, to 446 Pineview Road. I was born in 1965.

By that time there were quite a few yellow legal pads filled with cursive writing in pencil. Late at night after my brother and I were in bed, my father would settle down by the fireplace and write. The flow of words never stopped, and the young college professor seemed driven to get it all down on paper, as if doing so would purge the demons that caused his nightmares.

Around 1971 or 1972, my parents decided it was time to move their growing family to a new house. They purchased a couple of acres on Cardinal Crest Road and started building their dream home. We moved there in 1973. John was fifteen, and I was eight. While we built treehouses, roamed the surrounding woods with our .22 rifles or BB guns, and built a space capsule from the spare lumber left by the builders, my father continued writing. It was no secret that he was recording what he had experienced fighting in the jungles of the Pacific during World War II.

Eventually he asked my mother if she would start typing what was on the yellow legal pads. It wasn't something she was excited to do at first. But she did, first on a little Smith Corona manual typewriter and then later on an electric model, a Selectric that she and my father bought for $200.

My mother may have been unenthusiastic in the early stages of bringing what would become my father's book to life, but she certainly came around. She saw the power of what he was writing and the unblinking honesty of his story. I remember many summer afternoons with me sitting on the floor of the den, playing with the little green plastic Army men I had bought at the local dime store, while she clacked away on that electric typewriter in the laundry room. She was the one who told my father that his book should be published; he had simply wanted a written record of his wartime experience for the family.

It's true that he felt he had experienced something that needed to be shared, that it had been life altering and transformative for him as a person, and that writing it all down was something of a catharsis. But he also felt that he was telling his buddies' story.

I recently saw a copy of a letter that he had written to two of his Marine buddies in 1980. At that point his book was on the verge of being released. In that letter he said that he had spent the last several years obsessing about the most unpleasant years of his life, recalling events, names, and details of the most horrific things that had ever happened to him and his fellow Marines, because he felt driven to tell the world what they had experienced.

The book was written, he said in this letter, and he was ready to lay down his pen and get on with his life, to focus on his family and his career. Since he had it all down on paper, he felt that he had done what he had set out to do—divested himself of these things that were bottled up and trying to get out. Now he could forget about it and move on.

In the fall of 2021, while preparing for a podcast episode, I found an old letter tucked inside the pages of *The Old Breed: A History of the First Marine Division in World War II* by George McMillan. Dated June 21, 1982, this letter was apparently a response to the copy of my father's new book, *With the Old Breed*, that he had sent to McMillan for his review. Short and concise, it read:

> Dear Gene:
>
> You've written a good book. It reeks with the humility of a good infantryman, of one who has seen the worst of

> battle. It is honest and it is true. That photo of you on the dust jacket is GREAT, made me nearly weep with nostalgia, made me think of all the days I sat like that on my cot at Pavuvu. Something makes me think that the book is going to carve out a place for itself in WWII literature. You haven't heard the last of it. Let me know well in advance of the Bantam pub date. Maybe I can hit some kind of lick then. I'm honored you used old breed in your title and grateful for the dedication. Now write us another good book.
>
> Semper Fi,
>
> George

Shortly after the war ended, every man who served in one of the six Marine Divisions in World War II was sent a unit history that dealt with his particular division. Each was written by a Marine who served in that division. McMillan wrote *The Old Breed* for the 1st, and it is an immortal classic. That book was an indelible part of my childhood: opening up my father's copy, seeing his scribbled notes in his familiar cursive handwriting in the margins, and smelling the musty aroma of an old book sitting long on the shelf. It was, in a way, a blueprint for his own book.

It takes me back to when I was an adolescent, sitting on the floor of his study while he was at his desk. I spent hours looking at *The Old Breed*'s illustrations and pictures, fascinated by what my father and men like him had endured on those far-flung islands. To find a letter written by its author to my father lauding what he had just published was an amazing discovery. McMillan's prediction that my father's book would "carve out a place for itself in WWII literature" was, as it would turn out, incredibly prescient.

My father's manuscript, as it was originally typed by my mother and later by his secretary at the University of Montevallo, was around 1,100 pages. It began with his enlistment in the Marine Corps after his freshman year at Marion Military Institute and then purposefully flunking out of the V-12 officer's training program at Georgia Tech. He subsequently went into the Marines as an enlisted man. He goes through his training to become a Marine, his service in the Pacific theater at Peleliu and Okinawa, and then occupation duty in China before he finally came home to Mobile, Alabama, in 1946.

I remember my father sealing up huge manila envelopes containing his manuscript and sending them off to prospective publishers. One pleasant afternoon, probably in 1979, after I had gotten home from school and he had gotten home from work, we walked up the driveway to the mailbox, where we found a large envelope. "Well, that's probably a publisher returning the manuscript," he said matter-of-factly. He opened the package and pulled out a letter as we walked back down the driveway to the house.

It was, in fact, a rejection letter, the second one he had received. I didn't read it, but my father simply said, "Well, that's that."

Not long after, on another pleasant afternoon when I got home, my mother told me the exciting news that they had just heard from the third publisher, Presidio Press, that his book was to be published. They recommended that it be no longer than approximately three hundred pages, so this meant that the manuscript would be cut off at the point where the fighting on Okinawa ended. This they did, and in 1981 *With the Old Breed* was published.

For many years after I remember my father working on what came to be referred to as "the China manuscript." The idea was to make his China duty a book in its own right. While that story was certainly happier and more pleasant than *With the Old Breed*, my father didn't work on it with any sense of urgency. At that point my brother was long out of the house, and I was in college, then out on my own.

My father's nightmares now rarely occurred. The visions of dead Marines rising out of their rain-filled foxholes in the shell-torn mud fields of Okinawa, forlornly, silently, moving about in the lurid, eerie, greenish light of star shells swaying from their parachutes—the descriptions of which still move me to tears—seemed laid to rest.

With the Old Breed rolled on like a juggernaut, gaining accolades and recognition and garnering a reputation of being, in the words of military history scholar John Keegan, “one of the most arresting documents in war literature.” Paul Fussell called it “one of the finest memoirs to emerge from any war.” It has been compared to *The Red Badge of Courage* and *All Quiet on the Western Front*. And the list goes on.

It was perfectly understandable that my father had had enough of war. The cards and letters from readers and admirers the world over never stopped coming. The requests to speak to various groups or to be interviewed for a film or documentary about Peleliu or Okinawa were frequent and continued until the later years of his life. He felt obligated to go do these things until finally one day we told him, “You’ve done your part, Dad; if you don’t want to go, don’t.” Some World War II veterans happily donned dress uniforms with ribbons and medals and rode in the backs of convertibles in Veterans Day parades cheered by throngs of well-wishers, but my father just wanted to forget about all of it.

He passed away in 2001, and by that time his fame was well established. His second book, *China Marine*, was published posthumously in 2002.

Many years later his place in the annals of military history and American culture would be even further solidified, if that were possible, by recognition of his talents and contributions by Ken Burns and Tom Hanks. But that was much later. Not long after his passing, my mother and I were discussing a letter from an admirer who had just read *With the Old Breed*. It must have been a particularly moving letter; I don’t remember it, but I do recall my mother saying, “I think your father will be larger in death than he was in life.”

And so it has been.

At some point around 1999, my father began organizing all his papers, letters, and research material that he had accumulated over the years while he was writing his manuscript. He boxed up all this material and sent it to Auburn University, where it was placed in the archives. Among these papers was the original unedited manuscript of *With the Old Breed*.

Over the years my family had discussed bringing to light the parts of the original manuscript that were not published. We never pursued it until October of 2021, when my mother brought it up again. "I've thought about that too," I said, "but do you think there's really that much there that would add to the story?" She was convinced there was, and I decided to do something about it.

With the Old Breed has been around now for over forty years. While intimately familiar with the book and its origins, I really had no idea how much unpublished material from his original manuscript was tucked away in the files down there at Auburn University. I decided to write a companion piece to *With the Old Breed* that would be composed of that material, interwoven with my recollections, as his son, of watching that classic book come to life.

I obtained a complete copy of the original manuscript and thus began my mission.

PROLOGUE

Material from the unedited manuscript of *With the Old Breed* appears in bold.

One day when I was around three or four years old, I was sitting on the floor of the den of our house, looking out through the sliding glass doors to the patio during a heavy rain shower. The raindrops were hitting the bricks of the patio and splashing in every direction. Little ringlets redounded out from the center of each splash. My father knelt beside me and pointed out at the thrumming rain. "Look at that," he said. "See the way the water splashes when it hits? Those are called water babies. They're little elves splashing around in the water!"

In the spring of 1945, as American forces pushed the Japanese further south on Okinawa, my father and his fellow Marines were at the point of exhaustion. As they neared Shuri, the main Japanese defensive bastion on the southern part of the island, the fighting was as bitter and the environment as brutal as anything they had experienced yet. Sitting in his foxhole, on the edge of a ridge, my father could look out across a muddy, shell-torn field of death and destruction.

Directly below his gun pit was a flooded crater filled with a dead Marine. This poor man had been killed early in the fighting in that area. His grisly, skeletal remains created a horrific, vivid memory for my father. He remembered how the corpse lay with his back against the shell crater, still clutching a rusting BAR, his helmet resting against the side. The ghostly remains of his face under the cloth-covered helmet leered up at the sky as the rain poured down.

"His pack and web canvas ammo pouches for the big 20 round BAR magazines were all new and neatly adjusted.

"The man had been dead quite some time. In the rain, with the agents of decay rapidly at work, I saw the face vanish and rot away day by day.... The result was the most spine chilling and horrible expression imaginable.

"One night by the light of a star shell I looked down at the big BAR man and his awful, livid face grinning up at me in the pouring rain, and in the eerie light the white teeth, the jaws and the big black eye sockets formed a spectral visage beneath the helmet.

"The star shell flickered out. I shuddered in the rain. When another star shell whistled in and popped open, I could not bear to look back down at him.

Numb with fatigue, my father sat in the mud and filth, watching the raindrops splash on and around that corpse in the shell crater and remembering how, when he was a child, he was fascinated at how the rain splashed on and around a large green frog in a ditch in his family's backyard. His grandmother told him that elves made splashes like that, and they were called water babies.

In later years, after reading his book, I reflected on this horrific scene, and I wondered if the young college professor kneeling beside his younger son and gazing out at the water babies on the patio might have still been trying to forget that day near Half Moon Hill on Okinawa.

CHAPTER ONE

When the Japanese attacked Pearl Harbor on December 7, 1941, Eugene Sledge and his father, Dr. Edward S. Sledge (my grandfather), were bumping along a back road in my grandfather's Model A, returning from a hunting trip. They heard the momentous news announced on the car's radio. Although in the years since the indelible image of thousands of young men standing in lines at recruiting stations across the country has been burned into the American psyche, my father's military experience was not so immediate. My grandparents and my uncle urged him to stay in college and get commissioned into the Army as an officer. My uncle Edward was a graduate of the Citadel and destined for distinguished service in an armor unit.

My father was a freshman at Marion Military Institute. On December 3, 1942, he had enlisted in the United States Marine Corps.

"Pop, as a physician, had risen to the rank of Lt. Col. in the Army Medical Corps in World War I and knew the advantages of being an officer."

With his family adjuring him to avoid serving in the enlisted ranks, my father compromised and, when a Marine Corps recruiting team came to Marion, he signed up for the V-12 officer's training program. Thus began his career as a college boy Marine at Georgia Tech in Atlanta. Due to report for duty on July 1, 1943, he spent his last few weeks in Mobile with family and friends who had not already headed off to war.

"During June, I rode Cricket every chance I had—somehow, I knew it would be a long time before I saw that little horse again. Deacon, my spaniel, followed me everywhere. Mother, Pop, and I

spent a lot of time together, and I visited friends who had not already left Mobile for service in the armed forces."

Life as a college boy Marine, though easy, rapidly became intolerable. Half of the 180-man detachment, my father among them, deliberately flunked out so that they would then go into the Marine Corps as enlisted men. Soon enough he was headed to Marine Corps Boot Camp in San Diego, California. It was there that he would meet his drill instructor, Cpl. Doherty, and become a part of Platoon 984.

Growing up in the 1970s, we watched many of the television shows of the day that provided wholesome entertainment. One was *Gomer Pyle, USMC.* My father watched very little television, but when he passed through the living room one day during the episode of Gomer's enlistment, he stopped and watched with us. What followed has remained one of my cherished memories of those days.

Gomer had aroused the ire of Sergeant Carter, and the sergeant had Gomer put a bucket over his head and sing the Marine Corps hymn. We guffawed as Gomer sang under the bucket and Sergeant Carter shook with barely controlled anger before erupting into paroxysms of screaming and yelling.

"That reminds me of the 'bucket issue,'" my father commented.

"Corporal Doherty moved us out at quick march to a warehouse. At this warehouse we drew our bucket issue, an old tradition in the Marine Corps. We were each issued a large, heavy, galvanized bucket filled with numerous articles including soap, large wooden scrubbing brush, toothpaste, toothbrush, shaving soap, etc. Scuttlebutt had it that we had to pay for this bucket full of junk with our first month's salary while in boot camp."

From an early age, I had a fascination with firearms. My brother and I spent many hours in the woods behind the house shooting our BB guns, later .22 rifles and sometimes black powder muzzleloaders. We had many conversations through the years about the safe and responsible use of firearms. When I was a teenager, my father taught me to shoot a .30

caliber M1 carbine. I was particularly interested in this weapon because, as a mortarman, he carried one like it. In our backyard, he taught me to shoot "the Marine Corps way."

"Before dawn on a chilly December morning, we boarded USMC buses for the trip to the rifle range which was some miles away in the hills."

Their training began with "snapping in." This involved focusing on proper use of the sites, trigger squeeze, and breathing technique.

While I was kneeling in the shooting position and practicing the breathing and trigger squeeze, my father, with his red L.L.Bean handkerchief wrapped around his hand, would push the bolt. When we inserted a loaded magazine into the carbine and started shooting, I was impressed that his pushing the bolt back while dry firing was an excellent simulation of the actual recoil of the weapon.

As important as technique was, however, the thing my father instilled in me, forever after, was safety. He exhorted me to "keep the weapon pointed downrange at all times, to never point a weapon at anything you don't intend to shoot. Many accidents have happened with 'unloaded weapons.'"

After eight grueling weeks of intensive training, he graduated from Marine Corps Boot Camp on December 24, 1943. By that time in the Pacific, the great US juggernaut was heading ever closer to Japan. Guadalcanal and the rest of the Solomon Islands were now US territory. The US Army was winning victories in New Guinea, and the Marines had just secured Tarawa (at terrible cost) a month earlier in the Central Pacific. The 1st Marine Division, which my father was destined to join, was at that moment headed to Cape Gloucester on the western end of New Britain island, which they would invade on December 26, 1943.

"At this period there was a great deal of talk and speculation...'where do we go from here?' Scuttlebutt was rampant...one man had heard that we would be in the Pacific jungles within two weeks."

By the end of basic training, my father reflected that Corporal Doherty had done his job well. They were mentally and physically tough.

In the predawn darkness of Christmas Day 1943, Platoon 984 fell in for the last time with their seabags and rifles. They went down to a warehouse, and as each man's name and destination was called, he reported to a designated truck.

Corporal Doherty called out, "Eugene B. Sledge, 534559, full individual equipment and M1 rifle, infantry, Camp Elliott."

Most of these men were headed for the infantry. My father told me that at the time it never occurred to them why. They were destined to take the place of the increasing casualties in the rifle or line companies in the Pacific. They were going to be the tip of the spear—cannon fodder.

As the trucks rolled out, my father noticed Corporal Doherty watching them leave. Though he disliked his drill instructor, he did respect him.

There is no way to know what Corporal Doherty was thinking as he watched his new Marines roll by in the trucks on that chilly Christmas morning. I've wondered if he could have imagined that one of those Marines would go on to immortalize him in a highly regarded memoir.

My father's infantry training began at Camp Elliott, which was several miles north of the San Diego Recruit Depot, where he completed boot camp. It was then that he chose 60mm mortars as his weapons specialty.

A calmly confident blond sergeant, who my father remembered as "**about my size but slightly heavier**," addressed the men who had chosen to become mortarmen. He explained the effectiveness of the weapon in breaking up attacks on the company front and softening enemy defenses.

This man had seen action during the fierce fighting on Guadalcanal, and he explained the characteristics of the weapon. It was smoothbore and muzzle loaded. When the tube—or barrel—bipod and baseplate were assembled, it weighed forty-five pounds. Because of its high angle of fire, mortars were extremely effective against enemy troops in defilades or behind ridges that might provide cover from artillery. At that time in the Marine Corps, there were two, sometimes three, 60mm mortars in each rifle company.

They spent hours studying the weapon, how to set it up, how to tear it down, and how to take a compass reading on a target, then place an aiming stake in front of the gun to correspond to that reading.

"'In most cases,' said the sergeant, 'you will not see the target you are firing on but will depend on your observer to give you the correct compass reading and range and you then line your sights up on a stake just in front of the gun. After firing one or two rounds to register the gun, the observer will correct your fire. You must level the bubbles after each round—if you don't, the gun is out of alignment, and you may drop shells on your own people.'

Subsequent lessons dealt with bracketing fire, searching fire, traversing fire, and combinations of these."

When the men began training with live ammunition, they quickly realized what a deadly weapon they were dealing with. With each shell burst downrange, they could see steel fragments kick up dust in an area of nine to eighteen yards when the shells struck the ground. Three shell bursts covered an area of about thirty-five by thirty-five yards. When one man commented that he felt sorry for any Japanese caught in such a situation, the sergeant reminded him that the enemy would be throwing plenty of hot stuff back at them.

My father, a reflective man in his own right, realized at that moment that this was the difference between war and hunting. "When I survived the former, I gave up the latter," he said in later years.

He shared a story with me when I was a young man and had recently developed an interest in deer hunting. He was on a deer hunt with some family friends in some deep forest land somewhere along the Mobile and Tensaw Rivers after he had returned home from the war. It was a frosty morning, he was on a stand and heard deer being driven toward him in the pale light of dawn. A young buck that was on the run came crashing through the woods and stopped a short distance away from where my father stood. The other hunters and their dogs were fast approaching. The buck, a four point, stared wide-eyed right at my father. "It felt like ambush," he told me. "I wasn't about to shoot that deer. So, I stood out from my stand, held my arms up, and whistled softly at him. He turned tail and ran to safety." When the others caught up with him and asked if he had seen the deer go by, he simply told them no.

He did love being in the woods, but he'd lost the desire to kill. My own interest in hunting spanned a few years, but early on I arrived at the same conclusion as my father: I thoroughly enjoyed spending a day in the woods with a rifle or a pistol, but I was just as happy to shoot at a stick in the creek as I was trying to kill something.

My father and his fellow Marine recruits also learned about hand-to-hand combat.

Their instructor explained how when the sun went down in the Pacific islands, the Japanese always sent men into positions to try to infiltrate the lines. They were tough and they liked close-in fighting.

At this point, they were introduced to the Marine's foxhole companion, the Ka-Bar knife. The knife was one foot long with a seven-inch-long-by-one-and-a-half-inch-wide blade. The five-inch handle was made of leather washers packed together stamped with "USMC" on the upper guard. It was light and beautifully balanced.

The Ka-Bar that was issued to my father, and that was his constant companion throughout his combat service in World War II, lay on the bookshelf in his study. I sat in that room and had many conversations with him through my formative years. I would pick up his Ka-Bar and test its balance and weight. He would always say, "Careful, that thing is razor sharp. It's the most beautifully balanced knife you'll ever see."

"The instructor taught us how to hold the Ka-Bar, keeping the blade tip always pointed at the throat. 'Practice shifting the Ka-Bar from one hand to the other. Learn to toss it from one hand to the other but keep your eyes on your opponent at all times because he is gonna move in fast. By changing your knife from hand to hand you will confuse him. We practiced this with renewed interest."

My father quickly saw that survival depended on what they learned.

Despite the heavy and intense training regimen that turned them into battle-ready Marines, there were recreational diversions.

"In the afternoons after being dismissed we took a hot shower, cleaned our rifles, washed clothes, and 'shot the breeze' or got in a little sack time...or had a beer at the slop chute. Most of the conversation centered around women, home, and our training.

"On weekends a man could obtain a pass which gave him time to travel to Hollywood, Los Angeles, and other cities. I made frequent trips to the various zoos nearby.

"Weekend trips to Los Angeles began with catching a bus outside Camp Elliott. If your uniform wasn't sharp with shoes shined, as you passed the guard at the gate you were ordered to get it squared away or not leave camp."

That was a familiar sight every couple of weeks or so around our house growing up: my father sitting either in his study or in my parents' bedroom and polishing his shoes, then briskly buffing them with a brush to a bright sheen fit to pass any inspection.

"The bus carried us to the San Diego railroad depot. Hundreds of Marines, and an occasional civilian, boarded a train for the trip to L.A.

"One night a couple of the boys and I went to a burlesque theater which was supposed to feature chorus girls. I was sporting a brand-new suit of Marine dress blues I had recently purchased. (The Marine Corps didn't issue the dress blue uniform to us during World War II, but a man could buy his own from certain authorized dealers.)"

Those very dress blues hung in the cedar closet of a downstairs bedroom when I was growing up. On many occasions I would take them out, pull off the plastic that covered them, and admire their crisp perfection. They were still adorned with his ribbons and battle stars, the braided French fourragère around the left shoulder and the two chevrons of a corporal. It was always a point of pride for him that he was able to fit into them long after the war was a distant memory. He prided himself on maintaining a strict diet and regular exercise routine that prevented what he always referred to as a "potbelly."

"My buddies and I sat on about the tenth row in the side section. The girls, dressed like French can-can dancers, were beautiful. In

fact, I wondered what they were doing in a place like that. The music didn't do them justice.

"Finally, the master of ceremonies came on stage and announced that each girl would come offstage into the audience, choose a partner, and dance with him in the aisle. The boys all clapped and cheered at this. When the next number ended, the theater lights went on, and the twenty odd girls lined up across the front of the stage and looked over the hundreds of cheering uniformed fans. Each girl acted as though it was difficult to make her choice, which of course only increased the uproar.

"Finally, a tall, shapely, blue-eyed brunette looked me square in the eye and pointed to me. It must have been the dress blues! She slithered down off the stage and came up the aisle and beckoned to me. The troops all around me cheered and shouted at me. I hung back, insisting that she meant to dance with someone else. This delighted the young lady tremendously and when the uproar subsided, she said, 'I mean you Marine. You're cute.' Her sultry voice could have melted a glacier. The uproar around me began again, and my buddies shoved me out into the aisle. After the first dance my compatriots could stand it no longer and swarmed out into the aisle to have their turn. The M.C. finally coaxed all of us back to our seats with the promise of an extra-long show that night. When we returned to the barracks Sunday night my buddies razzed me about blushing so much when I danced with her.

"'Where did you take her after the show Sledgehammer?'

"'Nowhere,' I said.

"'You mean you didn't go the stage door to meet her after the show?'

"'No.'

"Groans of disappointment followed my answer.

"'You're hopeless Sledgehammer.'

"'Alright you guys, knock it off!' yelled the sergeant."

On November 20 to November 23, 1943, when my father was still in boot camp, the 2nd Marine Division assaulted the tiny coral atoll of Tarawa in the Gilbert Islands, thus opening Adm. Chester W. Nimitz's Central Pacific drive with the first of the "storm landings." As explained by Col. Joseph H. Alexander, USMC, my good friend and my son's namesake, in his superb treatise *Storm Landings*:

> "While there were many amphibious landings throughout the Pacific, only a few qualify as storm landings—the Japanese description of America's bold, frontal, daylight assaults into the teeth of prepared defenses.
>
> "For a variety of geostrategic reasons, these storm landings occurred in the Central Pacific from November 1943 to the spring of 1945. The list is short: Tarawa, Saipan, Guam, Tinian, Peleliu, Iwo Jima, and Okinawa.
>
> "The days of combining a tactical defensive with the strategic offensive ended with Guadalcanal and Bougainville. These later operations in the Central Pacific were assaults from start to finish. The landing force never relinquished the offensive. The battles were violent, relatively short, thoroughly decisive, always bloody."[1]

My father reflected on the most recent Marine Corps campaign and saw that the 2nd Division suffered terrible losses—3,381 dead and wounded. Its Marines killed all but seventeen of the 4,386 Japanese defenders of the tiny atoll. There was loud and severe criticism of the Marine Corps by the American public and some members of the military because of the number of casualties.[2]

"This was just heating up in the press when I got to Camp Elliott. We were all interested in what had happened and questioned our

---

1 Joseph H Alexander, *Storm Landings: Epic Amphibious Battles in the Central Pacific* (Naval Institute Press, 1997), 4–5.

2 Sledge, E.B., *With the Old Breed: At Peleliu and Okinawa*, Classics of Naval Literature (Naval Institute Press, 1996), 21.

instructors about it. Everyone agreed that there can be no element of surprise in attacking a tiny island in mid ocean. Losses would be high, but adequate numbers of amphibious tractors [amtracs, or LVTs for Landing Vehicle Tracked] could get troops successfully across the reefs that surrounded most of the islands in the Central Pacific. We hoped numerous amtracs would be available when we got overseas."

Mortar school and all aspects of advanced infantry training continued the entire time my father was at Camp Elliott. The last phase of special training received before embarking for the Pacific, and the real action, were swimming qualifications.

"In a large heated outdoor pool, we practiced endurance and distance swimming. There was a tower at the side which was supposed to simulate the deck of a troopship. It was about 35 feet high. We climbed the cargo net to the top of the tower and then jumped off, feet first, into the pool. When you surfaced, you had to remove your shirt, flip it over and trap air inside and use it as a float. We were told that no one could go overseas unless he passed his swimming qualifications. I know of only one man who couldn't meet the requirements, and whether he was given the chance to qualify later I never knew."

When I was five years old, my family joined a local swimming pool in Montevallo. While my father was never what I would have described as an athletic man, he was always fit and believed in vigorous exercise. My parents would take my brother and me to the swimming pool on hot summer days. While John and I, and our friends, reenacted scenes from *Voyage to the Bottom of the Sea* (a late 1960s undersea science fiction show with Richard Basehart and David Hedison), our father would swim laps as often as he could. At the time, I didn't give much thought to the fact that he was a very smooth swimmer and seemed very comfortable in the water. I'm sure all that Marine Corps training was coming back to him then.

CHAPTER TWO

Having completed advanced infantry training at Camp Elliott, my father and his fellow Marines were assigned to the 46th Replacement Battalion. This was a transient unit that simply ensured that new replacements were delivered to the Pacific Theater, whereupon each man would be assigned to the unit in which he would serve.

On February 28, 1944, they lined up to board a troopship in the San Diego harbor.

"I had seen many oceangoing vessels in Mobile Harbor, but the *President Polk* appeared to me to be the about the largest passenger ship I had ever seen."

A healthy appreciation and love for the Alabama and Florida Gulf Coast, including Mobile Bay and its teeming harbor, has always been with the Sledge family. As a youngster in Mobile, my grandmother, Mary Frank, would take my father to the waterfront where they would marvel at the bustling activity of a vibrant southern port. My brother John, in his book *The Gulf of Mexico*, wrote:

> "The American Gulf's smacks, luggers, trawlers, skiffs, and private charters were dwarfed by the oceangoing vessels that routinely crowded its harbors. Four- and five-masted lumber schooners, barks, white -hulled banana steamers, cargo ships, and tankers were all commonly

> seen moored together until the 1930s when sail power finally dwindled away."[3]

When we would visit our grandmother in Mobile in the early 1970s, we made regular visits to the waterfront. My father would drive me there in my grandmother's green and white 1959 Pontiac—I think it was a Star Chief—to take in the sights and smells. As John remembers in his book *The Mobile River*:

> "During the 1960s, for example, my grandmother often took me down to the docks to watch the stevedores at work. This was always a favorite outing. While other young boys dreamed of growing up to be firemen, policemen, baseball players, or soldiers, I wanted to be a stevedore and spend my days manhandling exotic cargoes from the holds of salt-streaked freighters."[4]

That February morning in 1944 made an impression on my father when he caught his first glimpse of the *President Polk*.

"The gang plank, leading from dockside up to the main deck, looked like it was at about a 45-degree angle, and was mighty long. "

The claustrophobic and fetid conditions of troopships had to be endured by thousands of young men who served overseas in every theater of the war. Even worse than these conditions were those endured by submariners. I well remember a trip my father, brother, and I made to visit the *USS Alabama* (BB-60), and the submarine *USS Drum* (SS-228) sitting beside her at the Battleship Memorial Park in Mobile. As we moved through the hot, tiny compartments aboard the *Drum* on that humid Mobile afternoon, I was duly impressed by the dazzling array of gauges, control levers, and shiny brass fittings. When we passed through one of the crew berths, my father whistled, shook his head, and remarked

---

3 John S. Sledge, *The Gulf of Mexico: A Maritime History* (University of South Carolina Press, 2019), 158.

4 John S. Sledge, *The Mobile River* (University of South Carolina Press, 2015), 1.

on the courage of the sailors who could live and fight in such a closely confined contraption.

On the *Polk*, the air was foul and the light dim. As soon as possible, they went topside.

"The racks shook and bounced when men climbed up and down, and when you stretched out, you were apt to get a boondocker in the face or a hand stepped on.

"An announcement prefaced by 'Now hear this, now hear this!' blared out over the squawk box instructing us to line up along certain gangways and passages leading to the galley. First chow in the ship's galley was an experience."

Amid the roar of ventilators, they ate standing at long folding tables. A sailor told my father that these had been used as operating tables for the Marine casualties the ship took on during one of the earlier Pacific campaigns.

The *USS President Polk* (AP-103) had stood by as a casualty-receiving ship for the shot-up Marines coming off Tarawa during that invasion in November 1943. In February 1944, she served again in that capacity, taking casualties from Kwajalein in the Marshall Islands back to the States. It was following that trip that the Marines of the 46th Replacement Battalion, my father among them, boarded her and headed for the Pacific.

In the wee hours of the next morning, they awoke to the vibration of the ship's engine. They were heading out. It was around 0500, and in the predawn darkness the deck grew crowded with young Marines wanting to catch a last glimpse of familiar shores. It was a hushed, subdued atmosphere as each man dealt with his own thoughts and grappled with the realization that they might never see home again.

"With the shout, 'gangway, ship's crew!' sailors scurried about their duties as we stumbled around getting out of the way. In short order, things were squared away, and the *President Polk* moved slowly out through San Diego harbor and bay.

"Later in the morning as the California coast became a thin irregular line on the horizon over the stern, the ship came into ground

swells that made us roll and pitch. I finally developed the ability to move about aboard a rolling ship with a minimum of holding on to railings, like an old salt. While the *President Polk* was rolling and pitching its way through the land swells most of the troops aboard laughed and joked about it being the best roller coaster they had ever seen. Before long, much of the laughter was diminishing and becoming groans of seasickness. Fortunately, I was never seasick, but some men were absolutely plagued with the malady even in the gentlest roll."

Later in life my father suffered from frequent stomach problems—spastic stomach, as it was termed by his doctor. He always kept a few Rolaids in his pocket. I remember the nightstand in my parent's bedroom where he always had his pocket change, key chain and leather belt loop (with a Japanese dog tag attached to it that Sid Phillips had picked up on Cape Gloucester), pocketknife, and a couple of Rolaids.

On a family beach trip to Destin, Florida, in 1974, my brother, father, and I took a four-hour trawling trip one morning aboard a forty-foot boat named the *Calypso II*. It was a sunny day, but the water was anything but calm as we headed out five miles into the Gulf. The seas that day were running five to eight feet. As my brother John recalled in *The Gulf of Mexico*:

> "Once out in open water, we were rocking with the green waves lifting and dropping the boat and shoving it in all directions. Dad, a World War II Marine Corps combat veteran whose sea experience included riding out a typhoon on board a supply ship, said it reminded him of being in the Pacific."

I was very worried about becoming seasick, even though I felt fine. My father told me not to think about it and slipped me one of his ever-present Rolaids. He seemed to be enjoying the pitch and roll.

The daily routine of life aboard a troopship crossing the ocean was marked by a monotony of diet and boredom.

The threat of patrolling enemy submarines was ever present, and a fully loaded troopship presented a very desirable target. It was for this reason that the men were strictly forbidden to throw any type of trash overboard, and anyone who disobeyed would suffer severe punishment.

"We were warned that even a cigarette butt, match or candy wrapper might be seen on the ocean by a patrolling submarine. Naturally everyone was very cooperative concerning trash disposal."

Daily activities on board included calisthenics and rifle inspections. Abandon ship drills were also conducted.

"Directions came over the squawk box, and each passenger and seaman had his station along the side of the ship where he would jump overboard if the order to 'abandon ship' was ever given. All the ship's personnel had large jacket-type life vests that they donned, and passengers wore a rubber inflatable lifebelt at all times.

"Several days later a shout went up from men on the bow that porpoises were escorting the ship. This meant land was near. I thought of Mobile Bay and the Gulf of Mexico as I watched five graceful porpoises play around the bow of the ship."

My father spoke to me often about the Gulf and how it had to be respected. It could be calm and docile, but it quickly turned rough and tempestuous. I remember his recounting how, during his time in the Pacific, he had sometimes seen the water as calm as glass.

"The sea was so calm at times that the surface looked like glass. I was always impressed by the utter vastness of the ocean. We once saw a whale in the distance, and several times we saw flying fish jumping from one wave to another. Other than that, it was an endless expanse of sea and sky from beginning to end of the voyage."

On March 17 the *Polk* passed through the Great Barrier Reef to arrive at New Caledonia. As the ship closed on the harbor, a pilot boat came alongside. He climbed the ship's ladder and went to the bridge to guide the vessel into the harbor of Nouméa.

"He looked like something from another era surrounded by swabbies in blue denim work pants, shirts and white hats, and ship's officers in khakis."

As they passed into the channel leading into the harbor, the deep blue of the Pacific Ocean turned to green. Any idyllic thoughts of an exotic seaport, however, soon dissipated as the vessel glided into its berth at a dock with long warehouses. This area bustled with activity as American military personnel, many on tractors, busily moved crates and equipment. Most of the shipping my father saw here was US Navy, but there were also foreign merchant freighters and civilian fishing boats.

CHAPTER THREE

The trip across the vast Pacific Ocean was finally over. My father and his fellow Marines walked down the gangplank and onto the island of New Caledonia. Piling their gear into trucks, they were driven through the central section of Nouméa. My father, always observant and mindful of detail, was delighted to see that the buildings reminded him of the older sections of Mobile.

The weather was cool and pleasant as they drove through hilly, mountainous country, dotted with palm trees, to Camp Saint-Louis, a tent camp that was to be their new home on New Caledonia while they continued their training. Once finished, they would be sent "up north" to the combat zone.

The training was rigorous and placed heavy emphasis on individual attention. The men were divided into groups of ten to twelve and worked with noncommissioned officers who were combat veterans. My father's instructor was a stout, red-headed corporal who had seen combat in the Solomon Islands. They called him Big Red.

Some of the most valuable training they received from Red was exposure to what Japanese pistol, rifle, and machine-gun fire sounded like. He also taught them to fire these weapons. Red put their groups of five into a five-foot-deep pit with an embankment in back.

As they later would find in combat, it was essential to learn the sound of Japanese fire coming at them and to be able to identify the weapon it was coming from. As the men took cover in the trench, Red blew a whistle, and several rounds were fired from each type of weapon. Then all the weapons were fired in long bursts. The men quickly learned to shift around to avoid the sizzling tracers that thudded into the embankment and then rolled down into the hole. This would turn out to be valuable training.

They engaged in more-thorough bayonet training, which emphasized not only the basic use of the weapon but actual techniques on how to win a bayonet fight against a Japanese soldier.

One of the artifacts my father had in his study when I was growing up was a Japanese bayonet. I recall one day closely examining the weapon. It was about sixteen inches long, well made with a wooden handle that had a hooked handguard. The blade was heavy steel and very sharp at the tip.

"You see this hook on the handguard?" he asked. "In a bayonet fight the Japanese used that to hook an American bayonet and twist the rifle out of his hands. It was a quick way to disarm our guys. It was pretty damn effective too."

I asked him if he had ever gotten into a bayonet fight with a Japanese.

"Hell, no," he answered emphatically. "I never let one get close enough to me for that. The Japs loved bayonet fighting, and they were good at it!"

Long marches through the jungles and swamps were also a large part of the training, intended to improve the men's conditioning. These marches were done with rifles and full packs and equipment, at a rapid pace, and resting was discouraged.

New Caledonia was nestled among many other islands, affording ample opportunities for continued amphibious training. Even then a naturalist and scientist at heart, long before he was formally trained as such, my father reveled in the natural surroundings of the camp.

"In the amphibious exercises we embarked in LCVPs [landing craft, vehicle, personnel], more commonly known as Higgins Boats, and landed on numerous beautiful, picturesque islets just off the coast of New Caledonia. Most of these were only a few hundred yards or less in size and teeming with vertebrate and invertebrate life, as well as lush vegetation. On the reefs and in shallows we found several

octopuses and a young example of a species of deadly poisonous sea snake."

Although no one had delusions about what they were training for or where they were going, the daily routine was occasionally interrupted.

"Liberty was merely a break in the routine. The pleasures Nouméa had to offer were available to officers only. It was an interesting old town that reminded me a great deal of the Gulf Coast. The civilians made themselves scarce, but one old French farmer told me how terrified the population had been when a large Japanese fleet had pulled into Nouméa and held amphibious maneuvers. He said they didn't harm anyone, but he kept his teenage daughters hidden anyway. I asked him where his daughters were now, and he grinned and shrugged, saying, 'I keep them hidden from all men in uniform, my son.' I smiled and told him he was a wise father."

On May 28, 1944, a little over two months after they landed on New Caledonia, the 46th Replacement Battalion packed their gear and embarked on the *USS General R. L. Howze*, a troopship that would take them north.

"There was a smoker on the fantail one afternoon, and men from the various branches participated in boxing and wrestling matches."

They were headed ever closer to the real war.

"Late in the afternoon of June 1, 1944, the ship dropped anchor offshore from Guadalcanal, and a unit of army service troops began unloading into Higgins boats for the trip ashore. Guadalcanal was a large U.S. base in 1944[;] as darkness fell, bright lights in several areas along the coast indicated the locations of camps and installations. After unloading some equipment, they hoisted the hook, and the ship got underway again."

They were headed about sixty miles northwest up the Slot to Pavuvu, the largest of the Russell Islands. As my father remembered it, the setting was idyllic, with coconut palm trees and clear, azure water. The peaceful setting that they sailed into on the *Howze* in June of 1944 was a drastic change from the ferocious life-and-death struggle that had been fought in the skies and waters of the Solomon Islands just months prior.

"We docked at a steel pier consisting of steel pontoons forming the pier and a causeway connecting the short distance to the beach."

From the deck of the *Howze* they could see the neat and orderly rows of tents and a network of coral roadways, all surrounded by coconut palm trees. Pavuvu was the home of the 1st Marine Division. My father and his buddies struck up casual conversation with some Marines on the pier. Although he wouldn't realize it until later, he was meeting veterans of the Guadalcanal and Cape Gloucester campaigns.

As they talked, the veterans told the new men that they had just left Cape Gloucester, on the western end of New Britain, in early May, then come to Pavuvu. They had been on Pavuvu about a month.

Brimming with excitement at finally arriving in the Pacific Theater, and actually meeting combat veterans who had been in direct contact with the Japanese, the new arrivals slept little that night. My father went out on deck to sleep in the open air, and he noticed that it was much hotter than it had been in New Caledonia.

CHAPTER FOUR

Around 0900 the next morning, June 3, 1944, my father made his way down the gangplank with his seabag containing all his personal gear. He headed toward a line of waiting trucks and saw some men, very tanned and in good spirits, waiting to leave the island.

"Some had Japanese weapons as souvenirs. I asked if there was anyone from H Company, 2nd Battalion, First Marines [Regiment], and two men near me said yes. I asked if Sid Phillips and Bill Brown were still on Pavuvu. The first man said he didn't know them, but his buddy spoke up and said, 'You know 'em, they're in the 81mm mortar platoon.'

"'Oh yeah,' replied the first. 'Bill shoved off for the States about a week ago and Phillips will probably go in a couple of weeks.'

"I would get to see one of my oldest and closest friends. Sid had enlisted in the Marine Corps right out of high school, gone overseas with the 1st Marine Division as a gunner on 81mm mortars, had his 18th birthday on Guadalcanal, and had made it through Cape Gloucester."

My father was in a group of about one hundred men, and a lieutenant counted them off into groups. At this point the officer told them their assignment: the 3rd Battalion, 5th Marines. They clambered into the back of a truck and were driven down the coral roads that twisted alongside the coconut-lined shore of Macquitti Bay. After passing several signs indicating different units of the 1st Marine Division, they arrived at the area belonging to the 3rd Battalion, 5th Marines. They debarked from the trucks and were assigned to companies by a noncommissioned officer. It was at this point that my father learned the unit he would become indelibly linked to for the rest of his life—K Company, 3rd Battalion, 5th Marines, referred to as K/3/5. I cannot remember how old I was the first time I heard that alphanumeric phrase, but I would hear it many times around our house as I grew up.

"We sat on our gear on the dirt company street for a few minutes and a lieutenant came along and formed us into three ranks and gave us 'at ease.'"

While most of the men were assigned to the rifle platoons of K Company, they were asked if any had special weapons training, meaning mortars or machine guns. My father was in a group of about fifteen who had this specialized training. They were taken aside.

"The lieutenant asked each of us what weapon we had trained with and if we wanted to be assigned to that type weapon in the company. Most of the guys said they were interested in doing so. Then he said, 'I need a volunteer to serve as a flamethrower gunner. This is a responsible position, and you will command the respect of everyone in the outfit. There are only two flamethrower gunners in each line company. It takes a tough man to carry this weapon.'"

At this point the officer looked at my father and asked him his weapon choice. Wincing at the thought of carrying seventy pounds of flammable jellied gasoline on his back for the rest of the war, my father answered that he had trained on 60mm mortars.

"The officer looked at the boy next to me and asked him if he would be interested in being a flamethrower gunner. He said he would do it, and the lieutenant said, 'Fine.' This boy was named Steele[;] he was seventeen years old, lean, and about six feet tall. Steele and I were to become close friends. Poor Steele was destined to become one of the men in K Company killed on Peleliu. He was trying to knock out a Japanese bunker with his flamethrower just after we got off the amtracs. I doubt if he ever saw a Japanese before he was killed.

"I was assigned to the second squad of the 60mm mortar section, and I began to get acquainted with the other veterans. Most of the

men were southerners or from the southwest. It seemed that almost every other man in K Company was a Texan. After I threw my gear down on my bunk all new men were told to report at the end of the company street. A blonde, suntanned colonel came out of a tent and gave us 'at ease.'

"He told us to sit on the deck and listen to what he had to say. He said we were members of the Fifth Marines [Fifth Marine Regiment], one of the Corps' oldest and finest infantry regiments. He said it was more decorated and had more battle streamers on the regimental flag staff than any other Marine Regiment. He said we had to do our best in everything to uphold this fine tradition."

There were tangible differences in being a new man to the outfit and being a combat veteran. The veterans of the Cape Gloucester and Guadalcanal campaigns were excluded from the daily working parties around Pavuvu that would transform it from a deserted tropical island littered by thousands of rotting coconuts into an active staging and training area for the 1st Marine Division. In addition to that, they quickly discovered that the ground, which initially appeared firm and solid, was soft and unable to sustain the tremendous amount of vehicular and foot traffic to which it was subjected by the 1st Division.

After the war my father spoke to me often about the lack of understanding from most civilians, and many servicemen from other theaters of operation, about the nature of not just combat but actual day-to-day life in the islands of the Pacific. But, as he remembered it, Pavuvu was on another level entirely.

"If it was difficult to explain to a civilian after the war, or servicemen who served in another theater of war, what life was like on a Pacific Island between campaigns, it was impossible to explain life on Pavuvu."

This place came to define the term *boondocks*. I can remember when I was in high school, and we would venture out on a field trip. Whenever we traveled beyond the city limits and into a less populated area, some classmate would always remark, "Oh, we're out in the boondocks now."

I usually never said anything, but I always shook my head and chuckled to myself.

Most work details involved improving drainage, pick and shovel work, and paving all walkways with crushed coral.

"The most detested of all working parties [was] collecting and loading rotten coconuts onto the big ten-wheeler trucks to be dumped into the swamp. I don't think I missed a single coconut detail in the 5th Regiment's area.

"The veterans were amused at the way we replacements went after the milk and meat of fresh coconuts with Ka-Bar **and bayonet. The sweet milk and crumbly meat seemed so delicious a treat that I stuffed myself on it—and I have never eaten coconuts since."**

Growing up, we never ate anything that was seasoned with coconuts. I remember one beach trip when we broke out some coconut-scented suntan lotion. At the first whiff, my father snorted in disgust. "God, that brings back memories," he said.

Predictably, my father did his share of complaining, for the first week anyway, about the work parties and austere living conditions. There was a veteran in K Company who became a close friend, and this man took him aside and explained to him that things could be much worse. He told my father that until he had tasted combat, he really had no right to complain.

Pavuvu did offer other distractions for my father, some pleasant, others far less so.

"Pavuvu had its interesting points to me in the form of bird life. It was spectacular to watch the flocks of about 30-40 large white cockatoos fly about the groves screeching at each other. However, Pavuvu was also infested with large rats. They hid by day in burrows throughout the grove and in the tops of palm trees. At night the rats ran through the tents, and if you had any food accessible, they got into it, as well as gnawing at almost everything else. We were advised to not eat while lying in our sacks because the rats might gnaw through your mosquito netting after you went to sleep. Different companies dealt with them

in various ways, but none of them dented the rat population in the least, so the troops gave up.

"Large fruit eating bats lived on Pavuvu and roosted among the fronds and coconuts of the palms. One night a great commotion took place in a palm by my tent, and something hit the canvas with a thud. From the scratching, squealing, and thumping about, a rat and a bat had gotten into a fight up in the fronds and fallen onto the tent. They finally separated, and the rat scampered off and the bat took wing."

Land crabs were another persistent pest on Pavuvu. They were ugly, hid by day, and roamed at will over the island by night. As my father recalled, they were loathsome creatures that had no fear of man or beast and would go anywhere. It was part of the morning routine for every man of the 1st Marine Division to shake the land crabs out of his boondockers before putting them on.

"When we returned from Peleliu, we killed over a hundred land crabs just in my tent."

The methods of ridding themselves of these filthy things will not be recounted here, but it didn't matter in the end.

"It was all an exercise in futility; the crab population seemed to get larger all the time."

Naturally, for young men in the prime of life and engaged in constant manual labor and combat training, chow, and the quality of it, was on everyone's mind. Because of logistical difficulties, things like fresh meat were a luxury. Everything was dehydrated—eggs, potatoes. Fresh bread was also rare, and what the bakers created was hardly worthy of the name. What the men got was usually infested with weevils, and sometimes worse.

"After Peleliu, replacements could always be seen picking the weevils out of the bread. I saw one boy with nothing to show for his effort but two little mounds on his mess kit: one of breadcrumbs, and one of weevils."

When I was eight years old or so, we were at the breakfast table, and I was eating my toast. It was not exactly to my liking, and I voiced my displeasure. My father patiently described to me eating bread during the war that had weevils in it and told me that I should be thankful for what I had and not complain. "We just looked at it like it was an extra source of protein," he said. I never complained about bread again.

"Refrigeration was something in another world as far as Pavuvu was concerned. A boat brought meat about once a week from the reefers on Banika, an island next to Pavuvu, but we had no ice. For me, 'a glass of ice water' became as symbolic of civilization as a beef steak, roast turkey, electric lights, or a house. On occasions we were issued a couple of cans of beer which we drank hot and were thankful of it."

Since formal showers and bathing facilities on the island were non-existent, the men had to wait each afternoon for the usual tropical rain showers, then run out into their company streets with a bar of soap in hand, lather as quickly as possible, and hopefully rinse before the rain abruptly ended, which often happened before some men could get fully rinsed.

"I devised a routine of catching runoff water from the tent in my helmet while soaping. It was necessary to stand on a board or in your boondockers to keep your feet out of the mud. However, a daily bath was a must in the hot, muggy climate in order to bolster sagging morale."

One of the most important things a man could have in this situation was a close relationship with his fellow Marines. Everyone had at least one buddy. Opportunities for entertainment were sparse.

"About the only entertainment was to go to the movies, so each man and his buddy took their ponchos and headed for the theater. There were several of them on Pavuvu—each of which was a clearing in the grove, rows of coconut logs for seats, and a projection booth on stilts covered with salvaged tentage. Each man always took a poncho, and sometimes a helmet liner, because it nearly always rained. We

sat around and shot the breeze for a few minutes with acquaintances from other companies before the show started.

"All types of movies from the finest dramas to the most ridiculous cowboy 'shoot 'em ups' were shown. The troops' comments on the movies were priceless if not always repeatable. Beautiful actresses always brought forth shouts and sighs of admiration. When I saw *Gaslight* starring Charles Boyer and Ingrid Bergman, the men around me were in a rage over Boyer's treatment of the beautiful heroine."

I recall watching *Gaslight* when it aired on a cable channel one night in the 1970s. My father was rarely one to sit down and watch a movie, but he did watch this one, or at least part of it. My memory of that evening is that he was very interested in the film and made quite a few remarks on Boyer's and Bergman's performances. He went to great trouble to explain to me the pernicious psychological game Boyer's character was playing. I don't remember him saying anything about watching this movie on Pavuvu, just that he was unusually interested in it.

"The old and worn-out projectors usually broke down at least once during each show.

"One night shortly after I arrived on Pavuvu, Sid Phillips and I attended a movie in one of the theaters near Division Headquarters. The projector kept failing during the early part of the film, and [the] audience was in no kind mood toward the booth or anybody in it. 'Get a replacement for that guy in the booth!' yelled one Marine. There were other shouts, and the harried operator stepped out on the platform behind the booth to explain. In the moonlight I could see an agonized expression on his face and his upturned palms as he said, 'You guys knock it off, can't you see I'm trying to fix this thing?' This was only met with more abuse, and the chagrined operator disappeared back into the booth. 'Put him in a line company!' yelled a man. 'Hell no, we'll lose the war!' yelled another. The projector squeaked to a start and the troops cheered loudly.

"The replacements sometimes quietly questioned the old men about the Japanese, their weapons, and about fear. There was little kidding about these subjects, and I found the veterans of great help

to me in describing from their experiences what we would have to face in the next battle, or blitz as they called it."

Though never a musician in the strict sense of the word, my father loved music and had a deep appreciation for it. When I was just four or five years old, I remember he would come home from work, have a beer, and strum his acoustic guitar. I do not remember any particular songs, but later he began to take an interest in classical guitar. He would sit for long periods and work at learning to play some incredibly complex pieces. Sometime in the mid- to late 1970s, he began to develop extremely painful tendonitis in his arms; he eventually had to give up playing classical guitar, but he never lost his love for music.

"Music was frequently our entertainment in K Company, as we were fortunate in having some talent, rustic though it was. Even though I love Bach, a battered folk guitar, a mandolin, and a fiddle, in the hands of former farm boys on Pavuvu, made some of the sweetest music I've ever heard. It was music from the heart—pure old American ballads the boys had learned from fathers and grandfathers. We all loved to hear and sing *Old Shep* and thought of the dog that every boy has had and loved as one of his closest companions while growing up."

My father would frequently mention *Old Shep* to my brother and me when we were sitting around the backyard with our German shepherd, Lady, after we had had a full day of roaming the woods behind our house with her.

"The liveliest music usually resulted from a little lubrication of the players with a couple of bottles of beer, opened with a belt buckle, or a canteen cup of jungle juice. This potent concoction would have made anyone bleary eyed. It was a simple formula—a little yeast, some canned fruit, some sugar, and water in a five-gallon GI water can.

Though not an avid drinker by any means, my father didn't let that stop him from enjoying a good social gathering. With his lively manner, incredibly sharp wit, and unequaled sense of humor, he was always a great addition to any party he and my mother attended.

"Although jungle juice was far too potent for me, I never missed a Pavuvu soiree in K Company. These went on and on into the night. If it got too loud, a few shouts of 'knock it off you guys!' had a quieting effect.

"As I left the party and hit the sack one night, I listened to the continuing merriment from up the company street as a violent thunderstorm suddenly came up. The singing and music gradually stopped, and finally everyone drifted back to their tents. A machine gunner who lived across the street from me...came walking slowly through the mud singing softly and melodiously 'Home Sweet Home' to the accompaniment of rolling thunder. I could see him clearly in the flashes of lightning; he wore only his dungaree trousers and socks and was soaked to the skin. I was cold sober, and my only thought, as the torrent poured down, was that he would have a heck of a time washing all that mud out of his socks. On Pavuvu, where being 'Asiatic,' drunk or sober, was the condition common to all, his conduct didn't strike me as unusual or funny. I just thought what a wonderful thing clean, dry, socks were, and fell asleep."

On many occasions growing up, I or someone else in the family would be complaining about something, and my father would simply say, "I'm just happy to have dry socks."

If isolation and remoteness were the goals of 1st Division leadership when they selected Pavuvu for a training base, they achieved their objective, possibly to a degree that they hadn't expected or intended. Letters from home were crucial to maintaining contact with their lives before the war.

"Some evenings were devoted to letter writing. Each man made his own flambeau of a bottle of kerosene with a piece of rope or cloth forming a wick. Many made little writing desks out of a wooden box with legs nailed to them. The composition of love letters became a polished art with some of the men. It seemed to provide some relief from Pavuvu's overwhelming loneliness.

"The shout 'mail call' always brought us out into the company street on the double. The company clerk would call out the names,

and the man shouted 'ho,' and the letter was flipped to him. The men's faces always lit up with smiles when they received mail. It was the one thing to look forward to on Pavuvu. When mail call was over and the last letter was delivered, the lucky ones went back to their tents, struck a match to the flambeau, and read and reread their letters dozens of times. If a man received a letter written on scented stationary, he might allow his buddies to inhale a whiff if their comments were not obscene. The unlucky ones at mail call always had sad expressions and stooped shoulders as they headed to their tents."

Even though Pavuvu offered its share of austere living conditions, the men—even those like my father, who at that time had not yet been in combat—understood that things could be worse and bore the conditions with resilience. The 1st Marine Division, the Old Breed, exemplified discipline and esprit de corps. Despite rain, heat, mud, loneliness, and falling coconuts, they were not under fire, and they were not sleeping in muddy foxholes—yet. The tough discipline and training they underwent every day were melding them into an elite combat unit. That was the first reason, in my father's opinion, that they were able to handle things as well as they did. The second, he believed, was "**the age of the men**."

I had many conversations with my father in which he mentioned that the 1st Division in World War II was extremely young. He himself was twenty. He told me once of an NCO he remembered on Okinawa who was twenty-three, and he said they all referred to him as an old man.

"Twice on Pavuvu I was sent on working parties to the nearby island of Banika. Located there was a big Navy hospital, a Marine base depot, and numerous other rear echelon units. Everything was in sharp contrast to what we had on Pavuvu. I saw the camp of an army infantry battalion that had supposedly been in the mopping up action on Bougainville. It seemed positively luxurious. The tents all had wooden decks, electric lights, and housed four men, compared to the six to eight men per tent with coral gravel deck on Pavuvu. There was also a big, barbed wire compound where Navy nurses lived, but they only associated with officers.

"Most of us looked on a working party to Banika as a chance to get pogey bait [candy], or some other delicacy, or to trade souvenirs. On one of the trips I made to Banika six or seven of us were to load supplies on an LST drawn up on the beach, and then stay overnight on the ship.

"After our work was completed [nearly all the LST's crew were ashore on liberty], one of the men managed to locate an unopened crate of fresh oranges which we sneaked up on the bow of the vessel in the darkness. There, the little group of K Company men gorged ourselves on oranges as we looked out on the dazzling electric lights of Banika and talked about home far into the night. We felt like kings eating such a rarity as fresh fruit. We had that singular comradeship and mutual respect that is forged among combat troops.

"After feasting on oranges, we divided the rest and stuffed them into our pockets and ponchos for our tent mates back on Pavuvu."

I can imagine my father and his K Company buddies talking quietly on the bow of a landing ship tank on the beach of Banika in the warm darkness, the lights of the island in the distance, the chirring tropical night sounds, and the occasional booming echo down below them in the empty hold of the vessel.

"Toward the end of July, the training schedule and working parties loading ships began to pick up in intensity. Showers, screened mess halls, and heads had been built by then, and camp construction was almost completed. Nearly every morning after reveille, the company was put through calisthenics and then double timed around the regimental area. Pavuvu was too small for training out in the wide-open spaces, so we ran around the same area to avoid colliding with other units. In the early morning darkness, shadowy figures clad only in khaki shorts and boon dockers could be seen peeling from the column of trotting men each time it passed near the company area. There they would lurk in the shadows and reenter the column as it came trotting by for the last round.

"Night working parties became more numerous around this time to load ammunition and equipment down at the steel pier. Doping

off became a polished art and some men expended more effort in avoiding working parties than they did in work. If you could successfully dope off on a working party or physical training, you felt like you had tricked the system and retained a slight amount of freedom in a situation of rigid discipline.

"On my side of the K Company street, our line of tents were back to back with a line of L Company tents. We had a mutual agreement with the L Company men, a machine gun squad, in the adjacent tent to mine. At any time during off-duty hours that a K Company NCO came down our street yelling, 'Outside for a working party,' we would dash through their tent into the L Company street and out of sight.

"This was not punishable during off duty hours but, of course, was impossible during regular duty hours. It was understood that the L Company machine gunners could do the same when one of their NCOs was out rounding up a working party. It worked very well because the tent flaps were tied straight out and all you had to do was crouch down and move from one tent to the other. It was comical to see my tent mates sitting or lying around on their sacks cleaning weapons, writing, or reading, and suddenly six or eight men would come dashing through the ropes in the back of our tent. They would jump around our sacks and over our mortar which was kept set up near our center pole and out into the K Company street. There they would peep back through the rows of tents and return nonchalantly when all was clear. We would do the same, crouching and dodging around tent ropes, jumping over sacks and over their machine gun set near their center pole. Sometimes a man tripped over tent ropes in the rush, and everybody, including the unlucky one, laughed and guffawed.

"One of the most hilarious things I saw during my entire enlistment was an occasion when the men from both tents tried to escape through the other's tent simultaneously. On this occasion I was scheduled for guard duty, so I was not subject to being sent on a working party. I sat on my sack and enjoyed the comedy. When the NCOs in the K and L Company streets yelled, the men in both tents sprang to their feet, bent low, and dashed out the rear of their respective tents. It looked like two opposing football teams at the snap of the ball when the mortarmen and machine gunners dodged, collided, tripped, stumbled, and fell over one another in the scramble. Some got to their feet and escaped, but the irate NCOs collared enough for their working parties and yelled, 'Knock it off!' at our uproar of laughter.

"Sometimes we couldn't escape, and once, about fifteen of us, with an NCO in charge, were sent to the steel pier at night to load ship. We had been caught by the company top sergeant lounging comfortably and confidently in our tents after nearly all the other boys had gone to the movies. There was much grumbling as we were sent off, but no one ever argues with the 'top.' This group was prime for doping off, and we did, beautifully. The NCO in charge of us was a Texan and knowing that I had a saddle horse back home, he walked beside me and carried on a spirited monologue about mustangs and quarter horses.

"As we wound down the dark coral roads past the different battalions, I noticed fewer footsteps behind us. I knew what my buddies were up to and envied them for it, but those of us being addressed by our Texan were a captive audience. He became more and more engrossed in his subject. When we reached the steel pier the NCO ordered halt by a pole with an electric light hanging from it. His face was a study in puzzled astonishment when he turned and saw that his fifteen men now consisted of a working party of four men.

"'That bunch of meatheads, always dopin off—ain't worth a damn. Wait till I get back and report this...there'll be a large case of the kick ass!'

"About that time the officer in charge of the ammunition trucks parked nearby walked over and said, 'Who's in charge here?'

"'I am sir,' said our corporal, saluting smartly.

"'I thought they were to send me a fifteen-man detail, Corporal.'

"'Well, sir, uh, there's a problem, some of them guys must've slipped off,' he said weakly.

"'What's the matter with you? Can't you handle your men?'

"'Yessir, but I uh…'

"'Never mind. Have these men unload what they can by 2300 and don't let this happen again or you'll be losing your stripes!'

"'Yessir,' the corporal said.

"The Texan cursed endlessly but was helpless to punish the miscreants. When we got back to the company area everyone had hit the sack and all was quiet."

My father and his buddies were soon to be assigned to another type of working party. The significance of this would not be realized until later, but it was one they would never forget.

"Several of us were sent one day to an area where dozens of empty oil drums were stacked near a small generating steam engine. A sergeant said, 'OK you guys, uncap each of those drums in that stack and clean 'em with this steam nozzle. Then recap 'em and stack 'em in this stack over here. Do it right, and no doping off. I'll be back in a little while. Bear a hand now.'

"We began doing as he had instructed. In about half an hour one of the guys working with me stacking the drums stopped, mopped his brow, and said, 'Boy, what I wouldn't give for a cold beer right now.'

"I looked out at the sunlight dancing on the ripples on the bay and replied, 'Me too. Why do these drums have to be cleaned with steam?'

"'That's a damn good question, Sledgehammer,' answered my buddy.

"'The others came over, and as the sergeant was not in sight, we sat down in the shade of a palm and lit up smokes.

"'This steam don't get all the old oil outta them drums anyhow.'

"'Well, you know what they say—there are two ways to do everything: the easy way and the Marine Corps way, and the Marine Corps

way is the hard way.' In other words, there is a right way and a wrong way to do everything—do it right and you will avoid trouble."

Many times, as a teenager, when I would inevitably complain about a chore my parents assigned to me, my father used this time-tested logic. Although it didn't prevent my complaining, I always ended up doing as instructed.

"We concluded that steam cleaning oil drums was idiotic under the broiling tropical sun; it was just busy work, and so we might as well make it easy on ourselves. We reasoned that fuel for tanks and amtracs would do just as well in the drums before they were steam cleaned as after, so we did as little as possible.

"Finally, the sergeant came back and dismissed us; we returned to the company area and forgot all about it—until we were on Peleliu in 115-degree heat, and we received our first water ration after landing. Tank fuel hell! Those drums had been intended for our drinking water containers."

Even on Pavuvu there were morale boosters. Bob Hope had been touring the Pacific and making various stops to entertain the troops. When he and his fellow performers stopped at Banika, he was told that on the adjacent island of Pavuvu, the 1st Marine Division was training for their next battle and would soon be back in combat. He and his fellow performers came over to Pavuvu.

They put on a show that my father remembered for the rest of his life.

Throughout the seventies and into the early eighties, whenever Bob Hope was on TV, my father would sit down and watch. I remember one night very well; during one of his performances, they showed clips from various shows he had done for the troops through the years. When they showed black and white footage of Hope performing this show on Pavuvu, my father, sitting in a chair with Holley, our dachshund, in his lap, leaned forward excitedly at the sight of thousands of tanned young Marines laughing uproariously as a young Bob Hope performed on stage.

"That's Pavuvu!" he exclaimed. "By God, I'm in that crowd somewhere!"

In the spring of 1980, Bob Hope played in a charity golf tournament in Birmingham. It was the Charley Boswell Celebrity Golf Classic, and from 1974 to 1988 it was "hosted by Charley Boswell to benefit the Eye Foundation Hospital."[5] Bob Hope commonly served as honorary chairman and was routinely part of the event. My father reached out to Bob through his publicity people, telling him he was a 1st Division Marine who had seen him perform that day on Pavuvu.

Arrangements were made, and at a certain point during the tournament, my father and I were taken directly to where Bob Hope was seated, waiting to meet us. It's a cherished childhood memory: a warm spring afternoon, my father and me hurried through throngs of onlookers right up to Bob Hope's area. My father had his copy of *The Old Breed*, the division history with a picture of the Pavuvu event and a description, under his arm. Bob Hope shook his hand warmly and signed his name to the picture, and they laughed and reminisced about the Marines on Pavuvu.

"Bob, this is my son Henry," my father said.

I stepped up to where he was seated. He warmly shook my hand and cheerfully said, "Hi, Henry!"

After a few friendly parting remarks between my father and Bob Hope, we left.

---

5 "Charley Boswell Celebrity Golf Classic," Bhamwiki, updated November 15, 2020, https://www.bhamwiki.com/w/Charley_Boswell_Celebrity_Golf_Classic.

CHAPTER FIVE

Amphibious landing exercises were conducted several times a week on the beaches and inlets around the island away from camp.

There was a method to their training and practice landings, and the men realized they were nearing their next operation and that everything they were being taught was deadly serious business.

"Sgt. Johnny Marmet, a Guadalcanal veteran, was the top-ranking NCO in the mortar section. After landing, he sent us orders from the front line, usually 30-40 yards ahead, by walkie talkie or sound power phone, so we could lay our guns to cover the company's front. We then put out aiming stakes on his compass readings and stood by to 'fire' on his order.

"At this point during maneuvers a halt was usually called for the officers to confer. The reaction of the enlisted man was comical. He first pulled off his helmet, mopped his brow because it was always hot and muggy, put the helmet on the deck and sat in it—it being a comfortable bucket seat. He then took a long drink of tepid water from one of his two canteens, placed his weapon across his knees, lit up a smoke, and whipped out a magazine from pocket or pack, and lost himself in deep concentration.

"Comic books were a favorite on these occasions. While sweating officers hurried about the groves and conferred in little knots scanning maps, giving and receiving orders by walkie talkie and 300 radio, or sending runners hurrying to and fro, the infantrymen sat motionless on their helmets at five pace intervals each with his eyes

glued to his comic book. There we sat under the palms, America's finest, toughest assault troops, each lost in the exploits of Superman, Joe Palooka, Li'l Abner, or Mickey Mouse. When the order 'move out' came, comic books were hastily stowed, helmets donned, weapons shouldered, and reality returned—only, however, until the next halt was ordered. Then out came the comics again.

"I saw this day after day during maneuvers before Peleliu, and repeated months later during the maneuvers in preparation for Okinawa. Such an escape from reality was too good to last. We were told that disciplined Marines were attentive and alert during maneuvers—no more reading during breaks.

"When it came to digging in, only two men could work on a mortar gun pit at a time; it was typically around two feet deep and just wide enough for the gunner and assistant gunner to crouch in with the mortar between them. So, Snafu and I dug awhile and then were relieved by the ammo carriers in our squad. Pretty soon out came the comic books and those not digging began reading. An NCO said, 'Alright you guys, stow them books.'

"'But Sarge,' someone said, 'only two can dig at a time.'

"'So what,' he growled. 'Then the rest of you pay attention to how a gun pit is supposed to be dug.'

"'But how do you pay attention to two guys digging a hole?' someone whined. 'We all know how to dig a gun pit.'

"'Shut up, stow them books, and pay attention to the digging, or I'll put you all on report!' he shouted and stormed off through the grove. We obeyed orders, and the squad sat around watching the men digging and making cracks about the intellectual level of sergeants and how we were all learning a great deal about the science of picks and shovels."

The pettiness and silliness of this can be appreciated by anyone who has spent time in manual labor jobs or even corporate America, working for a boss whose intellectual level is less than impressive.

"The words 'chow down' were always greeted with enthusiasm; although we were usually issued K rations on field problems, it at least meant a break.

"Along with a canteen cup, I carried a large USMC issue metal spoon tucked in the cover of one of my canteens. The Ka-Bar served as knife and fork. Cans were opened with a little issue can opener with a blade and a flat metal handle. I always carried one on my dog tag chain."

In conversations my father and I had about his time in the Pacific, he would use the terms *K rations* and *C rations* frequently. I asked him what the difference was between the two. What I remember most about that conversation was that the C rations were canned, and the K rations had two cigarettes and toilet paper. Since he was never much of a regular smoker, cigarettes were great for trading to other Marines for things that he wanted.

"When in the field for several days duration we were issued C rations. These being canned, they weighed more than K rations but also provided a larger meal.

"Frequently, on field problems and in combat the order to 'get your gear on we're movin out again' was passed along before rations were heated sufficiently, and we had to eat them cold and on the move—always with much grumbling and cursing. The odor of wet rations always reminded me of canned dog food."

One of the characters my father came to know at this stage was Gunnery Sgt. Elmo Haney. I have some early memories of hearing about this eccentric but iconic Marine. When I was in the second or third grade, I wrote a short story, complete with childish illustrations (I wasn't much of an artist), and one of my fictitious characters was named Haney.

He was, in every sense of the word, the "Old Breed."

"He was absolutely obsessed with the desire to bayonet the enemy.

"In the afternoons after returning to the company area dog tired and soaked with sweat I would take off my gear and relax a bit before taking a shower. Not Haney; he went straight to the tent, donned

his favorite unofficial Pavuvu uniform consisting of cut off khaki trousers, leggings, and boondockers, and have personal bayonet drill against a tow sack filled with palm frond ribs at the end of the company street near my tent. Many afternoons I sprawled on my sack and watched Haney go through the evolutions of bayonet fighting, while men walked past him going to and from the showers. He was oblivious of them, and they were careful to stay out of his way.

"Upon completion of his bayonet drill, Haney returned to his tent, sat on his sack, and entered into the ritual of cleaning his weapons. Then he stripped, took up his towel, a huge chunk of caustic GI scrubbing soap and his trusty brush, and headed for the showers.

"Once I asked Haney about his bayonet technique. He was absolutely delighted and explained every detail with enthusiasm. I could see that he would have me out there with him every day if I appeared too interested, so I had to slip past him to the showers until he forgot about me."

While he wasn't blind to the eccentric nature of Sergeant Haney, my father also appreciated that Haney was a living manifestation of the legendary old corps and a source of historical knowledge.

"The boys got a little peeved at him sometimes, chuckled about his eccentricities, but admired his years of service, energy, and drive. Naturally, sea stories about anybody like Haney were inevitable. But in his case the truth was so much more bizarre than fiction that the guys had no need to improve on his exploits."

When the men received individual training with the flamethrower, my father was soberly impressed with what a horrific weapon it truly was. We talked about this many times.

As he succinctly summed it up for me, "We could not have taken Peleliu without flamethrowers."

In November of 2001, my wife and I took some of my father's uniform items and artifacts to the National Museum of the Pacific War in Fredericksburg, Texas. We spent a few days touring the facility and getting to know Helen McDonald, the curator of exhibits. Gracious and accommodating, and deeply appreciative of the fact that I was making it possible for the museum to display artifacts that had belonged to Sledgehammer, she made it possible for me to operate the museum's WWII flamethrower late one afternoon after the living history demonstrations were over. One of the living historians took me out to a replica concrete Japanese bunker. I shouldered the tanks, pointed the nozzle at the bunker, and pressed the trigger. With a massive whoosh, in the early evening twilight, red flame squirted out of the nozzle, and I felt the searing heat on my face and arms. Afterwards, my clothes reeked of diesel fuel.

In World War II, all Marine officers had codenames. This was to prevent some overeager private from yelling, "Hey, Captain," or "Hey, Lieutenant," at night or in the middle of a firefight—thus giving away the identity of his officers, who would, of course, then become immediate targets of the Japanese. K Company's commanding officer was Capt. Andrew Allison Haldane from Methuen, Massachusetts—code name Ack Ack.

My father's first encounter with Ack Ack Haldane took place when the company was struggling along the muddy roads during one of Pavuvu's late afternoon thunderstorms after a day of training. In the gloomy twilight, with the rain pouring down, the men were tired, cold, and forlorn. As my father struggled to keep his balance in the muddy ruts made by tank treads and trucks, he saw a big man walking briskly along from the rear of the column.

It was Captain Haldane, and he began talking to my father. He exuded charisma and seemed genuinely interested in this young replacement from Mobile, Alabama. My father remembered that as they talked, the gloom seemed to disappear, and he felt a glow inside. Ack Ack said that it wouldn't rain forever, and soon they could get dry. As Captain Haldane moved along the column, he struck up similar conversations with the tired, wet men.

My father remembered Ack Ack as the finest and most popular officer he ever knew. He always spoke of him with reverential respect.

As July turned to August, the division was engaged in one amphibious maneuver after another. The commanding general, Major General William H. Rupertus, badly injured his ankle debarking from an amphibious tractor during one of these maneuvers. The accident caused a painful injury that put him on crutches, and my father saw it happen.

"During one amphibious problem I saw the Division commander and his staff debark an amtrac nearby to observe our movements. When the general hit the beach, he fell and twisted his ankle. He was only about thirty yards away from my squad when this happened."

One afternoon, following another amphibious maneuver, my father and his buddies saw a grim reminder that even in training, a Marine could lose his life.

"Late one afternoon while returning to the company area after debarking from the amtracs at the steel pier, we were halted to allow a vehicle to pass along the road. The usual talking, joking, and banter suddenly faded into silence as the ambulance jeep slowly moved past us up to the road. On a stretcher was a Marine's body covered by a poncho down to about midway between the knees and ankles. His name, unit, or how he was killed in training I never knew. But that grim stereotype—the stretcher, the poncho-covered form, the leggings, and the boondockers—was to become a common, everyday sight in combat.

"'What you reckon they'll tell his folks back home?' queried a man near me.

"'Don't know,' remarked another. Each of us kept his thoughts to himself as the company moved out silently."

As the invasion date of the next operation for the division neared, discipline and training both picked up in intensity. Unfortunately, much of the discipline bordered on harassment. The modern term for this would be *chickenshit discipline*. My father, however, had an aversion to coarse vulgar language, so in his manuscript he referred to it as "chicken discipline." While he swore pretty frequently, he generally avoided what we call "four letter words." The only time I ever heard him use the word *shit* was in a conversation I overheard between him and another gentleman who I believe was a Vietnam era veteran.

I don't remember how old I was but I had walked over to the university campus, close to our house, where my father taught biology. As

I approached the open door of his office in Harman Hall, I could hear him inside talking to someone.

He wasn't expecting me, and right before I walked in, I heard him say, "He got the shit knocked out of him by a close shell hit." I remember stopping in my tracks. He and I had talked so many times about his war experiences, but he had never said anything like this to me before, and I realized that in that moment he was talking to someone about a shared experience that I could never understand. As I walked on into his office, he looked up at me, and instantly his demeanor changed. "Hey, Big Shot!" he said happily. (This was the nickname he had always called me.) He then introduced me to his interlocutor, and we had a pleasant afternoon chat.

"It was the type of discipline the men referred to as 'chicken,' seemingly unnecessary orders or changing of orders while we were in the process of carrying them out.

"For example, clothing inspections became more frequent. Every item of clothing had to be clean and unpacked from my sea bag, folded, and displayed on my bunk while nervous NCOs rushed in and out of our tents checking and rechecking each man's bunk.

"Any errors resulted in our NCO being bawled out, and he then bawled out the offender. After they left us with an 'at ease, carry on,' we repacked all our clothing issue and waited for the next event.

"During one such inspection a new lieutenant fresh from the States paused at the rear of our tent obviously puzzled at the faint gurgling sound that was coming from the ground just behind the tent. The veteran company officer raised his eyebrows, gave a slight smile, and moved the new officer along, knowing there must be a can of jungle juice 'working' in its hiding place there.

"Inspections of the troops in full combat gear became more common also. During one of these just before Peleliu, Ack Ack demonstrated his usual compassion by ordering 'Company, fall out, platoon leaders continue inspection within tents,' as a Pavuvu downpour came up suddenly. After our platoon leader finished inspecting us in our tent and gave us 'at ease' and left, we sat on our bunks

and watched with disgust as the martinet who was the skipper of the company next to us inspected every man's weapon and gear, his men at rigid attention in their company street in a torrential rain.

"'Thank God for Ack Ack,' remarked one of my tent mates.

"'Amen,' we all said."

By early September, the harassment and chicken discipline had ramped up in intensity, and the men reached new levels of frustration and exasperation. The austere and primitive living conditions of a lonely island like Pavuvu exacerbated this. While some of the newer men grumbled mightily, the seasoned veterans realized that it was all part of the plan to keep the troops in fighting shape.

My father and I talked about some of this, and he told me how the Marine Corps wanted them angry, frustrated, and mean as hell before they were about to go into combat.

He spoke often about rear echelon and service troops. He realized that these men were doing their jobs and that as combat infantrymen, he and his buddies depended on these men greatly, as did the entire war effort. But it was inevitable that there would be feelings of frustration, if not outright bitterness, toward these troops and their more desirable living conditions. This was a major factor later, on Peleliu, when some of these men would venture up into the frontlines looking for souvenirs, such as Japanese swords, rifles, or bayonets.

"The living conditions of men in the rear areas looked pretty good to us as infantrymen. It all tended to widen the gulf of understanding between combatants and noncombatants. What they took for the necessities of life we looked on as luxuries. If we weren't tired, wet, muddy, hot, cold, thirsty, hungry, or under fire, we felt well off. I griped as loudly as any about our living conditions and discipline."

It was only later, after surviving the brutal conditions of Peleliu and Okinawa, that he realized these deprivations equipped and prepared them to deal with the "**psychological and physical shock and stress**" of deadly combat.

One of the most important things a man could have in this environment was friendship. As the invasion of Peleliu loomed nearer, my father saw this in stark clarity.

"Just prior to Peleliu a mysterious replacement joined the company. This man was quartered by himself in a pup tent in the grove near my end of the company street. His head was shaved and a guard with a loaded Thompson submachine gun stood watch over him in shifts day and night. The prisoner went out on some training exercises, but when we returned to the company area to remove our gear, shower, chow down, and enjoy a few hours of leisure before sack time, he returned to his pup tent and guard. There he took up a heavy pickax and pounded away at a palm stump and sweated away the weary hours until taps. He was, naturally, the source of much curiosity as well as pity.

"'What's the story on that guy?' asked a buddy of mine.

"'I know a guy over at battalion who claims he overheard the colonel say this fella got a general court marshal and was sentenced to hard labor for striking an officer aboard ship coming from the States.'

"'Well, whatever the hell he did they damned well threw the book at him, that's for sure.'

"'Yeah, the word is nobody is supposed to talk to him, and if you do it's your ass.'

"'Well, I pity the poor kid, but I reckon I'll steer clear of him,' came the reply.

"Thus it went, and I never knew any more about the mysterious replacement and never knew anyone who did. I did not see this tragic unknown after D Day on Peleliu. Someone told me he was killed shortly after we hit the beach. As far as I knew, he never had the blessing and benefit of the one and only thing that made life bearable to a man in a combat unit—a friend."

CHAPTER SIX

Map 4: Peleliu, 1944
Main US advance
Front line, with date
Mangrove swamp
PACIFIC OCEAN
PELELUI
Kongauru I.
Ngesebus Island
Akarakoro Point
Amiangal Mt.
Hill 80
Kamilianlul Mt.
Ngabad I.
Umurbrogol Mt.
Umurbrogol Pocket
Ngarekeukl
Ngardololok
Asias
20 Sep.
18 Sep.
17 Sep.
16 Sep.
15 Sep.
22 Sep.
1 Mar. RUPERTUS
1 Mar.
5 Mar.
7 Mar.
Beach White 1
Beach White 2
Beach Orange 1
Beach Orange 2
Beach Orange 3
Beach Purple
Ngarmoked I.
N
2000 yards
2000 metres

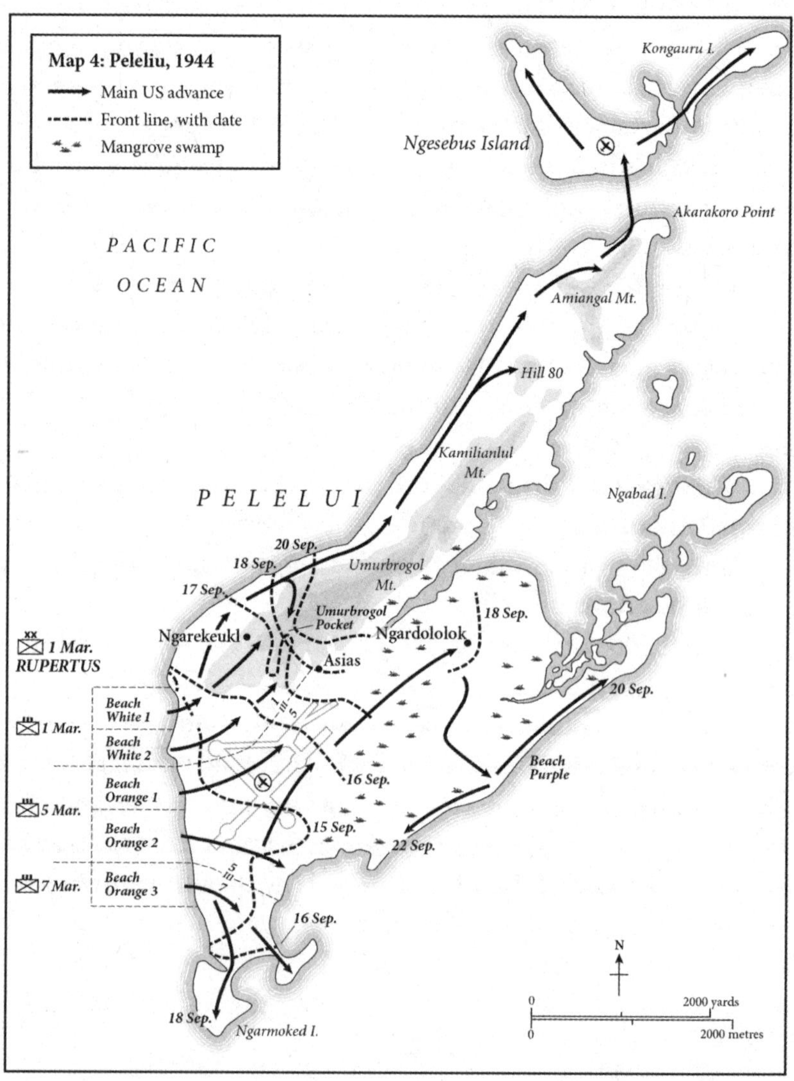

On August 26, 1944, K Company, along with the rest of the 1st Marine Division, completed training on Pavuvu and boarded ship to head out. Each rifle company that was slated for the assault waves of their next operation—meaning the first ones on the beach—would load onto an LST (landing ship, tank) that would also be carrying the amphibious tractors the Marines would ride into the beach. These machines were down in the tank deck of the LST. K Company would be aboard LST 661.

My father and his fellow mortarmen felt fortunate when they discovered that they would berth in a troop compartment in the forecastle with a hatch entrance onto the main deck. Many of the other platoons had to accommodate themselves on the main deck under and around LCT 858 (landing craft, tank) and the other landing boats and gear that were stowed there.

They weighed anchor and sailed out of Macquitti Bay toward Guadalcanal, where the division would conduct more maneuvers in the Tassafaronga area. Several days were spent on this additional training. As for Pavuvu, without a doubt no one was sorry to leave it, but compared to where they were headed it was a paradise. Sadly, many would not come back.

Even though the area around Tassafaronga bore no resemblance to Peleliu, every effort was made to improve all aspects of their operational readiness.

"Marine and Navy fighter planes bombed and strafed the areas inland to the landing beaches and lent an aspect of grim realism.

"During the landing exercises our officers on LST 661 found that if we were ordered below to the tank deck to load into our assigned amtracs before the machines had warmed up their engines, we all became violently nauseated from the exhaust fumes. The big exhaust fans opening from the tank deck topside might ventilate the tank deck adequately for Sherman tanks and their crews, but not for open amtracs packed with men. Fortunately for us, D Day at Peleliu we were sent below only after the air in the tank deck was cleared of heavy fumes. Some of my buddies who were in other LSTs later told me that they weren't so fortunate and went ashore at Peleliu thoroughly sick from fumes."

I remember every time we started the car in the garage, my father insisted on making sure the garage door was open and regularly reminded us how deadly exhaust fumes could be. I can only imagine a fully loaded tank deck of an LST, choked with the exhaust of so many amtracs and their seven-cylinder, 250 hp radial engines.

But it wasn't all serious. They indulged in some lighter moments.

"A three-foot iguana fell from a tangle of vines, and we tried to catch the big lizard by surrounding him in an open grassy area. He escaped by running between one of the men's feet and climbing into a tangle of brush. The man swung his bayonet and yelled and jumped straight into the air when the big lizard headed for him—ironically, he turned out to be the only man I ever knew who insisted that he was not afraid in combat. None of us ever believed him."

At last, training on Guadalcanal was completed, and final preparations and combat loading were finished. The assault companies of the division, embarked in thirty LSTs, hoisted their hooks on the morning of September 4 for the 2,100-mile journey to what would be my father's baptism of fire.

"Our average speed was about 7.7 knots. The faster troop transports, seventeen of them and two LSDs [landing ship dock—averaging 12.1 knots] left on the 8th."

Although only a couple squalls interrupted an otherwise uneventful voyage, that did not mean there weren't moments of excitement.

"During one dark, rainy night a buddy and I were assigned to a bow 40mm gun tub during the midwatch (midnight to 0400) to aid the sailors in standing watch. Radio silence had been ordered between ships in the convoy, and we were to phone the bridge if we sighted anything. We [had to] keep a sharp lookout so that we kept proper distance from the LST off our bow. We had to phone the bridge of our ship twice when the dark bulk of the stern of the LST in front of us suddenly appeared through the rain-drenched darkness. The engine room responded immediately each time, and our ship slowed to avoid ramming the one ahead of us. I was glad when my watch was up and we could go below, get a cup of hot joe and hit the sack."

Although my father didn't remember the first time they were told the name of their objective, they had been given some rudimentary information about the island. Although there is some discussion on this now, Peleliu was deemed necessary at the time to secure General MacArthur's right flank as he advanced through the Southwest Pacific toward his ultimate and sacrosanct goal of returning to the Philippines. They had seen models and maps of Peleliu in their training and knew that it had a large and heavily used airfield. In fact, in the best of times for the Japanese Empire, Peleliu was a hub of naval aviation, serving as a vital link between the area of the Philippines, approximately 500 miles to the west; Yap, roughly 240 miles to the east; and Truk, Japan's main central Pacific naval base, 1,089 miles from Yap.

US strategic planners feared that Japanese airplanes, flying from Peleliu, would pose a threat to MacArthur as he advanced toward the Philippines. In fact, after a series of US Navy carrier plane strikes in the Philippines and the Palau islands earlier in 1944, it was evident that Japanese air power was not as strong as originally thought. For this reason, Admiral Halsey suggested that the invasion of the Palau islands, which included Peleliu, should be cancelled. Adm. Chester Nimitz, Halsey's boss, removed any possibility of this, however, by stating that since the invasion convoy was already underway, it was too late to call off the operation, a move that could have stoked Japanese morale by enabling them to claim that they had defeated an American invasion attempt.[6]

The Palaus form the westernmost part of the Caroline Islands. They consist of several large islands, including Babelthuap and Koror in the north and Peleliu in the south, about an hour-long boat ride away. Over a hundred smaller islands are sprinkled along the chain. Except for Angaur—which lies about six miles south of Peleliu—and a couple of small atolls in the north, all the Palaus lie within a coral reef.

When I visited Peleliu in 1999 for the fifty-fifth anniversary of the battle, I flew into Babelthuap and was then driven to a hotel on Koror, where most of the approximately eighteen thousand Palauan islanders

6 Richard B. Frank, email message to author,7/26/2023.

live. At that time, the only way down to Peleliu was by boat. Once on the island itself, I met up with a top-notch group of historians, experts on the battle, and family members of veterans, including my friends Col. Joseph Alexander, USMC; Eric Mailander, an expert on the battle who had visited six times previously; Nick Russo, whose father had fought at Peleliu in F/2/1; and David Watkins, whose father, Bruce Watkins, was a platoon commander in E/2/1.

This was the fulfillment of a dream. I remember telling my mother when I was a teenager that I wanted to go there. What drew me wasn't just the thought of seeing this tiny island where my father fought; it was also the knowledge that the island was still littered with the rusted detritus of the battles that had been fought there in 1944.

At that time, all I knew of Peleliu was that it was small and remote. Only a few hundred locals lived there, and from what we had been told, they usually did not venture up into the steep cliffs, caves, and rocky recesses of the Umurbrogol Mountain, collectively known as Bloody Nose Ridge, where the bitterest fighting took place. It was said that at night the wind whistled and moaned through the canyons and caves of Bloody Nose Ridge, and the islanders believed that ghosts prowled the old battlefield. Whether that was true or just local legend passed down through the years I never learned, but it certainly added to the mystique of the place. I had to go see it for myself.

We didn't have to venture far inland from the landing beaches to see unexploded hand grenades, artillery shells, and the remains of fighter planes, amtracs, and tanks. One of these tanks was a Japanese Type 95 that had been knocked out in a swamp just inland from the northern landing beaches. Over the years the swamp had dried up. The only parts of the tank still visible were the tracks and bogey wheels on one side—still charred black from the flamethrower that had helped knock it out.

Peleliu is only about six miles long from north to south and two miles wide, and it's shaped like a lobster claw with two elongated extensions of land. The southern section, flat and wide, was where the Japanese had constructed the airfield. Hangars and some buildings lay on the north side of the airfield. This southern section projected eastward from the flat ground and transformed into several coral islets and mangrove swamps.

The northern section or arm of the island was longer, also extending eastward. It was dominated by the Umurbrogol Mountain ridge system, which was, in fact, a set of five coral ridges in parallel. Apart from the airfield, most of the island, including the ridges, was covered with thick jungle scrub growth before the battle. There were also some areas of palm trees and open grassy areas, but the thicker vegetation obfuscated the actual nature of the terrain. To gather as much photoreconnaissance of the island as possible, the US Navy sent in submarines to take photographs. Unfortunately, they did not show the true nature of Peleliu's topography. Aerial photos were no better.

"The submarine *USS Seawolf* in late June 1944 had obtained photographs that gave some information about the island. In July the submarine *USS Burrfish* attempted to send in small underwater demolition teams by rubber boats at night."

Underwater demolition teams, or UDTs, were the precursor to our modern Navy Seals.

"Because of bright moonlit nights, Japanese radar, and constant air and sea patrols, the sub had to remain submerged in the area for two weeks. One dark night a five-man team paddled ashore on one of the beaches to be used in our assault. These incredibly brave men obtained valuable information. However, data on the depth of the water, type of shoals and bottom was not gained until UDTs examined the area under protection of naval gunfire just prior to the landing."

In the Peleliu operation, the 1st Marine Division's attack plan was a combination of both problems and lessons learned from previous amphibious operations—notably Tarawa and Saipan. This was because of the natural coral reef all along the beachhead (six hundred to seven hundred yards), which could not be negotiated by LCVPs. Troops, equipment, and supplies would have to go across the reef in amtracs. The Army's 81st (Wildcat) Infantry Division was assigned to the invasion force to capture Angaur, the little island immediately south of Peleliu.

Total 1st Marine Division strength when they departed Pavuvu was 16,459 officers and men, not counting the reinforcements. Of these, only about 9,000 were combat infantrymen. The division's three infantry regiments were the 1st Marines, 5th Marines, and 7th Marines. The artillery regiment was the 11th Marines.

It was believed by the division's top brass that the ratio of the attacking force would be close to the desired mark of roughly three to one.

"There wasn't any way to form a complicated plan to seize an island 2 x 6 miles in size. The only thing up for choice was which beaches to use. The southwestern side of Peleliu was a jumble of inlets, coves, and swamp, choked with mangroves and heavily studded with Japanese defensive positions. The northern beaches were impractical because less than a few hundred yards inland was the high ground of Umurbrogol Mountain.

In fact, the Umurbrogol contained more than five hundred heavily fortified and interconnected caves that would enable the Japanese to exact horrendous casualties on the Americans.

Invasion planners had decided that the division's three regiments would land abreast on the western beaches along a front that was approximately 2,200 yards long. The landing beaches were assigned color-coded names. From left to right, the 1st Marines would land on White Beaches 1 and 2, the 5th Marines would land in the center on Orange Beaches 1 and 2, and the 7th Marines would land to the right on Orange Beach 3. My father's battalion, the 3rd of the 5th Marines (3/5), was to land on Orange Beach 2. Their mission was to push straight across the island to the eastern shore. There was always at least one unit held back in reserve from the main landing force. For D Day on Peleliu, this was 2nd Battalion of the 7th Marines (2/7), about one thousand men.

"None of the Division or III Corps brass [the III Amphibious Corps was composed of the 1st Marine Division and the Army's 81st Infantry Division and was commanded by Gen. Roy S. Geiger] apparently realized the unwillingness of our division CO, Major General William Rupertus, to use Army troops to help us on Peleliu.

This developed into outright refusal to use Army help later on the island."

The commander of Japanese forces on Peleliu was Col. Kunio Nakagawa. His forces consisted of approximately ten thousand troops of the 14th Division—hardened and experienced veterans from the fighting in Manchuria.

"In addition, there were elements of the 53d Independent Mixed Brigade and also Japanese Navy Guard Force units and some service and labor troops. Many of Nakagawa's men were seasoned combat veterans of fighting in North China and Manchuria. They were indoctrinated with the strict Bushido code of the warrior and took pride in their fighting ability without regard to personal safety. Some of the noncombatant naval forces and Korean labor troops were less fanatical, but the combat troops effectively forced them to resist us aggressively, and few succeeded in surrendering."

The Japanese defensive strategy at Peleliu was a preplanned "defense in depth." They had intelligently profited from lessons taught them by Marines in the Solomons, Gilberts, Marshalls, and Marianas.

Earlier battles across the Pacific in these islands had seen the Japanese defenders resort to massed Banzai charges. While certainly terrifying to face, they always hastened victory for the Americans because of the huge casualties the Japanese sustained.

"Here, they were to conceal their strength and dispositions, resist to the last ounce of strength and extract the maximum cost in blood from their opponents. By July 1944, the Japanese high command had realized the futility of trying to annihilate the U.S. invaders on the beach. American assaults against well-fortified beaches had succeeded because of the devastating preparatory bombardments. Therefore, complete reliance on beach defenses was futile. After the invasion of Biak by MacArthur's soldiers during the New Guinea landings, the Japanese commander had not thrown away his troops in suicidal Banzai counterattacks. On the contrary, he had them dig in, forcing the U.S. soldiers to knock them out individually. The

fighting dragged on for weeks and denied the use of the airfields to American forces in time to assist in the invasion of Saipan."

So, effectively, Biak was the first evidence of the new "defense in depth" Japanese doctrine. Historian Edward Drea discovered that this tactic was developed during that battle, not preplanned.[7]

At Saipan, the Japanese had intended to stop the Americans on the beach and concentrated their forces accordingly. This led to severe fighting for the first several days, including Japanese counterattacks with tanks, but all this failed. Their remaining forces just did the best they could for the rest of the battle, aided by the difficult terrain.

"The Japanese had prolonged the fighting on Saipan for about three weeks, although there they finally did stage a Banzai attack which cost them 4,311 dead and ended the campaign a couple of days later.

Thus, Peleliu was to see "defense in depth" employed by the Japanese as an established doctrine.

With its topographically complex ridge and cave system, Peleliu afforded limitless opportunities for defenses like those Nakagawa was ordered to construct. The result was a maze of mutually supporting positions in ridges, caves, crevices, and ravines that had weapons of all calibers and types.

In 1999, as we explored a cave and its field of fire onto a ravine in the Umurbrogol, my friend Eric Mailander, with a map in one hand, explained the potential for the Japanese inflicting casualties on US troops trying to reduce such an objective. "This Nakagawa guy was a tactical genius!" he declared.

"The beaches were sown with mine belts extending inland 100 yards to impede U.S. landing forces. The approaches to the beaches were dotted with offshore obstacles. Anti-tank ditches were built and covered by weapons in casemates and pillboxes. Barbed wire was strung along the beaches. Artillery was entrenched in all dominating features of the terrain and zeroed in on the beaches. On flat terrain

7 Frank, email message to author.

inland, well camouflaged pillboxes and other defenses were placed. One steel-reinforced concrete blockhouse contained sixteen mutually supporting automatic weapons.

"If we survived the landing, and consolidated the beachhead, the Japanese had very effective measures planned for the defense of Peleliu. They were ordered to fall back to previously prepared positions covering the ground between them and the beachhead. If we knocked out these positions, last ditch resistance would drag on from the extensive natural crevices and cavities and the well-prepared cave positions in the Umurbrogol ridges of northern Peleliu. This ridge system consisted of the most incredibly rugged terrain encountered by Americans in the Pacific.

"The highest elevation reached 300 feet, and tunnels were separate or connected in networks with hollowed out rooms six feet high and ten feet across. There were rooms for food, storage, ammunition, medical supplies, and living quarters."

D Minus 1

On September 14, 1944, LST 661 and the rest of the convoy carrying the 1st Marine Division glided to a stop in the calm waters near Peleliu. The men felt a change in vibration through the vessels' deck plates as their engines shut down. After evening chow, my father and Private Steele, the young man who had agreed to carry a flamethrower back on Pavuvu, leaned against the deck rail of their LST and talked quietly about what they would do after the war.

They watched as the red ball of the sun sank below the horizon, and my father reflected on how Pacific sunsets were even more beautiful than the many he had seen on Mobile Bay. He wondered if he would live to see another one.

"Poor Steele, that was to be the last sunset he would ever see. I have always been glad for his sake that it was so beautiful."

As the evening grew darker and the vessels around them melted into the gloom, a voice came over the loudspeaker: "Now hear this, now hear this. All troops lay below to quarters. All troops lay below to quarters."

My father and Private Steele headed to their compartment on the forecastle. A work party went off to draw rations and ammunition. A lieutenant came in; he looked tense and worried as he gave the men at ease.

He told them that the fighting would be rough but fast—four days, maybe three. He exhorted them to keep their heads down going in on the amtracs, and when they stopped on the beach, to get out and away from the amtracs as fast as possible. They had to stay out of the way of the landing craft because they would need to get back out to pick up more troops. He also reminded them that tanks would be coming in behind the infantry. As if it needed to be said, the lieutenant told them that the Japanese would be plastering the beach with mortars and artillery. With a nod to the mortarmen, he told them to make sure they had the canister containers of high-explosive rounds untaped and in their ammo bags ready to use when they were called on to deliver fire on the company front.

He concluded by telling them to make sure their canteens were full and to have plenty of salt tablets. "Hit the sack early," he said. "You will need the rest. Good luck and carry on."

After the officer left the compartment, the men sat on their racks, smoking and cleaning their weapons. They also mused about the expectation that Peleliu would be a short battle. Most felt confident because the division leadership seemed convinced that this would be a short operation. One of the consequences of this overconfidence was that many of the news correspondents in the invasion fleet chose to not even go ashore.

There were thirty-six correspondents in the convoy, and many never went ashore at all. Only six stayed through the early phases when victory was far from certain.

"Of the latter group, one was killed. In my opinion this is one of the primary reasons why the campaign on Peleliu is almost unknown and certainly not understood by many historians."

Even though the morale of my father and his fellow Marines was excellent, and they were physically toughened from months of training, they fervently hoped it would not be a protracted battle.

"There were skeptics among us though. 'Who is he tryin to snow?' growled one veteran. 'Remember that potbellied congressman back in 1941 who said the Navy could blockade Japan and the war would be over in two weeks? He was all fouled up, wasn't he?'

"'You said that right,' answered another man."

One of my most prized possessions is the combat pack that my father carried throughout the entire war. When I was growing up, he kept it (along with many other items of equipment he carried) on the top shelf of the closet in his study. Many times, I would stand on a stool and bring it down to look at it. It was made of stiff canvas, not that large, and it still bore the remnants of dark green paint that he had daubed on it for extra camouflage, as I remember him explaining to me. His name was stenciled in light green along the bottom strap. Once, when I was about ten or eleven, I asked if I could carry my schoolbooks in it "because the guys in my class might think it's kinda cool."

"No, Big Shot, I don't think so," he answered patiently.

Marines traveled light. In most cases, their packs contained only the bare necessities, like their poncho, socks, extra ammo, and rations. They also had writing materials, toothpaste and toothbrush, and family photos, along with some letters.

"Orders were to cut off the address on our envelopes in case they fell into enemy hands. This was a joke because Tokyo Rose announced that our division was going to hit Peleliu."

Headgear consisted of a steel helmet with camouflage cloth cover, herringbone twill cotton dungaree jacket and trousers, canvas leggings, and field shoes or boots known as boondockers. My father also carried a green fatigue cap in his pack. This cap I still have, and it is displayed proudly in my den along with his other things.

He also carried a pistol belt with a pouch containing a combat dressing, his two canteens, a compass, and a pouch with two carbine clips.

"My web pistol belt did not have the pouches stitched on it for clips of M1 Garand ammo as was worn by riflemen."

On his belt he also carried his Ka-Bar in its sheath, a grenade hooked over it by the spoon, and a heavy bladed knife like a meat cleaver sent to him by my grandfather, to be used for chopping open the crates that 60mm shells were packed in.

"This was a very useful tool, because the heavy crates with wire braces around them were hard to get into in a hurry."

Hanging on the wall above my desk is his Ka-Bar and leather sheath, mounted to a wooden plaque.

Since the carbine that he carried did not have a bayonet lug, he did not carry a bayonet. Even though entrenching tools would be useless on Peleliu because of the sharp coral, he carried one attached to his pack. His buddies were dressed the same as he, with different cartridge belts and weapons.

Since my father was a mortarman, he carried a carbine. Some carried .45 automatic pistols. He himself would carry a .45 later after my grandfather sent him one, but that would be after Peleliu.

"Riflemen carried the M1 Garand rifle, bayonet, and cartridge belt with 8 round clips in the pouches. Officers usually carried a .45 automatic, carbine, or .45 Thompson submachine gun. Their packs were slightly smaller from those of enlisted men, and they usually carried a large canvas map case and field glasses. No insignia of rank was worn by officers or noncommissioned officers in a rifle company. All officers were addressed by their code or nickname.

"Medical Corpsmen carried a pistol or carbine and a pouch with medical supplies. They wore no red cross or insignia distinguishing them as hospital corpsmen but looked simply like Marine infantrymen. The Marine Corps had learned on Guadalcanal that any mark of rank or medical specialty was sure to draw attention from Japanese snipers."

Eventually the dim overhead bulbs in the troop compartments were turned off, and the men hit the sack. My father thought of home and family as he tried to get to sleep in the hot compartment. As he told me, he wondered, "Would I be able to do my duty; would I be wounded or killed?"

Despite his pounding heart, he fell asleep reciting the Lord's Prayer.

D Day, September 15, 1944

Before dawn, an NCO came into their compartment and barked, "OK, you guys, hit the deck!" The men got up and pulled on dungaree trousers and jackets and their boondockers. They shaved and headed to chow. This consisted of steak and eggs, a tradition learned from the Australians.

"Just as I started to leave the galley and go topside, it was announced that Tokyo Rose had sent a radio message saying something like, 'Hello to you American boys all over the Pacific. I want to announce that the 1st Marine Division, the brave conquerors of Guadalcanal and Cape Gloucester, is preparing to invade Peleliu Island. The heroic troops of the Imperial Japanese Army, however, have a big surprise for the Marines.'

"We all looked surprised. Then we cursed and laughed at Tokyo Rose. 'No doubt now the Japs know where we are headed,' said the man next to me. Usually, Americans in the Pacific took her announcements with skepticism, but not this time.

"I returned to the forecastle compartment. All over the ship K Company men were loading their weapons and squaring away their gear, and the ship's crew was manning battle stations."

As dawn began to break, many of the men went topside to the weather deck. There they gathered in little groups, quietly talking, smoking, and gazing out across the calm sea at the thin outline of Peleliu. My father sought out Cpl. Merriell A. "Snafu" Shelton of Louisiana and stayed close by him. He was the gunner on their mortar and a veteran of Cape Gloucester. The veterans knew what to expect, and this was comforting to the new men.

"The pre-assault bombardment commenced with ships and planes joining in. The island looked like a low elongated object on the sea. Smoke began to appear from shells and bombs exploding on it. Planes were bombing, firing rockets, and strafing with increased intensity. The big battleships were firing thundering salvos from their big turret guns; cruisers and destroyers joined in with their smaller calibers. The LST's crew were dashing about with their helmets and

life jackets on and manning their anti-aircraft guns. We stood around like spectators at a big show.

"As we watched a plane fly over the island a few puffs of smoke appeared from Japanese anti-aircraft guns. I thought how lucky those pilots were if that was all the fire they had to face. Suddenly, the plane turned into a flaming red ball and went down out of sight. Someone near me said, 'Jesus, did you see that? Them poor flyboys, they didn't have a chance to get outa that plane.' I got weaker in the knees and felt sick and prayed silently for the crewmen of the plane."

This plane was most likely a US Navy Grumman TBF Avenger torpedo bomber, which had crews of three—pilot, radioman/bombardier, and turret gunner.

As the squawk box blared out for the men to gear up and stand by, my father and Snafu hurried to their compartment to get to their bunks and get their gear on.

LST 661 was a hive of noise and activity: The 40mm and 20mm gun crews were busy firing their weapons; the empty shell casings were clattering on the deck around them or passing noisily through feed chutes; the deck plates vibrated as down in the tank deck the amphibious tractors were starting their engines. Snafu had their 60mm mortar (all forty-five pounds of it) slung over his shoulder, and my father shouldered his carbine and heavy mortar ammo bag.

They made their way down a ladder, encumbered by their personal gear and weapons, to the tank deck where NCOs were directing the men to each of the amtracs. The machine he and his squad mates were ordered to board was an older LVT-2—with no drop tailgate ramp (like the newer LVT-4)—so they would have to climb over the sides, exposing them to enemy fire. In my father's case, it would almost be fatal.

The huge bow doors yawned open, and the exit ramp went down. The amtracs' engines were roaring and belching exhaust fumes. Exhaust fans overhead in the tank deck were whirring, trying to clear out the fumes through vent stacks topside. Glaring daylight streamed into the tank deck through the open bow of the ship as the first amtrac lurched out and clanked down the sloping ramp.

"Several tractors went out and our turn came. My squad began its tiny role in the whole series of carefully synchronized steps that made up a complex amphibious assault. I had put my ammo bag on the floor of the tractor between my feet, and we were all occupied with trying not to fall down. The tractor hit the water, and then it floated free and settled like a big duck. We relaxed a bit and looked up at the swabbies on the ship's gun tubs and along the rail. Some of them waved and so did some of us. I would gladly have traded places with any of them.

"A small boat came alongside, and an officer yelled something to our driver, and he headed us along with the other tractors from the initial LST launching line about 6,000 yards from the beach to the rendezvous area to form the line of departure, which was about 4,000 yards from the beach. The intensity of the bombardment was rapidly increasing as we slowly (4.5 knots) churned past ships of all descriptions firing all their heavy weapons at the island. Dive bombers were making continuous runs over the beach. We arrived at the rendezvous area and the amtracs formed up into waves. Each was under the command of a wave commander, bearing the wave number on a flag, in a fast open boat."

Air support during the Peleliu landings was provided by no fewer than eighteen US Navy aircraft carriers: four fast carriers (CVs, the largest), four light carriers (CVLs), and ten escort carriers (CVEs).[8]

"Out in front of us was a line of armored amtracs, next was the first wave of troops, and then our line of amtracs making up the second wave of troops. Behind us other waves of tractors formed. Further back Higgins boats from troop transports slowly circled with the supporting waves of troops who, for the trip over the reef, would transfer to the amtracs that had taken us in. In front of the line of armored amtracs were various craft firing on the beach.

8 Robert Sherrod, *History of Marine Corps Aviation in World War II* (Combat Forces Press, 1952), 255.

"The most awesome sight of all from the standpoint of sheer massive power were the great battleships with all their monstrous guns protruding from each turret, firing 14" and 16" salvos."

My father said, "It was like a thunderclap every time one of those went off."

On a trip to the *USS Alabama* in the early 1970s, as my father, brother, and I walked around the gun turrets on the deck, we marveled at the massive barrels of those sixteen-inch guns. "We would see those shells in groups of three arcing overhead," he said as held up his hand with his thumb extended. "The shells looked about the size of my thumb as they went over."

The odors of explosives and diesel fuel permeated the normally clean salty air. They had to shout to be heard over the gunfire. The big vessels shifted to the flanks of the amtrac formations. They sat waiting for some agonizing moments for the final signal to start toward the beach. Finally, the navy wave commander gave them the signal, their amtrac driver revved the engine, the treads churned water, and they started in.

"Everything in my life was prior to or after that awesome moment."

They were the second wave ashore.

"The LCI rocket boats, mortar boats, and Patrol Craft moved ahead of the first line of amtracs almost to the reef. The fleet began firing white phosphorous shells to screen the amtracs from Japanese observers."

As the preceding two waves got close to the reef, close shell hits began dropping in and raising massive geysers of water.

"I saw a large shell explode off the port quarter of a Patrol Craft to our front. As the geyser of water leaped up the navy gun crew of the 81mm mortar on the port side hit the deck as one man but were immediately back on their feet firing away."

"When that first shell hit," my father told me, "I realized my place was back home with my mother." The island, as he described it, seemed "**marked by a continuous sheet of flame from left to right for the entire length of the beach, backed by a thick wall of smoke.**"

It wasn't white smoke, like what rises over a campfire, but angry black smoke, the kind that comes from exploding shells and burning vehicles and structures, and maybe from things hit and burning that weren't meant to burn.

"I remember thinking, My God," he said, "none of us will ever get out of that place alive."

"The lieutenant motioned for us to get our heads down as the Japanese shells began to hit closer. There was a violent jolt as the amtrac lurched upward and out of the water. We were thrown violently against each other and the sides of the amtrac. The treads crunched and scraped against the rough coral as we moved out of deep water onto the reef. The gunner on our tractor started firing his .50 caliber machine gun, but I could hardly hear it. I felt detached and forlorn as I watched the empty shell cases fall on the steel floor. Something rattled above the din of the bombardment, and I hoped it was the falling brass cases. I looked up at the gunner, but he was ducking down and away from the Japanese machine bullets which were rattling and pinging against our amtrac's armor. We moved off the coral into an area of deep water, and the tractor floated again."

My father looked toward the front of their amtrac from his position near the rear and saw their lieutenant reach for something. It was a half-pint whiskey bottle.

It all seemed unreal. But it was real, and it was happening to this compassionate young man from Mobile, Alabama, who loved riding his horse back home, his family and dogs, and going on hunting trips with his father. The lieutenant held the bottle out to my father, but he refused it.

They took a close shell hit to their right front. As their engine stalled, they jerked to the left and bumped into the rear of another amtrac, which was either hit or stalled. They sat, the tractor heaving up and down in the turbid water. The Japanese gunners were getting the range on them. My father looked forward and could see the driver wrestling frantically with the control levers trying to get it going again. Shells were shrieking in faster and faster. Sgt. Johnny Marmet leaned toward the driver and shouted something. They heard the reassuring surge of the engine and got going again as water from shell explosions drenched down on them.

What Sergeant Marmet said to the amtrac driver was made clear by my father. "Johnny stuck the muzzle of his tommy gun into the driver's cab," my father told me, "and yelled, I was close enough to Johnny, I could hear him yell, 'You get this goddamn tractor movin' again or I'm gonna kill your ass!'"

"We continued to be thrown roughly about as the amtrac alternately crawled over rough coral and floated free in deeper water. Only an amtrac could have made such a trip. The fact that it wasn't knocked to pieces by the coral was proof of its durability."

As the waves of landing craft moved closer to the beaches, the Navy dive bombers and fighter planes took their strafing and bombing further inland. At the same time, the naval gunfire lifted off the beach area and moved inland. Shell fragments moaned through the air.

"A Georgia man was next to me in the rear of the tractor. Ski was a Gloucester veteran and had answered many of my questions concerning what we might expect on Peleliu. He was as anxious as I was and peered over the edge of the amtrac as we jolted across the reef. I nudged him and looked up at him. He leaned and yelled, 'The first wave's on the beach. Don't see no Japs.' A shell hit nearby, and Ski jerked his head down. At least they had not come up out of their pillboxes and met the first wave on the beach with bayonets, as some feared.

"I peered over the side of the amtrac. I could see two armored amtracs parked on the inland edge of the beach firing their 75mm guns. Men of the first wave were up and down, scurrying and dodging among the shell bursts. Some lay still. Beyond the beach in the direction we were headed was a sort of wide defilade which was possibly a tank trap. We had been told that this landmark would be on our left flank when we landed, but we were now headed directly for it. Due to the heavy fire, our driver had veered farther to the left than scheduled.

"'Get down!' yelled the lieutenant as machine gun bullets cracked overhead. I jerked my head down."

A Marine yelled to stand by. My father felt for the reassuring weight of his weapons and gear and made sure his chin strap was buckled. Their amtrac crawled out of the water and up the sloping beach, its engine roaring and track grousers draining water. The men in the back struggled to keep their balance as it lurched to a stop. An NCO yelled the inevitable "Hit the beach!"

"We piled out over the sides as fast as we could," my father said. "Snafu went over first, and I was right behind him; I planted both feet on the left side of the amtrac to leap out, and just as I did I remember this line of white tracer fire—the Japs used white tracers—came right past my face. At eye level, it almost grazed my face."

He continued, "Well, I jerked my head back like a turtle, and then I fell down onto the beach. When I fell off the side of the tractor I just fell onto the sand in a heap—mortar ammo bag, canteens, carbine, Ka-Bar—it was certainly not the way John Wayne hit beaches."

He wasn't the only man to have difficulties hitting the beach; Pfc. Bill Leyden, a K Company rifleman and later one of my father's closest friends, recalled, "The amtrac went up the beach, and lurched back, and at the same time the ramp fell down [Bill was in an LVT-4 with a drop tailgate] and we all went rolling right out, with sweaty faces, because the heat was unbearable, and rolled right into the sand."

The reference to iconic movie star John Wayne was to be expected; so often while growing up, when my brother and I would be watching a John Wayne WWII movie, my father would stop and chuckle as he passed through the room. Inevitably he would say, "The Duke'll straighten 'em out."

As my father tried to untangle himself and his gear after the near miss from the Japanese machine gun burst, he felt a strong hand on his shoulder. As he told me, "A corpsman came crawling over because he thought I was hit, and he put his, he put his hand on my shoulder to roll me over, and I thought 'Oh my God, it's a Nip,'...because they would sometimes come out of emplacements right after amtracs landed if they could, so I tried to get my Ka-Bar out, and luckily I couldn't, because I guess I would've carved up the corpsman."

By this time the Japanese were starting to respond to the assault with a heavier volume of return small arms fire and counterbattery fire. The air was thick with whirring pieces of shrapnel, dirt, and debris. Behind my father and the other men who landed with him, their amtrac spun around in a cloud of exhaust smoke to head back out for more troops. He began to move off the beach.

In his words, "All up and down the beach shells were going off, amtracs were getting hit on the beach before they could let the guys out. You could see guys falling all along the beach because of the extremely heavy small arms fire, and artillery and mortar fire."

He saw bodies being blown into the air. Out on the reef he saw some Marines trying to get out of a smoking amtrac. The Japanese had the range on them and bracketed them mercilessly with machine guns and mortars. Some of the men were getting hit and falling into the water. My father told me how helpless he felt seeing their buddies trying in vain to help them in the knee-deep water.

They moved inland. "We got in off the beach as far as we could go," I remember him saying, "and hit the deck in the sand, and just before I hit the deck, I happened to look down, and my right foot missed no more than by six inches a Japanese mine that was in the form of a five-hundred-pound bomb buried in the sand, and it had a metal pressure plate on the top of it. A little way down the beach I saw a boy step on one, and he just, it just atomized him, he just disappeared."

It seemed at that point that the Japanese gunners were more concentrated on the incoming waves than on the troops moving into the jungle scrub beyond the beach.

"I ran over to where R.V. [Burgin] was standing looking to our front and flopped down at his feet. 'You'd better get down!' I yelled as bullets snapped and cracked all around.

"'Them slugs are high, they're hittin' in the leaves, Sledgehammer,' he answered nonchalantly without looking at me.

"'Leaves, hell! Where are the trees?' I yelled back at him.

"He started, looked to right and left. Down the beach, barely visible, was a shattered palm and nothing near us was over knee high. Burgin hit the deck with haste. 'I must be crackin up, Sledgehammer. Them slugs sound just like they did in the jungle at Gloucester, and I figured they were hittin' leaves,' he said with chagrin.

"Off to our left a little distance two Marines were throwing grenades and firing Tommy guns into the fire port of a well-camouflaged, low bunker that I had run right past and hadn't even seen."

Having survived the viciously opposed landing and first stages of the battle on the beach, my father suddenly craved a smoke. He called out to his buddies for one. My father took some good-natured ribbing, especially from Snafu Shelton, about his previous opinions on smoking, which he took with his characteristic good humor.

"Tanks began landing with the fourth wave, and I marveled at the crews as they opened their hatches, got out under fire, and removed waterproofing tape from around the turrets as though on maneuvers. The tanks had a rough time, too, crossing the reef. The Japanese fire was so heavy that over half of the Division's thirty tanks suffered from one to four hits during the ten minutes they required to cross the reef."

More and more Marines were piling in behind the troops already on the beach, but my father and his fellow K Company men were still not seeing anyone to their right, as they should have.

"Underwater obstacles and heavy Japanese fire had caused some of the amtrac drivers to steer to their left and land 3/7 troops behind us instead of on our right flank.

"Fortunately, the Japanese were either not aware of it at the time or too dazed by the pre-assault bombardment to attack us there. If they had, it would have put the Division's entire right in a precarious position.

" K Company 5th Marines and K/7 finally got disentangled. Casualties were reported. Steele was missing. He was reported last

seen with his flamethrower on the beach moving on a Japanese pillbox with some men from the 7th Marines."

As they moved into the scrub growth inland from the beach, a Japanese machine gun, concealed in the scrub, opened fire.

"I watched with admiration as one of our light machine gun crews to my right rear opened up on the Japanese machine gun. The men of our machine gun crew were out in the open, flat on their bellies, with no hole for protection, trying desperately to locate the enemy by the source of his tracers. Another Japanese gun joined in, and he was a little to my left front. His first burst sent slugs snapping just overhead."

My father found a vacant shell hole and crawled in. Enemy mortars began dropping rounds all around them.

"I was midway between dueling machine guns. The lieutenant dove for my hole but found it big enough only for one, so he flattened himself on the coral with his face about a foot from the edge of my hole. He had the most forlorn look, peering enviously at me, and his mustache twitched each time a shell went off with a crash."

Virtually their entire unit was pinned down under extremely heavy enemy fire. No movement was possible. Smoke and dust filled the air. This barrage was one of the first my father endured just after the landing.

As he gritted his teeth, sweating and praying, he pitied the lieutenant who was lying exposed on the flat ground. Even though the officer was a Cape Gloucester veteran, he seemed as terrified as my father or any of the other men experiencing their baptism of fire.

"Finally, the company moved forward. The riflemen moved ahead as skirmishers, and my mortar squad moved along in dispersed formation behind them ready to set up and give mortar fire when called upon."

At this point they were starting to see casualties headed back to the beach, where they would be evacuated out to one of the ships lying offshore.

As K Company moved through the sniper-infested scrub inland from the Orange Beaches, it was imperative to be on the alert constantly. When they halted in an open area, my father saw his first dead enemy soldiers.

A couple of fellow Marines showed up and began checking them over for souvenirs. As they went about this methodically, the mushroom steel helmets of the Japanese soldiers clanked and rattled after the Marines removed a folded flag and then tossed the helmets on the coral.

This image of a combat-hardened Marine casting aside a Japanese helmet reminds me of one time my father and I went to a gun show. We came to a table displaying, among other items, a Japanese steel helmet. I don't remember what the price tag on it read (it was exorbitant), but I well recall my father's reaction. "Good God!" he exclaimed incredulously. "We used to kick those damn things around like tin cans!"

"In the blue sky directly over us a seaplane, acting as spotter for naval gunfire, flew slowly back and forth parallel to our front. The plane frequently banked and turned so the man in the rear cockpit, the observer-gunner, could fire his single .30 caliber machine gun at Japanese positions out in front of us. He meant business, but the tat-tat-tat of his one .30 cal machine gun was almost comical to us after watching the roaring dive bombers pouring out rockets, bombs, and thousands of .50 cal machine gun bullets from their multiple guns. The fellows around me watched the float plane and laughed heartily.

"'Give 'em hell buddy!' someone yelled.

"'Boy, he's having a ball, ain't he?' said another with a grin.

"It felt good to laugh after what we had been through, and we kept it up until the order 'get your gear on, we're movin' out!'

"We shouldered our loads and moved into the thick, scrub forest again, heading in the direction of the airfield at about [1030]. The riflemen ahead periodically ran into Japanese defensive positions, and we stood by to give mortar fire support if needed.

"I had never seen plant growth like the scrub forest before. It reminded me of the thick scrub one would encounter in dry regions of the western United States.

"Visibility was limited to a few feet. We lost contact with I Company, 3/5 on our left, and with 3/7 on our right. It was equally hard keeping contact with the platoons of our own company. There were no landmarks in the scrub we could use to get oriented. Japanese

snipers kept up constant harassing fire. The crack of their rifles and whine of ricochets off the hard coral and trees was unnerving. An occasional shell fell nearby in the scrub.

"Fortunately, most of the communications men were able to wade ashore and join the battalion in the afternoon. My squad moved slowly through the dust covered, thick growth, the men keeping about a 5-pace interval. At such times you felt terribly lonely, and there was a strong temptation to sidle up to your buddy so you could watch for snipers together and exchange a few comforting remarks.

"'Don't bunch up, keep your five-pace interval,' the NCOs kept saying. As a buddy sardonically summed it up to me, 'Sledgehammer, where there are two or three gathered together, there are always Jap mortar shells.'"

The temperature was climbing, and so was the humidity. The men sweated profusely. They ate their salt tablets and took frequent drinks of the water in their canteens.

"Shortly after noon the attack was stopped by a Japanese line of mutually supporting pillboxes and trenches with automatic weapons.

"The word came, 'Mortar section, stand by!'

"I moved nearer to Snafu so [that] when he set the gun up, I could drop the shells down the tube. The firing up ahead became intense. A platoon of tanks moved past us to support the company. We received no orders to fire as the Japanese small arms snapped and cracked overhead. Our tanks were firing their machine guns constantly and working over the enemy with their 75s. We waited impatiently, anxiously listening to the heavy fire fight.

"'Why the hell don't they let us open fire and help the rifle platoons? There are bound to be plenty of targets we could hit,' I remarked to Snafu.

"'It's them damn officers, Sledgehammer. None of 'em know how the hell to use mortars, so we sit on our cans and don't do a damn thing while the company catches hell.'

"With the aid of the tanks, the Japanese positions were knocked out, but contact with 3/7 on our right was lost."

There followed a period of disorientation for my father, who was not sure where K Company was located.

"This was not unusual for an enlisted man in the confusion of the battlefield."

The bottom line was that the inability of 3/5 to make contact with the 7th Marines on their right created a gap that could be exploited by the Japanese if they counterattacked at the right place. My father and his squad mates were ordered to move up into a clearing, where they joined the rest of K Company.

"Nearby a Sherman tank was parked, and I watched a sweaty, dirty Marine stand beside it catching water in his open mouth as it poured from a bullet hole in a five-gallon water can strapped on the side of the tank. So like, yet so unlike, a child at a water fountain. It struck me not as amusing but as pitiful.

"I saw several rifle pits nearby, each with two dead Japanese sprawled in them."

Around that time Japanese mortar and artillery fire began to increase. The intensity indicated a probable enemy counterattack. Most of it went over them to their rear.

They moved to the edge of the scrub a short distance away. It was around 1650 and as they looked out across the airfield toward Bloody Nose Ridge, they could see vehicles moving amid clouds of dust.

My father told me that he "looked at Snafu and said, 'What are those amtracs doing out there at the base of the Jap ridge?'

"He said, 'Hell, you idiot, those aren't amtracs, they're Jap tanks!'

"Well, I mean my blood turned to ice water, because I didn't want anything to do with a Jap tank."

American Shermans took them under fire.

This was, in fact, a well-coordinated armor/infantry counterattack by Colonel Nakagawa consisting of seventeen Type 95 Ha-Go tanks from the 14th Division. However, the Japanese tanks with their quarter-inch armor and 37mm guns were no match for the heavier American M4 Shermans of the 1st Marine Tank Battalion and their 75mm guns.

My father and Snafu got the order to set up their gun behind them across a trail. Word came of a possible counterattack.

The men had the utmost confidence in their officers and NCOs, but with the lack of contact with other units and the "rumbling chaos" of the day's events, as well as the ever-present threat of snipers, my father admitted to a feeling of being lost. As Snafu set up the 60mm mortar, he readied an HE shell from a canister in his ammo bag.

"A couple of the ammo carriers got more shells ready to pass to me. Our observer across the trail with the riflemen yelled back a fire order and Snafu sighted the gun in the direction given, leveled the sight bubbles, and called the range and charge to me. I grasped the shell in my left hand and pulled the safety pin to arm it."

As Snafu yelled the fire command, my father exulted that they could now provide fire support to the company.

He raised a shell to drop it into the mortar tube. Suddenly a burst of machine-gun fire swept by my father's hand.

"I jerked my hand down and Snafu impatiently yelled 'Fire!'"

A Sherman tank fired its 75mm off to their right rear. My father could see it through the hot, hazy air in a clearing behind them.That shell hit close on the same trail they were on. The next thing they heard was a Japanese 70mm field piece from that spot returning fire on the Sherman tank. Once again, he tried to drop the 60mm shell down the tube of their mortar, and once again the machine gun opened up on them. As the tank and the Japanese field gun fired at each other, they realized that the tank was mistaking them for Japanese, and they could be hit by friendly fire.

"The men across the trail were, of course, ducking the same machine gun fire, but I had the uncomfortable feeling that the gunner had me singled out, because he fired every time I raised up.

"'We're pinned down by that tank,' someone yelled from the crater."

Someone across the trail called for the mortar to be secured.

"With relief I put the safety pin back on the nose of the shell. I saw an NCO directing a man who had volunteered to contact the tank to move to our left and then back to the tank. He crawled off.

The tank obviously thought we were Japanese infantry along the trail with the field gun.

"We hugged the hot coral and waited apprehensively, each moment expecting the tanker to start blasting away at us with that deadly 75. Finally, the word was passed, 'All clear.' Our volunteer messenger had made it and saved our lives."

The firing from their left finally let up—the Japanese counterattack had been broken. My father lamented the fact that, because they were pinned down by the Sherman tank, their mortar had not contributed at all. After the tank had knocked out the enemy field gun, it secured its 75mm and clanked off to another area. My father and his buddies went down the trail to get a look at the Japanese gun that been dueling with the tank. Its crew lay dead around it.

"Just as the men set about field stripping the Japanese dead the order came, 'K Company move out! Let's go, you bunch of souvenir hounds!' growled a sergeant.

"'Where is the guy that saved our hides by contacting that tank?' asked a man near me.

"'A sniper got him,' answered an officer. 'Poor guy, he made it to the tank and had to climb up on top of it to talk to the crew because the outside phone was knocked out."

Sherman tanks had a telephone mounted to the back of the tank so that infantrymen could communicate with the crew inside.

"'The tankers said that about the time they unbuttoned the turret the Nip sniper hit the guy in the leg. He fell off the tank but climbed right back up and told the crewman we were from 3/5. The sniper hit him again and killed him.'

"We were all saddened by his death and agreed that he certainly had probably earned the Navy Cross by sacrificing his life to save so many of us. I had known the man, although not well.

"He was easy to spot in the company on D Day, because he wore a mottled, camouflaged dungaree jacket and not the green herringbone type worn by the rest of us. To top it all off, he actually

discarded his helmet and went ashore through that fire storm wearing a felt campaign hat!...

"The Marine campaign hat with its large bronze globe and anchor emblem was, sadly in my opinion, to become the trademark of the post WW2 era D. I. But, to us, during the war it symbolized the Old Corps."

In later years my father bought one of these hats, complete with a large bronze Marine emblem pinned to the front. In colder weather he frequently wore it when he was out in the yard with the dogs.

Since the two battalion's flanks were not in contact, they had been abreast of each other on the same trail, but no one knew it.

"What I know now is that most of the heavy Japanese shelling prior to the tank attack passed over and to the rear of my company because we were so far forward and on the same trail as the Japanese field gun. By about 1600, 3/5 had pushed three to four hundred yards ahead of the 7th Marines on our right, and the 7th was firing on our battalion. From my observations we were still under fire by them when the Japanese tank attack struck the Division line to our left."

The veterans were hoping for a banzai attack, but the coordination and discipline of Japanese movements across the airfield were superb.

"When they attacked, the Marines poured it on them; the Japanese infantry was either wiped out or withdrew. The tank drivers firewalled their throttles and raced at the Division lines, fortunately right where most of our anti-tank weapons were concentrated. Our Sherman tanks, artillery, infantrymen with bazookas, and even a Navy dive-bomber tore up the Japanese tanks so completely that the exact number could not be determined. A couple overran our lines but were knocked out anyway. I saw the beginning of all this action when the Japanese tanks first moved out from the ridge and barracks area across the airfield. We were then ordered to repel a counterattack and became pinned down by the Marine tank behind us.

"A tired, sweaty runner hurried by us with his helmet tilted back on his head and nervously clutching the leather sling of his M1 rifle slung over his shoulder.

"'What's the hot dope?' asked a mortarman.

"'It ain't good! Nip barrage knocked out battalion CP—CO got hit. Some guys killed and wounded. Ain't made contact with the 7th Marines yet!'

"He hurried on, picking his way through debris and scrub, to find our company CP We looked gloomily at each other.

"We moved and halted aimlessly through the scrub in dispersed formation, dodging shells and sniper fire while the officers tried desperately with faulty radio contact to reestablish contact with other units."

The battalion at this juncture late in the afternoon of D Day was effectively lost. This had to be rectified before nightfall.

"We came across little knots of Marines from different units. All looked haggard and tired. Some I recognized from boot camp or infantry training. Inquiries about various mutual friends were the main topic of conversation. It was depressing to see how many of us had already been hit that day.

"We continued moving and halting until about dark, when we were ordered to prepare to dig in for the night. At that time all three of the battalion's companies were still separated in the growing darkness, so the word was passed for us to prepare for defense from attack from any direction. Entrenching tools began to clink against the rocky ground."

We had a WWII entrenching tool out in the garage when I was growing up. Recognizing what it was, I asked my father about it. Although it was not one that he had carried but rather one he bought at an Army Navy surplus store at some point, we did talk about the importance of digging a foxhole in combat. He specifically referred to Peleliu and said, "That damn coral on Peleliu was so bad—there was no digging in most of the time. About all you could do was pile rocks and logs around you."

"Each man was told by an NCO exactly where to dig in, so we couldn't just search around for a good hole. The Guadalcanal and Gloucester veterans were apprehensive about the company's position

but didn't say much. However, the usual air of confidence we newer men associated with them seemed lacking.

"It had gotten quite dark when suddenly an order was passed along: 'Get your gear on, we're moving out. Knock off that chatter. Keep a five-pace interval and don't lose contact with the man in front of you.'

"'"Good God! Are you nuts?' exclaimed someone in the darkness. 'Any Marines that see or hear us are bound to think we're Nips and open up on us.'

"I followed Snafu as we began to move slowly along in extended file through the hot darkness. Barely audible was his grousing and grumbling in his distinct accent about the stupidity of a whole Marine rifle company moving around at night. As the self-appointed tactician and military analyst of the mortar section, he seemed more disgusted than afraid."

My father said many times that whenever Snafu was displeased with a situation and felt that it could be better handled, he would inevitably say, "They need to get some more damn troops up here!" As my father told me, "He was usually right."

"The only sounds in our area were our boondockers crunching on the coral, the gentle slapping of a bayonet scabbard against some man's leg, and the sloshing of the tepid water in my canteens. Occasionally, a man tripped on a log or limb and cursed softly. This was always followed by 'Knock it off!'

"We could hear firing as an occasional shell passed overhead, and there we were groping along in the darkness. When we moved through open woods, I could just make out the dark forms of the men plodding along ahead and behind me. Up ahead, star shells from our ships began to appear in the sky over the airfield. They burst with a muffled 'pop' and a bright flare suspended from a parachute illuminated a considerable area with an eerie greenish light."

"The scrub thinned out as we moved along and finally reached the edge of the airfield. The chalk white coral reflected the pale light

of the night sky and little groups of K Company men preparing to dig in. Johnny Marmet came by and said, 'Snafu, dig in your gun here and stand by to register in, on the double!'

"We threw down our gear, broke out our entrenching tools, and commenced digging the gun pit. To our relief we found that the site was composed of crushed coral that was not solid rock, and we were able to actually dig in—a rare bit of luck on Peleliu. It was hot work, and I became drenched with sweat.

"'I'm going to take ten, Snafu,' I said.

"'Take ten like hell, Sledgehammer. If the Nips commence shellin' us, you'll wish this damn hole was ten foot deep.' This put new energy into me, and we soon finished the approximately one-and-a-half-foot deep gun pit. Once, as I glanced up, I noticed three officers about a dozen paces from us studying a map with a tiny flashlight.

"'Hey Snafu, who is that square jawed guy?' I asked. Snafu glanced at the group and said, 'That's Lew Walt! Hey you guys,' he called to the mortar section men digging in nearby. 'There's Lew Walt over there. He must be squaring' away the lines.'

"The boys began to discuss Col. Walt's well-known exploits while he was CO of 3/5 during the fight for Aogiri Ridge [renamed Walt Ridge] on Cape Gloucester.

"'I figure if Lew Walt moved us out of that jungle and out here on this runway, then everything's squared away like it ought to be,' Snafu said confidently.

"Farthest away of all Col. Walt located K Company. We were about a hundred yards southwest of I Company, or three hundred yards south of the airfield, to which he ordered us to move and tie in with I Company on our left and 3/7 on our right.

"The three companies had been in the thick scrub about a hundred yards apart. It was about 2300 when K Company reached the airfield.

"Although Japanese infiltrators were all over the place that night, no counterattack hit the lines in our area.

"I longed for Pavuvu. The three-hundred-yard night move to the airfield seemed awfully long to me, but our K Company officers were reoriented by then.

"I could see a dark, low line of trees against the skyline to the south and east. Our mortar section ammo carriers were dug in, two men per hole, around the gun pit some yards out as security for the gun if Japanese slipped past the riflemen, also dug in two men per hole, forming the first line."

It was good to have experienced veterans around. This instilled a sense of security and confidence in the new men who were learning on the job despite their months of excellent training.

"I kept Snafu busy answering questions about the various noises around and over us since he was a Gloucester veteran. He simply answered my questions and gave me direct orders regarding the operation of the gun.

"While 3/5 had been groping about in the jungle and finally moved onto the airfield, we could hear periods of heavy firing to the north in the 1st Marines' sector, out on the airfield, and to the south. All this thunderous bedlam resulted from enemy counterattacks which Marines stopped cold. Shortly after dark the Japanese had hit the line where the 1st and 5th Marines tied in, with infantry and two tanks, but both the tanks were destroyed.

"Our battalion was extremely vulnerable, but things did not heat up for us until later in the night. Infiltrators gave us trouble most of the night. Two counterattacks were beaten off by 3/5 in the early morning hours. These came from the south and were aimed at reducing the 5th Marines' salient stretching across the airfield. At the time all these attacks were marked by heavy firing."

With the gun pit dug and the 60mm mortar registered in, my father and Snafu could take stock of their situation as their first night on Peleliu wore on. They drank the last of the water in their canteens. The 1st Division had taken heavy casualties that day, and many veterans said the fighting so far was as bad as anything they had seen.

"The beach head was not as large as the high command had planned. Casualty figures were grim from any perspective."

As the night wore on, shells continued to periodically arc over their position.

"Our artillery, the 11th Marines, had emplaced some 75mm guns to the rear of our regiment and had joined the ships' guns in harassing fire against the enemy. Japanese fire was increasing too, and as we crouched peering out into the ghostly light of the flares, Snafu methodically identified each sound as U.S. or Japanese, caliber, and often whether the weapon was nearby or far from us. It was amazing how often he was correct.

"It was confusing to me, but I learned rapidly. Most men developed this ability to identify sounds encountered in combat.

"Enemy artillery shells came in screaming or whistling. The smaller the caliber the higher the pitch. Our 75s went 'swishing' over on their deadly mission, joined by big naval shells which rumbled along like locomotives in the distance. Enemy mortar shells, mostly the big 81mm and 90mm, emitted an almost inaudible, soft 'wissh-shh-shh' as they approached.

"Mortar shells were almost upon you without warning. The sound of the explosion seemed to be double and began with a grinding and crunching noise like some demon clawing its way to freedom from inside the shell, followed by a loud, dull BANG. Steel fragments rushed out and tore through the air with a whirring, ripping sound that caused even the most stout-hearted to cringe. That terrible murmuring voice of an incoming mortar shell, so insidious, seemed like the ghostly summons of some witch to enter oblivion. Each shell seemed to say to me, 'maybe next time."

One of my favorite Snafu stories when I was growing up was the way Snafu would curse contrasted with how my father would pray. He said, "The worse the shelling got, the louder I would pray, and the louder Snafu would cuss."

"Even the bravest souls I knew admitted that a barrage could induce one to seek cover and protection.

"The crackle of small arms fire and the bang of grenades added to the racket D Day night. Over in one area a few rifle shots would be joined by a machine gun and the bang of grenades, then another, and then more rifles as it spread along the line. Often the firing sputtered itself out as quickly as it began, but it frequently grew in intensity and spread, joined by mortars and finally our artillery swishing overhead. Then I could hear some fear-strained voice shout 'Corpsman.'"

A man commented on the intensity of the Japanese fire in that area, and Snafu responded that they must be prepping for a counterattack.

"I heard later that the Japanese did just that, but they were detected before getting as far as the airfield, and our artillery broke them up.

In the early morning light, word was passed that they had to move out and attack across the airfield.

"Many of us had no water, and ammunition supplies were low. We hoped supplies would come up before the attack. We were thirsty, and we could not go much longer without water."

A concentration of heavy machine-gun fire swept over their gun pit.

"First, I distinctly heard three separate shots—crack—crack—crack—as the bullets passed over, quickly followed by the report of the gun. 'That's a Hotchkiss [Japanese Hotchkiss-type heavy machine gun],' said Snafu as we ducked our heads. No sooner had he uttered the remark than the gun fired a long burst and tracers streaked over us, and the slugs cracked as they went over, not more than a foot above ground level.

"Whether those Japanese heavy machine gunners were laying down harassing fire supporting another counterattack, or whether they actually observed our position by the muzzle flashes from our mortar or saw us by the light of the star shells, we couldn't know."

My father knew that as soon as this machine gun fire ended, they were going to have to prepare to attack across the airfield. The thought of this filled him, and all the Marines who would have to do it, with dread.

CHAPTER SEVEN

D Plus 1—September 25

In the murky light of dawn, the temperature quickly began to rise. Men began asking about water.

"It was reassuring to see our friends dug in around us by the daylight instead of the eerie light of the star shells. Their illumination had been a blessing throughout that dreadful night though, and it probably discouraged large scale counterattacks by the Japanese."

The order came to move out, and they squared away their gear. A buddy called out that they had found a well. Several men, including my father, rushed over to check it out.

"A large log with short branches on it slanted from the upper edge to the bottom."

Just as my father lifted his helmet to take a drink, a corpsman ran up saying that the water could be poisoned. There were groans of frustration.

They headed back to their positions as the order came to have their gear on and stand by. At that point, water, rations, and ammo reached them. The water was in five-gallon cans. One of my father's buddies helped him pour some into their canteen cups.

"It just so happened that we had been together on that detail assigned to steam out the oil drums on Pavuvu."

The water in their canteen cups was brown from rust residue and stank of oil and fuel. It was practically undrinkable, but it was all they had.

They moved into the jumping-off position for the airfield attack.

"I passed a Marine machine gun position in a company of 2/5 that had killed about fifteen Japanese during a pre-dawn counterattack.

The dead Japanese were strung out in front of the gun, and all had one or more disc-shaped mines tied to their bodies. The Japanese closest to the gun position had an unexploded grenade in his right hand.

"'Thanks to our flares and star shells I managed to see this bunch and rack 'em up before they rushed us in the dark and set off those mines,' the gunner told me.

"'Let's go Sledgehammer,' someone yelled.

"I passed a small crater with a man in Marine battle dress sitting in it with a small portable typewriter on his knees. We halted nearby, and I watched in admiration as the correspondent typed furiously away, with shells whistling over and bursting with increasing frequency in our area."

Once they were in position, they hit the deck to wait for the preparatory barrage on the area across the airfield and the distant hills. It was a tense time because they knew that as soon as it ended, they would have to move out.

"The Japanese shelling of all the 5th Marines' sector prior to our attack got a direct hit on the regimental command post situated in a big abandoned Japanese trench. Several high-ranking officers were casualties. The much-admired Maj. Walter S. McIlhenny, who had been CO at Gloucester, was severely wounded and evacuated."

Louisiana-born McIlhenny's name was heard often around our house growing up. He retired from the Marine Corps in 1959 as a brigadier general and later founded the McIlhenny Company, which made Tabasco sauce. My father and General McIlhenny, who wrote the foreword to *With the Old Breed*, had many late-night phone calls during those years.

After lying prone on the hot coral for what must have seemed an eternity, an officer shouted, "Let's go!" Four battalions—from left to right, 2/1, 1/5, 2/5, and 3/5—moved out in dispersed formation.

The Umurbrogol Mountain system bristled with heavy weapons and Japanese observers who could call mortar and artillery fire down on the Marines without mercy. My father, running and crouched as low as possible, could see men moving ahead of his squad.

"I had noticed heat waves shimmering over the surface of the hot coral before we started across, but smoke and dust from the barrage now limited my vision."

In conversations in later years, with both me and the many people who came to visit him, he described the Japanese tracer fire snapping by him on both sides at chair-rail height as they asked about crossing the airfield.

In 1999, Eric Mailander took me to the spot on the airfield where my father and K/3/5 had crossed. It was an oppressively hot day, just as it was in 1944. Everyone hung back a discreet distance when I said, "Guys, I just want to be alone for a few minutes." I reached down and took a handful of the hot, white coral in my hands. I squeezed it between my fingers and watched the chalky dust catch in the hot breeze. I gazed around and tried to imagine that day for him, and I realized that my life—that I even had a life—was a miracle.

As the Marines began to trot and then break into a run, enemy fire picked up in intensity. Halfway across, my father stumbled and fell forward as Snafu got hit by a shell fragment and went down with a grunt.

"As he went down, he tried to brace the heavy mortar slung over his shoulder and grabbed his left side."

My father crawled over to him and made sure he was OK.

One day in my father's study, I pulled his web pistol belt and leather holster out of the closet. This was the very belt he had worn through combat. He looked thoughtfully at me and the belt as I held it in my hands.

"See how thick that material is? Strong enough to stop a shell fragment. I remember when we were crossing the airfield on Peleliu. As we were running across, a shell exploded right beside Snafu. We both went down—I heard this piece of shrapnel fly through the air. It went right over my head. When Snafu went down he made kind of an 'omph' sound—you know, because it knocked the wind out of him. I crawled over to him and saw he was OK and I saw this inch square piece of hot metal that had hit him—right in his web belt—he was wearing one just like that one. And you could see how the material was all frayed from it, but it stopped that piece and probably saved his life.

"But I picked up that piece of metal and had to juggle it in my hand because it was so hot"—my father mimicked the motion of bouncing a piece of hot metal in his hand—"and Snafu was trying to yell to me to put it in his pack. 'Course it was so loud I couldn't hear him, but he motioned with his hand to do that, so I did, and then we got up and got on across."

By the time they made it across the fire-swept airfield, they had gone several hundred yards. My father always said, both to me and in his many interviews, that crossing that airfield was the worst experience of the war.

As on D Day, the temperature was soaring toward 105 degrees—even in the shade. It would later hit 115. Men began falling out from heat prostration. Corpsmen tagged them for evacuation.

My father told me that as they panted and tried to catch their breath after the run across, a Gloucester veteran, a man who had already seen plenty, looked at him and wryly remarked, "That was rough duty, Sledgehammer—I'd hate like hell to have to do that every day."

Once on the eastern side of the airfield, they moved through mangrove swamps as snipers fired relentlessly. They dug in for the night with their backs to the sea. My father's mortar was set up about fifteen feet from the shore next to a sheer rock bluff that dropped about ten feet to the water. Despite the hard coral, they were able to scratch out a gun pit. Darkness began to fall; the men noticed that the jungle was so thick that most of the other men were out of sight after they dug in.

My fascination with World War II was not limited to the Pacific Theater. My father and I also had many conversations through the years about the European theater during which he compared various tactics used by the Japanese—and with which he obviously had experience firsthand—to tactics used by the Germans, which he had read about extensively. "The Germans were fine soldiers," he said, "and I wouldn't have wanted to have to fight them. But at the end of the day, they would bed down and get their rest. The damn Japanese were moving around at night, all the time, and they never let us get any rest."

After my father and his fellow Marines had dug in late in the afternoon, they prepared for another long, hot night by adhering to a fairly standard procedure: They registered in the mortar and made sure all avenues of approach to their positions were covered, either by their gun or by machine gun or rifle fire. Then they tried to replenish themselves.

"Chow consisted of whatever a man chose from the K rations in his pack. My canteen cup of dehydrated coffee that night was awful, because of the polluted water."

The password for the night was whispered to everyone, and it always contained the letter *L* because the Japanese couldn't pronounce it properly.

"As usual some character near me repeated it too loudly, and his foxhole buddy chided, 'What the hell you yellin' about.... You tellin' the Nips the password, or you tellin' us?'

"'Pipe down you meathead, you probably can't even remember the password.'

"'The hell you say.'

"'Knock it off you two,' came the stern order of an NCO. This kind of banter went on incessantly and actually kept our spirits up."

The men were informed where other units were in relation to them. They lit up smokes and placed weapons where they could get to them quickly during the night, then the glow of cigarettes winked out in the darkness as someone called out that the smoking lamp was out.

In each hole, one man would settle himself as best he could to try to get some rest while his buddy was on watch, alert for any sound or movement in the darkness. At such times a man wanted his Ka-Bar and .45 pistol close at hand.

"I spent many a night with my Ka-Bar in one hand and my .45 in the other," my father told me. That night, their second on Peleliu, was pretty quiet. An occasional Japanese mortar shell exploded nearby. The sea lapped gently against the base of the rocks behind them. They fired a few rounds from the mortar to discourage movement.

Suddenly my father became aware of two men dug in behind them at the edge of the cliff moving around.

"One raised his hand and pitched a grenade over the cliff. The spoon clanked as it fell on the coral, the primer went 'pop' and in a few seconds the muffled 'bang' as it went off. We could hear water splashing down from the explosion. Japanese soldiers began sloshing around in the knee-deep water at the foot of the cliff.

"Word was passed among those of us in the immediate area, 'Hold your fire.' One of the men rose cautiously from his foxhole and began firing his M1 rifle at the Japanese over the cliff. We kept our eyes glued to the cliff's edge because a Japanese might pop up at any point.

"The man, who I won't name, moved back and forth along the cliff edge firing down at the Japanese. I knew him only casually. He was a Gloucester veteran, and the men had told me that the strain of that jungle campaign had been too much for him, and that he had cracked up. However, he went after the Japanese with a vengeance that night. Little did I guess that a few nights later the strain of Peleliu would get to be too much for him, and he would die a tragic death."

The Japanese were trying to infiltrate the Marine lines, along their front and along the shore behind. Small arms fire and the bang of grenades echoed through the night. Fire discipline and letting your comrades know you were out of your hole became of paramount importance.

"In the case of this man, he had passed the word to us as to what he was about to do and we all knew it, while also keeping an eye open for any strange movements which we would assume were Japanese prowling around.

"Throughout the night, he ran up and down the shore's edge firing at Japanese sloshing around at the base of the low cliff, and some of the men tossed grenades down at them. At daybreak on September 17 we ate chow hurriedly and squared away our gear. We stood by in preparation for moving out of the swamp area to relieve 1/5.

"One of the men saw a Japanese floating face down in the shallow water and climbed down the low cliff to check him out. Several

of us went over to help. As the Marine dragged him through the water over to the bank, I remarked that the uniform looked more like a Marine dungaree jacket than a Japanese uniform. When we heaved the corpse up out of the water and lay it on its back, there on the left breast pocket was the Marine Corps emblem and U.S.M.C. The man had a bullet hole between his eyes.

"'That bastard,' snarled one of my buddies, 'he's got on a Marine dungaree jacket.'

"'Check his pockets and see if he has any maps or dispatches that G-2 can use,' ordered an NCO.

"While this was done, one of the men delivered a profane denunciation of any Japanese who wore any U.S.M.C. issue uniform. The corpse carried nothing of importance, but it did prove what we had heard about Japanese infiltrators wearing Marine clothing."

The order came to gear up and move out. After hoisting their loads, they filed slowly along, headed out of the thick swamp. When my father passed the foxhole where his buddy Robert B. Oswalt had been, he was saddened to learn that he had been killed the day before.

They moved along at a five-pace interval through the thick swamp. In the distance was the sound of heavy firing, and they were headed toward it. The temperature was quickly climbing.

"We moved along a sandy roadway through open vegetation and halted alongside a file of Marines resting on the sand. We exchanged news, and they said they were from 2/5.

"The sound of small arms fire was heavy, and we could hear Japanese mortar and artillery shells exploding. Our own artillery was giving support to our troops up ahead. The 'whoosh, whoosh, whoosh' from our 155mm Long Toms passed overhead. These guns were firing airbursts—set to explode over the treetops above the enemy out in front. A large, oblong, dense black cloud of smoke with a flash of flame and a tremendous 'karump' explosion characterized each one. Fragments went straight down and nearly always killed or wounded anyone below who did not have the overhead protection of a pillbox or bunker. Thus, an open foxhole offered little protection

against air bursts. These were the deadliest of all our artillery shells against exposed troops.

"On this occasion the Long Toms threw out a few shells up ahead, and then three went off very near us—probably between us and the troops we were moving to relieve.

"'Those sky bursts are getting pretty close,' I remarked to a member of my squad resting next to me.

"'Aw, Sledgehammer, you're just nervous in the service,' he chuckled. He had no more than spoken the words when there were three earsplitting explosions. Two slightly to our front and one directly overhead. It was like a giant thunderclap on top of my helmet. Fragments zipped and whirred down kicking up sand all around us. I looked up and saw three elongate black clouds of smoke—one directly overhead. Men cried out, 'I'm hit! Corpsman!'

"'Short rounds, short rounds!' The man in the file next to me who I had been talking to grabbed his thigh and grimaced. His buddy pulled out his Ka-Bar knife and cut his pants leg away to reveal a severe wound. He pressed a battle dressing over it and yelled, 'Corpsman!'

"The corpsmen had their hands full with wounded all around us. An officer was on his radio calling the artillery to knock it off.

"'K Company, move out on the double!' came the order. We picked up our gear and trotted forward hoping the officer got through to the artillery. To everyone's relief, no more of those terrifying sky bursts came in short."

They finally emerged from the swamp in the area east of the airfield. They found what shade they could in the scrub growth at the edge of the airfield.

Soon they could make out the southern edge of Bloody Nose Ridge, which at that point was to their left front. They were moving up to relieve 1/5 and would tie in with the 1st Marines. They would then have to attack northward along the eastern edge of the ridge complex.

It was September 17, D+2, and this relief movement was made very difficult by shellfire from the Japanese on their left front, which slowed the process and caused casualties among 1/5 as they tried to displace.

My father, as he always did when seeing fellow Marines under heavy fire, pitied them.

"The relief continued, and 1/5 went briefly into regimental reserve.

"The famous Peleliu 'gas attack' occurred at about this time. As we waited for orders to move forward, I sat on the hot coral at the edge of the airfield and talked with an artillery observer. He had on a set of headphones from which a small line was connected to a larger wire. He had firmly attached his wire to a stout root so he did not pull the connection of the two wires apart. We exchanged news, between his calls for fire orders to his battery which was sending shells over against the Japanese positions on the ends of the ridges ahead of us.

"'The 1st Marines are catching hell against that high ground,' he said. Japanese artillery and mortar shells were falling in certain areas around us where the enemy observer saw tempting targets. I suddenly noticed a couple of large shells exploding with greenish yellow smoke out across the airfield to our rear.

"'Are those Jap spotter shells for registering on a target?' I asked.

"'I don't think so, never saw anything like those,' answered the observer.

"Men began yelling—some word was being passed in reference to strange shells. The observer and I got the word immediately.

"'Gas! Gas! Gas attack!'

"Because of the heat, the observer and I, like most others, had already discarded our bulky gas masks and canvas carrying cases, as we had everything else not considered essential. At the alarm, we sprang up and looked wildly about for gas masks. I spotted one that had been dropped about a dozen paces from me. I made a dive, scooped it up, ripped open the snaps of the case, and jerked out the mask.

"As I put the mask to my face I saw the observer, still wearing headphones, sprinting toward a mask some distance from him. Suddenly he was jerked off his feet, and for a moment his body was suspended in midair horizontal to the deck. He had reached the end of his wire connected to the root, and it jerked him off his feet. He

hit the deck in a minor cloud of dust, ripped off the headphones, and grabbed up the gas mask.

"I donned and adjusted my gas mask. Men all around us were running helter skelter looking for masks—a few had kept their own. Finally, 'All clear, false alarm,' came the word—to our great relief.

"The artillery observer and I removed our masks and grinned at each other sheepishly. We laughed about how he got jerked off his feet, and about how fast I got a mask on. But it had not been the least bit funny. Those had been some horrifying minutes. It was the closest thing to panic I saw during the course of two of the bloodiest campaigns of World War II. Friends of mine throughout the Division told me after Peleliu that they too had scrambled around looking for masks. The alarm had apparently been widespread."

This story, when I discovered it while researching my father's unpublished writings, surprised me. I had so many conversations with him over the years and when *With the Old Breed* was published that I felt as though I had heard it all before—but I have no memory of ever hearing about the "Peleliu gas attack."

It was the job of 3/5 to attack that afternoon through the low ground along the eastern side of Bloody Nose, while 2/5 was to clean out the jungle between their right flank and the eastern shore.

As they began to move forward, heavy flanking fire opened up from Bloody Nose Ridge on the left. They hugged the ground for cover.

This was their first taste of Bloody Nose Ridge, and they felt for their comrades in the 1st Marines who had been in that meat grinder from the first day on the island, and who were facing it head on right now.

"My mortar was situated out in the open area bordering the airfield. The ground was crushed coral from construction of the runways, so we were able to dig a fairly good gun pit. We registered in with HE and then prepared the flare shells for the night."

A short while later, my father and several others were ordered to head to the rear to unload an amtrac bringing up water and supplies.

"I took up my carbine and we moved toward the airfield. There was a little small arms fire and only an occasional shell."

A few minutes later the amphibious tractor came rattling up, its radial engine rumbling, and clanked to a halt. The driver greeted them and climbed down from the cab. They had to unload it as quickly as possible before Japanese observers started shooting rounds into their area. As the men gazed down into the cargo compartment of the amtrac, they were amazed to see, wedged under a stack of ammo crates, a fifty-five-gallon drum of water.

Several profane remarks were expressed on the genius of supply officers, but they set to work to unload the supplies on the double. Japanese mortar shells began to whisper in.

"We managed to get the heavy, 55-gallon drum of water out of the amtrac by tying both ends of a heavy rope to cleats on one rim of the tractor cargo compartment, running it under the drum and around it and back over the same side of the tractor to which the rope was tied. We tugged on the rope and sweated until the drum slowly rolled up the rope sling, over the side, and hit the coral with a thud. I had seen this technique used to load heavy pine logs on trucks in Alabama—except the pulling was done by a yoke of oxen instead of a half dozen sweaty Marines."

After they finished unloading the amtrac, each man took up some supplies, and they returned to their positions. They stacked what they couldn't carry, and more men were sent back to bring up those supplies. When they got back to the company, they began to prepare for another night.

They were dug in next to 1st Lt. Edward "Hillbilly" Jones, K Company's machine gun platoon leader, and Sgt. John A. Teskevich. These two K Company men were very familiar to me growing up, as my father spoke of them often. I well remember my parents discussing their twilight foxhole conversation in later years.

As darkness fell, things were quiet in their area except for outgoing artillery fire. Hillbilly and Sergeant Teskevich, known as the Mad Russian, crept over and sat on the edge of their gun pit. Hillbilly was second only to Ack Ack in popularity and was highly respected.

"Perhaps it was because he had come from the ranks and not from Officers' Candidate School as a '90 day wonder' that we thought so highly of him."

In the quiet, reassuring words of Hillbilly, asking my father about his family in Mobile and expressing optimism that they would prevail in the coming weeks of hardship on Peleliu, my father found a sense of peace and solace.

"I told him I felt ashamed of how scared I was," he described to me.

"'And I remember Hillbilly said to me, 'Don't worry about it, Sledgehammer. Everybody else is just as scared as you are—it's just that you don't mind admitting it.'"

Sergeant Teskevich was a different kind of character than Hillbilly, but he was equally respected.

"He was from the industrial northeast, and had an accent as hard as nails. He was not a large man but was muscular and had obviously spent his youth in hard work. He was a capable NCO, loved the Marine Corps, and did his job well. He told us of some of his previous life and talked about how he thought the war would progress."

As I remember my father telling it, "It had gotten quiet, and suddenly I heard, in a voice as clear as me talking to you right now, a voice say, 'You will survive the war.' And I looked at Hillbilly and Teskevich, and they looked at me, and I said, 'Did you guys hear that?'

"And they looked at me and said, 'Hear what? I hear a machine gun off to the left.'

"And I said, 'You guys didn't hear somebody say something?'

"And they said, 'No, we didn't hear anything like that.'"

In that moment, as the twilight turned to darkness on Peleliu, my father felt that the voice he heard was a sign from God that he would make it through. He was very skeptical of people seeing visions and hearing "voices," and he said so many times throughout his life, but he also didn't doubt what he experienced right then. Hillbilly and Teskevich were both later killed on Peleliu.

My mother and I spoke about this not long before she passed away. "I think your dad found a lot of comfort in hearing that voice, and it helped him through such a hard time in his life."

"After Hillbilly and Teskevich left the gun pit, darkness had settled and the ships began firing star shells. We could see the ridges bathed in the eerie light to our left. Over on the left flank of our battalion I heard a high-pitched voice yell, 'Nippon Banzai!' I could see Snafu grow tense.

"'You suppose that's the big Banzai attack?' I asked.

"'Naw, just some Marine yellin' at the Nips,' he said unconvincingly. A burst from a Marine machine gun answered the yell, and then some small arms fire erupted in the area. A few grenades went off, a hoarse cry [of] 'Corpsman', and then relative silence. It must have been a single Japanese infiltrator or a small raiding party.

"Then the nightly routine commenced: the password, star shells, our artillery whistling over, Japanese raids and infiltrators, bursts of small arms fire, 'Corpsman,' the bang of grenades. Calls for mortar flares and HE on the company front, heavier artillery fire, on and on until dawn."

This was the third night on the island, and certain realties of the infantryman's life were becoming painfully obvious. My father expressed it to me about as eloquently as one could.

"One of the things that a frontline infantryman faced was filth. Filth and fear went right together. By the third day, either you or your foxhole buddy told the other one that he stunk. And, of course, you both stank—from the terrible heat, the sweat, absolutely no way to get yourself cleaned up."

We've all known people who relish the opportunity to get away from their work routine for a few days, be it on a camping trip, hunting trip, or some other adventure, and enjoy not having to shower, shave (although I don't know too many people who even bother with that anymore), or attempt to wear nice clothes (also becoming increasingly less common)—in other words, roughing it. This was unthinkable to my father. Many times, I heard him say, "I don't know why in the hell a man would enjoy intentionally enjoy not getting cleaned up or shaving. I had to go over thirty days like that on Peleliu." In all the years I knew him, I never saw him skip a shower, and I never once saw him unshaven.

The next day was September 18, and the battalion was going to continue moving north on the eastern side of the Umurbrogol.

"My memory of the events of September 17 and 18 are blurred; my only recollection is of being under heavy fire.

"The number of HE shells we fired, and whether it was search and traverse or for effect on one or more particular points, depended on the situation. Our air-cooled .30 cal light machine gun squads fired on areas in front of the platoons they were attached to support. (Our heavy-water-cooled .30 Browning machine guns were usually used when we set up defensive positions.)

Never one to aggrandize himself, my father always emphasized how, as mortarmen, they supported the riflemen, who were the spearhead of any attack. But when the riflemen came under heavy fire, as frequently happened, they depended on supporting fire from the mortars and machine guns. Under enemy fire the rifle squads would move forward in short rushes toward an objective.

"In this case [if there were opposition] we shelled the area to knock out the Japanese holding up the rifle squad."

Riflemen, machine gunners, mortarmen, bazooka and flamethrower gunners, tankers—everyone caught hell on Peleliu.

"Our company cooks acted as stretcher bearers in combat because in those conditions we ate C & K rations if we ate at all under fire. If the riflemen took their objective they dug in (often impossible in Peleliu's coral), and we moved forward with the mortars and came up with them to set up in a hole or defilade again and help repel any possible counterattack. The machine guns set up with crossfire patterns across the company front.

"During World War II the Marine Corps was frequently criticized for its 'hell for leather' rash aggressiveness, but our successes are a matter of history. We had to capture islands as quickly as possible,

because our supporting fleet, if delayed by a prolonged battle, might be subjected to Japanese air and surface attack."

As Richard B. Frank pointed out to me, the quick execution of these operations, though costly at times, had the effect of keeping the Japanese continually behind in reaction time. Their defensive strength later in the Solomons, New Guinea, and across the Pacific was consistently weaker than it would have been otherwise. Through island hopping, we gained key locations like Manus, Majuro, and Ulithi at minimum cost.

Because of the heavy artillery and mortar fire from the Japanese, the attack was called off. The 1st Marines continued battering against the ridges while 2/5, and then my father's battalion, behind them moved east onto the smaller prong of the lobster claw and across the causeway road. At that point they were moving away from Bloody Nose Ridge.

When some of the men expressed their pity for their comrades in the 1st Marines, my father realized that at some point every battalion of every regiment would be thrown into Bloody Nose Ridge.

"For the past two days every time 3/5 moved along the eastern side of the ridges the Japanese opened up with such heavy artillery and mortar fire that we were absolutely pinned down. Then our planes, ships guns, artillery, and 81mm mortars would plaster the ridge to permanently silence any of the enemy's fortified positions.

"As soon as we started to move again the same furious hail of Japanese shells fell on us with the same deadly effect. It was as though the only thing the terrific, massed firepower of our supporting weapons accomplished was to chip away some coral rock on Bloody Nose Ridge.

"The Japanese pulled back into their caves and waited, and as soon as we moved, they poured the shells on us again. They exposed neither weapons nor men needlessly and had excellent fire discipline. Marines were out in the open in most cases."

It was in this scenario that the tactical genius of Colonel Nakagawa took its terrible toll on the attacking Marines—and would continue to do so for much longer.

"It was that insistence [from the high command] on quick victory at Peleliu that cost us so much. In fact, the 1st Marines' line was

not able to move much farther beyond the point where it had been on September 18, despite four more days of fruitless frontal assaults from the south that cost prohibitive casualties.

"The truth was that nothing like the Umurbrogol Mountain defenses had ever been encountered by Americans in the Pacific war. If the high command didn't know it at the time, it was obvious to some of us in the ranks that something was wrong.

"The Japanese troops in the southern end of the ridges had been ordered to hang on to their positions there regardless of attacks, so they could employ these positions to shell the airfield and deny U.S. forces the use of it as long as possible. The Five Sisters, for example, a huge coral mass with five sheer walled peaks containing numerous caves, was fruitlessly attacked by the 1st Marines with heavy loss. It was successively attacked by the 7th Marines and the 5th Marines. The defenders always inflicted heavy losses on Marine units but continued to hold out. The Five Sisters was finally knocked out by Army infantrymen two months later, about one month after all Marines had left Peleliu.

"There was bitterness about being over-aggressive against Bloody Nose. I certainly heard it voiced vehemently by the men around me."

On September 18, the 5th Marines moved onto the smaller lobster claw. The hot, humid conditions continued to be a struggle.

"I carried a little Gideon's New Testament in my breast pocket, but it stayed soaked with sweat during the early days."

This Bible has long been an object of fascination by admirers of *With the Old Breed.* Through the years, everyone from the well-known historical documentary filmmaker Ken Burns to actor Tom Hanks, and many others, have seen my father's Bible as one of his most fascinating artifacts. It will soon be enshrined in the Library of Congress in Washington, DC.

"There were numerous patrols throughout this area; most were uneventful, but one made such an impression on me. It was commanded by 1st Lt. Hillbilly Jones, assisted by Hank Boyes."

In an interview many years later, I heard my father describe a conversation with Hank Boyes at a 1st Marine Division reunion—probably in the 1980s—in which the two talked about this patrol.

As he related to me, "'Hank told me, 'Sledgehammer, what I knew about that patrol out into the mangrove swamp was that it was basically supposed to be a suicide patrol. I couldn't tell you guys that at the time, but we were basically being sent out there to probe their positions and draw their fire.' Well, when he told me that, my knees just went weak."

The patrol consisted of riflemen, BAR men, a machine gun squad, my father's mortar squad, a Doberman Pinscher war dog, and the dog's handler. In all, it was about forty men.

"Many of the veterans commented on the firepower we had, and large number of machine guns being taken."

According to an NCO, intelligence reported a significant number of Japanese troops, possibly two thousand or more, on the other side of the swamp, and it was believed they might try to get back to the defensive positions of Bloody Nose Ridge. It was K Company's job to hold them up until air strikes, reinforcements, and artillery joined them.

"The words of one of my Camp Elliott instructors rang in my ears, 'There are basically two types of patrols, the reconnaissance patrol and the combat patrol. The recon patrol was usually made up of a few men, who move out with a single mission—to seek information. The recon patrol tries to avoid contact with the enemy.

"'The combat patrol usually consists of platoon or more strength, with machine guns and mortars attached. Its mission is to contact the enemy and test his strength or occupy and hold a strategic position against any enemy attack.'

"As we picked up our gear and filed out through the company front line, I wished I had not remembered what my instructor had said."

As they passed through the last friendly position and headed out into the unfamiliar, thick jungle growth, my father discovered what it meant to feel lonely and vulnerable. He also began to understand his attachment to K Company.

Scouts went out as they moved as quietly as possible, always looking for snipers. The only sounds they could hear were the occasional clinking of canteens and weapons, maybe a man suppressing a cough here and there or a muffled curse when a man tripped on a tangle of mangrove roots. Further away they could hear the battle rumbling on Bloody Nose Ridge. It was swampy terrain, lots of tidal inlets and pools choked with mangroves and pandanus trees.

Despite the thick tension from heading into potentially hostile territory on a combat patrol, my father still found time to see the natural beauty of his surroundings.

He was duly impressed by a pair of man-o-war, or frigate, birds perched at the top of a tree they passed under. The male extended his seven-foot wings and clicked his beak reproachfully at these strangely clad intruders. It reminded my father of watching the same species of bird fly over Mobile Bay in more peaceful times. Another man exhorted him to keep up.

I remember going to the Dauphin Island Sea Lab with my father when he would take his ornithology classes there on field trips in the spring. On one such trip, probably around 1974 or 1975, as we rolled south along the causeway between Mobile and Dauphin Island, we saw a couple of huge birds perched on a power pole. As we passed below, they flapped their enormous wings and took flight. "Frigate birds!" my father exclaimed. "Look at the wingspan on those things! Man, I remember one time seeing those things up close on Peleliu!"

On my trip in 1999, one particular day stands out in my mind very clearly. It was hot and humid, although not nearly so much as during the battle. Eric Mailander had a compass with a built-in thermometer that read 85 degrees, although it felt much hotter. We were exploring an area known as the Coral Badlands. Most of our group had departed for home the day before, and it was just him, Sean Prizeman, me, and one or two others. We found a machine gun nest still occupied by its rusted Browning .30 caliber water-cooled weapon. In the breach was the decayed remains of an ammo belt. Not a breath of air stirred, and the sunlight filtering through the tree canopy overhead dappled the ground.

The only sounds we heard, other than the coral crunching under our boots, were the plaintive calls of several jungle birds, and they only added to the haunted atmosphere. When I returned home a few days later and described this to my father, what interested him the most was the jungle birds.

"A little further on just as we were signaled to halt, I saw a Japanese corpse that had not been dead long. I knelt beside the body and looked it over carefully to be sure it wasn't booby trapped. The soldier, with superior private insignia on his collars, had been a knee-mortar gunner, and he wore, in addition to the usual equipment, a canvas web vest with pouches containing the 50mm shells. His mortar lay beside him. I picked up the weapon and examined it. It was brand new, the beautiful, blued steel shining and well kept, with no wear on the outer surfaces.

"'You could sell that to some pilot for a hundred bucks, Sledgehammer,' said a buddy. I remarked that it would make a good souvenir, too. The heat was oppressive, and when I thought of the weight of the equipment I had to carry, a knee mortar weighing several pounds stuck in my pack would get pretty heavy. I held the Japanese mortar toward my friend and said, 'It's too heavy to carry around, you want it?'

"He shook his head and said, 'No thanks ole buddy, this man's Marine Corps issues me all the gear I can tote, and then some.'

"He was right. Souvenirs this big were the treasures of rear area troops, who, like scavengers, picked the fought over area clean of enemy equipment after the infantry had passed through. I reluctantly dropped the weapon."

On the bookcase in my father's study by his Ka-Bar was a 50mm Japanese knee mortar shell. I was fascinated by it growing up, and he told me all about the weapon and its effectiveness. The shell had been emptied of its powder charge and rendered safe, of course, and I don't recall ever hearing where he got it from or how. I wonder if he picked up the shell on that occasion.

"The knee mortar was designed to cover the area between grenade range and the larger caliber Japanese mortars. From what I saw,

the Japanese employed knee mortars extensively, and they had about nine of them in each rifle company. They fired them rapidly and accurately and inflicted a lot of casualties with this weapon. It was a difficult weapon to locate and knock out because when things got too hot for him the gunner hid, or simply picked up his handy weapon and moved to another position and commenced firing again. We had a lot of respect for those shells that made that peculiar 'twanging' sound upon bursting."

It was late in the afternoon when the patrol halted near an abandoned Japanese bunker made from coconut logs and coral. It would serve as their command post, and the men dispersed to dig in around it. The ground where my father dug his gun pit was only a few feet above water level and about thirty feet from the bunker. Densely tangled mangrove roots limited their visibility to just a few feet on three sides of their defense perimeter.

"No one was to fire any weapon unless ordered to do so."

Darkness settled in as they prepared for a long night in their holes. It began to rain, and they listened to the drops splashing out in the swampy darkness. The crushing feeling of being expendable almost overwhelmed my father.

"I thought of the utter futility of it all if a large body of Japanese stumbled onto us; if we were lucky, they wouldn't come through our area; if they did, we might be wiped out."

The long night dragged on. They were as alert as they could be, but all they heard were night jungle sounds. Occasionally there would be a splash, like something falling into the water.

"However, the noise seemed to be caused by some type of wild creature."

Shortly after midnight, the man who, on one of the first nights on Peleliu, had ran back and forth shooting the Japanese in the water below them had a mental breakdown and began yelling. They tried to restrain him, inject him with multiple doses of morphine, and even punch him in the face to knock him out. But nothing quieted or calmed him. As a last resort, he was struck with an entrenching tool and killed. It was tragic and disturbing to all the men that night, but there was no choice. If he gave away their position to any nearby Japanese, the patrol would have been wiped out.

"There we were, a patrol of about forty US Marines out in a pitch dark, rain-soaked mangrove swamp on a dangerous mission trying to keep our position secret from God only knew how many hundreds of Japanese, and this man was out of his mind and screaming like a maniac."

The next morning Hillbilly decided to take the patrol in. Everybody's nerves were shot from the previous night, and Hillbilly made a tough decision that my father and the other veterans of the patrol appreciated. They called Major Gustafson on the radio, and, respecting Hillbilly's judgement, the major sent a relief column with a Sherman tank to bring them in.

"G-2 found out later that the Japanese battalion—about a thousand men—that we had been sent out to delay in the swamp had moved to the ridge several days earlier, around D Day. This was not known when we made the patrol.

"We made several other patrols on the eastern coast, the Purple Beach area, during the next couple of days. On these occasions a skeleton crew rotated on the mortar in the company area, and the rest of the mortarmen went on patrol as riflemen. These were uneventful, as we encountered a few Japanese stragglers. I found some Japanese maps and an artillery spotting telescope which I turned in to G-2. The abandoned enemy defensive positions in the area were formidable, particularly along the beach."

One of the Japanese artifacts I remember looking at in my father's study was a brown leather officer's map case. It was in excellent condition, and all I remember him ever saying about it was that a Japanese officer had used it to carry maps. This is one artifact that got away from the family at some point. I wonder if he picked up that map case in the Purple Beach area.

"The main topic of conversation in the company at this time was the scuttlebutt regarding an offer by the CO of the Army 81st Division to help us on Peleliu. The 81st Wildcat Division had just captured neighboring Angaur in a tough four-day fight. That island

lacked a fringing reef and much in the way of coral ridges, but the doggies had learned and fought well against stiff Japanese resistance, and their commander had offered the assistance of his now experienced infantry to the 1st Marine Division on Peleliu.

"I talked to a radioman in battalion CP and he said he heard that some of the rifle companies in the 1st Marines ain't got no more than platoon strength left.... 'They been all shot up makin' frontal attacks against Bloody Nose and them damn caves,' said a company runner sitting next to me during a break on a patrol.

"'Yeah,' said another man, 'I got a buddy that talked to an NCO casualty that said the Army wants to relieve 'em but General Rupertus says we don't need no help from the Army.'

"'Like hell we don't—just look at the casualties we've had in 3/5. If the 1st Marines are worse off than us, you know damn well they done shot their wad and need relief.'

"'But the Division CO says our Division can finish securing the island in a few days without no help. Maybe he's just striking for a medal, or glory,' said the runner. I heard other remarks, not printable, about the refusal of Gen. Rupertus to accept help offered by the Army."

"At the end of the first week our entire division had suffered nearly 4,000 casualties—about one thousand more than the 2nd Marine Division lost on Tarawa. During this time 1st Marine Regiment had lost 1,672 men, or 56% of that regiment's strength. The Division's heavy losses troubled the [Third] Amphibious Corps Commander.

"On September 21, Gen. Roy Geiger visited the CP of the 1st Marines to get a clearer picture of the situation. He concluded the '1st Marines were finished' and said that regiment should be relieved and replaced by an Army regiment."

"Gen. Geiger was not inclined to impose his will on Gen. Rupertus, but he finally felt it necessary; he realized the 1st Marines were shot to pieces and the 5th and 7th Marines who had suffered heavily would need help."

The 5th Marines scoured most of the Purple Beach area and set up defensive positions in case the Japanese attempted to land reinforcements.

"This was a real threat because there were thousands of fresh Japanese combat troops on the Palau islands north of Peleliu that might be floated down on barges to reinforce Peleliu."

Roughly ten days after the start of the battle, the exhausted remnants of the 1st Marines were relieved by the Army's 321st Infantry of the 81st Division. The meat grinder of the Umurbrogol had exacted a bloody toll—and the battle was far from over. As the 1st Marines moved into the relatively quiet Purple Beach area, my father and his buddies in K/3/5 boarded trucks to be taken to a position straddling the West Road. They would then attack north along the western side of the ridges.

"When I passed the 81mm mortar platoon of 2nd Battalion, 1st Marines, I was delighted to see Wes Tatum. He was an Alabamian, and Sid Phillips and Bill Brown from Mobile had been in his squad during Guadalcanal and Gloucester. I had met Wes on Pavuvu. 'Boy, I'll tell you, ole Sid and Bill really missed a tough one when they got sent back to the States before Peleliu, didn't they?' he said. We talked a few moments, and then we had to move out."

The date was September 25, D+10. Although the 1st Marines were now out of the fight, twenty more grueling days would pass before the 5th Marines were relieved. They would be just as depleted from their time in the ridges.

When they boarded the trucks, they headed south along the East Road, then northward along the West Road. As they drove past the airfield, they were amazed at the terrain's transition from a combat zone to an American airbase. Clean-shaven rear echelon personnel eyed the filthy, bearded, and bedraggled infantrymen curiously as they drove by on the trucks. My father described it as being animals observed in a circus parade.

Farther up West Road, the truck convoy jolted to a halt. The ridges were on their right, a section that, at that point, was in American hands. As they unloaded, they met the soldiers from the 321st Infantry, 81st Division of the US Army.

CHAPTER EIGHT

Assault on Ngesebus

"The 7th Marines had taken over the old line of the 1st Marines across the southern end of the ridge and bending north along the ridge, bordering West Road. The doggies pushed north along the flat area between the ridge and the coast. This was the area in which the 5th Marines debarked from the trucks after leaving the southeastern coastal area [Purple Beach] on September 25."

As my father and his fellow Marines passed through the army lines, they could hear the chatter of Japanese machine guns and see bluish-white tracers passing high above them. The men up on the ridge were pinned down.

"The witty, likeable sergeant [John Teskevich] with whom I had had the memorable conversation the night he and Hillbilly came over to my foxhole was killed on September 25 while riding on a tank directing its fire. He was shot in the abdomen. What a waste. We all greatly regretted his death.

"Our battalion turned right at the junction of the West Road and East Road, headed south along the latter and dug in along Hill 80 just at dusk. Because of the terrain, the company's positions front to rear did not have much depth. The front line, holes about five yards apart, two men each, was placed along the edge of the white coral East Road.

"Machine guns were set to crossfire in the thick jungle across the road to our front. My mortar gun pit was situated in an open

flat area no more than twenty-five feet behind the front line. Not an enviable position for a weapon that spouted bright flame each time a round was fired at night. The company CP was situated in a little depression to my left rear.

"By the time we got set for the night darkness was gathering, and the whispered order 'smoking lamp is out' came from the company CP.

"Snafu was furious—he hadn't had his 'after digging in' cigarette. So, while I drank a cup of K ration bouillon and ate a can of cheese, he unintentionally provided me with some good entertainment. He crouched and huddled himself over his knees, tried to pull his poncho over himself and light a cigarette—cursing and grumbling vehemently all the while. All he managed to do was get tangled in the poncho and lose his book of matches. Finally, he found his matches, and I draped the poncho over his huddled form. With immense relief he finally lit the cigarette, and what looked like little smoke signals wafted out from under the poncho as he continued to shift around to be sure the glow of his cigarette was hidden from Peleliu's ubiquitous snipers."

Someone ordered my father to carry a five-gallon water can over to the CP. When he got there, Ack Ack was intently studying a map by the dim glow of a tiny flashlight. A 300-radioman sat nearby calling for artillery fire. Struck by the scene, my father sat down on the water can to take it in.

This has always been a poignant story and one of my favorites from *With the Old Breed.* I can picture it so clearly in my mind—my father sitting on that water can and looking at his skipper with admiration in the faint glow of a shielded flashlight as twilight descended on the ridges, his camo helmet cover pulled out from the back of his helmet and draped over his neck, his grimy, oily hands on his knees, the quiet voices of the radioman and Ack Ack. I wish an artist could paint it because it would have made a wonderful picture. Knowing the respect my father had for Ack Ack only makes it more meaningful.

"Shortly after dark I heard something out on the road to our right. 'Halt, who goes there!' came the challenge from a Marine. Silence, and then the challenge was repeated. Next followed a long burst from the Marine light machine gun, the red tracers streaking down the road to the right. Then silence again.

"Later we found, lying in the road, a group of about a dozen dead Japanese. This was the group the machine gunner had fired on just at darkness, when they approached along the road apparently not suspecting Marines in the area. The first six or eight Japanese were strung along in Indian file and each had the crown of his head shot away. They must have been exactly lined up with the machine gun to have been hit that way. Some of these Japanese were dressed as aviators with goggles, leather helmets, and flight suits. They were definitely not infantry.

"Our battalion made a successful attack on what was called Hill 80 early in the morning. We went on across the narrow part of the island to the swamp beyond Hill 80."

They were getting some Japanese fire from just across the channel on Ngesebus Island. This had to be neutralized. The Japanese also might send down reinforcements from Babelthuap and Koror in the northern Palau Islands, and Ngesebus would be a natural debarkation point, as, from there, they could then get across to Peleliu. An airstrip on the little island might also prove useful.

In fact, on the night of September 22, about six hundred Japanese of the 2nd Battalion, 15th Infantry Regiment came down from Babelthuap and did get ashore on Peleliu to reinforce their beleaguered comrades.

"The Japanese had full confidence that they could defend Peleliu against us and slipping in reinforcements would certainly prolong the whole affair. At some point during the early days of fighting, I don't remember exactly when, the Japanese somehow sent out propaganda leaflets urging us to surrender."

Robert Leckie corroborated this in his memoir *Helmet for My Pillow*. My father saw copies of this leaflet and quoted it as saying:

> **"'American Brave Soldiers! We think you much pity since landing on this ileland. In spite of your pitiful battles we are sorry that we present only fire, not even good water. We soon will attack strongly your Army. You have done bravely your duty.**
>
> **"Now, abandon your guns and come in Japanese military with white flag (or handkerchief), so we will be glad to see you and welcome you comfortably as we can well.'**

"We found copies of this, and I read the thing myself. The men passed them around and made many profane remarks regarding its content.

"On September 27 our positions were taken over by soldiers and we moved northward along the road."

They would hit Ngesebus the next day. As far as the airstrip was concerned, it was determined after the island was taken that the sand on that strip was too soft to accommodate the heavier American fighters and torpedo bombers like the Vought F4U Corsair, Grumman F6F Hellcat, and Grumman TBF Avenger.

They dug in for the night in a sandy, open area on the northern peninsula among shattered palms and prayed that this amphibious assault would not be a repeat of the Peleliu landing.

The next morning, they geared up and prepared to board amtracs that would take them across the five-hundred-to-seven-hundred-yard channel to Ngesebus.

In 1999, we set aside an afternoon to explore Ngesebus. Eric Mailander had corresponded with my father in great detail about some of his experiences on the island. There were specific sights we hoped to find, so this part of our adventure was highly anticipated. Some of the most gut wrenching and visceral combat my father saw occurred here. Much of it he and I had talked about.

In preparation for the assault, they had naval gunfire as well as excellent Marine close air support based on the Peleliu airfield. This was to be a superb example of close air support for the Marines as they approached their objective. The Corsairs were from VMF-114. Known as the Death Dealers, they were under the command of Maj. Robert "Cowboy" Stout from Wyoming—a six-kill ace formerly of VMF-212 in the Guadalcanal days of two years earlier when the war in the Pacific was on the knife's edge for America.

About six-foot-one with an easy-going manner and movie-star looks that rivaled Errol Flynn, Cowboy Stout was the perfect leader for the aviators of VMF-114. Their skill and tenacity were on full display as they pressed home their attacks bombing and strafing the beach. Their services were much appreciated by the infantrymen like my father who were about to land on that beach.

"While the amtracs revved up their engines, the ships thundered forth a rain of big shells on Ngesebus, and the Corsairs circled overhead preparing for their strafing runs, the infantry who were to do the fighting waited nervously."

The infantrymen, my father among them, sweated in their gear as the blue Corsairs, radial engines roaring, made strafing and bombing runs on the beach that they were about to hit. The idling engines of the amtracs added to the noise.

This was the first time air support for the landing force consisted exclusively of Marine pilots—in all other landings, there had been Navy and sometimes Army pilots, but not at Ngesebus. Their performance was one to behold as they plastered the beach with guns, bombs, and rockets.

Cowboy Stout's wingman was Lt. Glenn "Bud" Daniel, also from Wyoming. Two excerpts from his logbook state, in the truncated language of Marine aviators, what my father saw happening in front of him:

1. 9-28-44 FG-1, 14016 1.5 hours bombing and strafing for Ngesebus landing.
2. 9-28-44 FG-1, 14016 1.5 hours bombing and strafing for Ngesebus landing.

In his own war diary, Lieutenant Daniel wrote this about that mission:

> "Sept. 28—covered Marine landing on Ngesebus Island—bombed with 500 lbs. bombs and strafed.
>
> CP of 1st Division, also big wigs including Gen. Rupertus really pleased."[9]

At the appointed time, the amphibious tractors revved their engines and moved out into the water.

"The water was shallow, and the amtrac moved across the reef and did not become waterborne."

The amtrac my father was in, an LVT-4 with a drop tailgate, lurched up the beach and jolted to a stop. It thumped down and the men scrambled out.

As they moved inland, they were fired upon by a Japanese sniper. As my father described to me, "I remember just when we hit Ngesebus—it was right when we got to the edge of the airstrip—me and a buddy huddled behind a rock because one of their Nambus had cut loose on us. There was this crack—it sounded like a broomstick being snapped, and my buddy cried out, 'Oh God, I'm hit!' See, it was a bypassed Jap sniper. So I dragged him around the rock out of site of the sniper. But we still had to worry about the Nambu firing on us."

"The machine gun was firing cover for Japanese to the front, but I knew the sniper [behind] had his eye on us and would fire again and keep it up to inflict as many casualties as possible until some of the men back on the beach killed him. Fortunately for the two of us my guess was right."

My father called for a corpsman, and Kent Caswell came over.

"Another man also came over to see if he could help with the casualty."

My father always cautioned me about the sharpness of his Ka-Bar knife when I picked it up and looked at it in his study. As he remembered,

---

9 Glenn "Bud" Daniel, *Cowboy Down: A WWII Marine Fighter Pilot's Story* (CreateSpace Publishing, 2014).

"When my buddy was wounded by that Jap sniper on Ngesebus, he was lying there, and Doc Caswell was tending to him. And another Marine was going to help get my buddies pack strap out of the way so Doc could help him. He put his Ka-Bar blade under that strap and jerked it up, and that thing was so razor sharp it just came straight up and cut Doc's face to the bone."

As the mortar section moved further inland, they came to what appeared to be a Japanese bunker or pillbox. It was, in fact, an air raid shelter that had been strengthened into a fighting position and covered in sand. They were ordered to set up their guns on the inland side to fire on the enemy at the company's front.

"Gunnery Sgt. W.R. Saunders came by and we asked him if he knew of any Japanese in the bunker."

The men noted that the structure seemed undamaged, but Saunders assured them that it had been cleared with grenades thrown through the ventilators. My father and Snafu began to set up their mortar about five feet from the bunker.

"While Snafu and I were getting the mortar set up, I could hear something behind me in the pillbox. It was Japs in there and I could hear them talking to each other in excited voices, but not very loud. I heard metal rattle against the grating on one of the vision ports in the side of the bunker. They were trying to get a rifle barrel through there. I grabbed my carbine and yelled to Burgin, 'There're Nips in that pillbox.'"

Burgin at first didn't believe my father and said, "Sledgehammer, you're crackin' up." Fortunately for all concerned, however, he took him seriously and moved over to the ventilator port directly behind my father. It was a small square opening, about six by eight inches covered with iron bars about a half inch apart.

There was a Japanese soldier right there, and Burgin shot him at point blank with his carbine. This caused a stir among the other Japanese inside the structure.

My father told me, "We were all on the alert when the shooting started. A Jap threw a grenade out the entrance to my left, and I yelled,

'Grenade,' and dove for cover behind the sand breastwork that protected the entrance. It was L shaped to protect the entrance from our fire. The Japs tossed out a few more grenades, but they exploded and none of us got hit; we were all hugging the deck. I remember most of the guys crawled around to the front and were staying low so the Japs inside couldn't see them or shoot at them. [John] Redifer and [Vincent] Santos jumped on top. Burgin yelled to me, 'Look over that wall and see what's in there, Sledgehammer.'"

My father was closest to the entrance at the end of the bunker. As he said to me, "I was trained to follow orders without question, so I looked over that wall down into the bunker." It almost cost him his life. No more than five or six feet away was a Japanese machine gunner, crouched over his weapon.

"I was staring right into the muzzle of his machine gun. As soon as I saw that, I jerked my head down so fast my helmet almost flew off because my chin strap wasn't buckled. As I did, he fired a quick burst from his machine gun. The rounds went right over my head through the sand that was piled up to that protective wall by the door."

In July of 2006, I flew to Texas and visited Burgin. As he showed me around Lancaster in his red pickup truck, he reminisced about the war, including the action at the bunker.

"I told Sledgehammer to look over that wall. The man only had thirteen days combat experience. I should have looked myself. The Jap machine gunner fired a burst and almost took his head off. He ducked, thank God."

"Do you remember him saying anything?" I asked.

"Yeah, I heard him say in kind of a hoarse voice, 'I'm ok, I'm alright.'"

After the Japanese soldier loosed a burst at my father, he crawled around to the front of the structure.

"I jumped up on top with Santos and Redifer," he told me. Redifer and Snafu got in an argument because Redifer said that the Japs had a machine gun, and for some reason Snafu disagreed. "It was just one of those unreal things," my father said to me. "We were twelve Marines or thereabouts, with a bull by the tail, that bunker and all those Japs inside it, and Snafu and Redifer arguing with each other about whether there was a machine gun in there. We knew we had to keep them in the bunker because we didn't want them to get out into the bushes or the undergrowth where they could cause trouble for us. Redifer and I were close enough to the door that we could have dropped grenades down into the opening."

Many times, my father told me how the Japanese would take American grenades and throw them back at the Marines who threw them first.

"When you threw a grenade at a Japanese soldier at close range you had to make sure it went off before he could pick it up and toss it back at you."

"A lot of guys would pull the pin on a grenade, let the spoon pop off, and then hold it and count to two, because our grenades had a four second delay from when the spoon popped off to when they exploded. The damn tragedy was a lot of times they would go off prematurely, maybe because of a defect from the factory."

As my father and Redifer crouched on the roof of the bunker, Japanese soldiers were grouping up just inside the entrance to charge out. My father said, "I remember we looked down and could see three or four Arisaka rifles with bayonets. Those damn bayonets looked ten feet long. Redifer took his carbine and held it by the muzzle and used the butt to knock 'em down." As he described it to me, my father reenacted the motion of a carbine being worked up and down.

"Well, Santos was behind us, and he yelled out that there was a ventilator pipe sticking up through the roof and it didn't have a cover on it, so he dropped his grenades down into it. Redifer and I handed him our grenades and he dropped those down in there, but we kept watch at the door so none of them could escape."

They could hear the grenades explode below them with muffled bangs. At first, they thought no one could still be alive inside, but very quickly a couple of more Japanese grenades were tossed out. My father and Santos dropped to the roof for protection, but Redifer got some fragments in his arm because he held it up to shield his face.

A runner went back to the beach to get a tank or amtrac with a 75mm to help. My father and his buddies pulled back to some craters about thirty-five to forty yards from the bunker. As they waited, three Japanese soldiers ran out of the structure.

"Each of them had his rifle with fixed bayonet in one hand, and they held up their pants with their other hand. They were headed for the thicket where they could take cover." The Marines cut them down with their carbines.

About this time, they heard an amtrac—an LVT(A)-4 with a 75mm on it—clanking toward them. It lurched into position, and another cluster of Japanese ran out of the bunker. They, too, were cut down in a hail of carbine fire from the Marines, as well as the amtrac machine gunner firing at them with his machine gun.

"They just all went down in a tumble, packs, helmets, rifles, just all in a tangle when they went down," he told me.

"While firing at the Japanese we heard the 'zip' of .45 cal slugs from a Tommy gun on our right rear. It was Cpl. Farmer from G-2 trying to get in on the kill. We yelled at him and bawled him out and told him if he wanted to get into the fight to come up where it was and not endanger our lives by firing from the rear.

"Poor Farmer, he fatally shot himself later while carelessly fooling around with an Arisaka rifle on the last day of the Okinawa campaign."

The amtrac fired three rounds from its 75. The entry hole in the side of the bunker was about four feet in diameter. Dust, coral, and concrete fragments were still clattering down when a Japanese soldier staggered into the opening.

"He was grim determination itself as he drew back his arm to throw a potato masher grenade [a grenade attached to a wooden handle] at us."

My father had his carbine already up, his sights on the man's chest, and began squeezing off shots.

I was sixteen when *With the Old Breed* was published, and I read it when we received the first copies from Presidio Press. Though I knew the story well, I'll always remember the feeling I had when first reading about how my father's bullets tore into this man's chest and the look of agony he saw on his face.

Over the years, I have asked many people, what is it about his memoir that they find so compelling? Almost all of them have answered, "His humanity." I saw that when I read this passage as a teenager, but it was more than that to me. He had just killed a man at close range, and he was not shy in describing the revulsion he felt at the inhumanity of war.

I felt a tremendous sense of pride in him for not only bravely doing his duty but still retaining a semblance of decency amid the horror of it all.

The men fired steadily on the bunker while Cpl. Charles Womack, a big husky man from Mississippi, got into position with his flamethrower.

The flamethrower did its job: The Marines heard screams from inside, and then things quieted down.

"We heartily thanked the amtrac crew and they drove their clanking, rattling monster back toward the beach."

A count of the enemy bodies, both inside and outside the charred, smoking bunker, revealed that they had killed seventeen Japanese.

"Whenever there was a lull in the fighting the men would always 'field strip' any Japanese they had killed or found lying about."

My father removed a bayonet and scabbard from a dead Japanese at this time. I have it mounted on a plaque on my wall to this day. I also have a short-handled knife, with a very sharp, shiny blade with a wooden cover. I noticed it on the bookshelf in my father's study one day, and I asked him about it.

"That's a hara-kiri knife," he said. "I got it off one of the dead ones from that bunker on Ngesebus."

As the Marines collected themselves after this intense close action, ammo and grenades inside the bunker popped off and exploded from the heat of the fire that had been started by Womack's flamethrower.

"Redifer said he wondered where the Japanese machine gun was that had fired at me. Snafu said there hadn't been any machine gun, that Redifer was going Asiatic. This started their argument anew."

Redifer took a flashlight and a cocked .45 pistol and went into the charred and blackened structure. He was going to prove his point to Snafu.

"He was a Cape Gloucester veteran and should have known better, but he went anyway."

Snafu's sardonic comments were offered up in his characteristic Louisiana bayou drawl.

"'Go on in that dark pillbox where you can't see nothin', you dumb jerk. Some Nip is gonna carve up your can and then I'll have to come in and drag you outta there.' Redifer grumbled curses at him.

"It seemed to us that Redifer had been swallowed up by hell itself. After a brief period, he shouted that he had found the machine gun. He said there were a lot of dead Japanese in there. Finally, he came out triumphantly carrying a light machine gun—.30 caliber, the type the Japanese mounted on their observation planes. Snafu had to admit he was wrong. We took turns examining the gun, myself in particular! It did not look as big as it had been the first time I had seen it looking into its muzzle."

The weapon was, in fact, a Lewis machine gun. Sean Prizeman from Illinois was on the trip in 1999, and he researched this weapon and sent my father some information on Lewis guns in a letter in November of 1999—a few months after our trip.

"Redifer counted seven Japanese bodies in the bunker. These, plus the ten killed outside, put the enemy casualties at seventeen. If they had rushed the twelve of us before I happened to hear them talking in the bunker, they would have had the element of surprise in addition to numerical superiority. We had been assured by Gunny that the pillbox was out of action, so we had not been very cautious."

It was fortunate for all of them that my father insisted he heard Japanese voices in the bunker even when Burgin told him he was cracking up.

In October of 1999, Eric Mailander contacted some of the Marines who were involved in that action.

George Sarrett was an assistant gunner in the 60mm mortar section. We'll see much more of him, especially on Okinawa. He remembered the pillbox on Ngesebus—it was "in the open and had several firing ports in it." The LVT (A)-4 fired on it, "at least two times" by his count, and on the beach side. During the action, he recalled, "about four Japs ran out, one with his pants or leggings on fire. Santos shot him in the rear!"

Vincent Santos, another close friend of my father, was a 60mm gunner. His assistant gunner was John Redifer. Santos recalled that the 75mm on the LVT(A)-4 "fired on the beach side of the structure." According to him, "they fired at least four rounds at the structure—they did not penetrate both sides." He remembered "about four Japs running out—one almost made it." He also spoke of "baffles protecting the door to the pillbox and an air vent on top." At one point they tried to "put grenades at the firing ports near the round bars, but the Japs kept putting canteens on front for added protection."

Apparently, Santos must have gone into the knocked-out bunker after it was all over. He stated that he remembered "a dead Jap gunner slumped over an aircraft machine gun, and when I pulled on the barrel the Jap 'popped' from being so bloated." Was this the machine gunner my father had the face-to-face encounter with?

Finding that bunker was a seminal moment in my journey of retracing my father's footsteps across Peleliu. Eric Mailander, Sean Prizeman, Ron Leidich, Ray Fournier, Col. Joe Alexander, and David Watkins were there with me.

When we first saw the structure after half running and half stumbling through the sun-dappled jungle, I'll never forget Eric's exuberant whooping and yelling. It had eluded him on previous excursions to Palau, but not this time.

As he hacked at the vines and roots that clung to the concrete of the bunker with his machete to make it more accessible, he stood by that spot where my father had been when Burgin told him to look over the wall and said, "Henry, if your father had been a split second slower, you would have never been born!"

I took my own machete and hacked out a chunk of mossy concrete from that spot of the wall, right about where my father was when the burst from the machine gun plowed a furrow and rained dust and dirt down on him. It is one of my most prized possessions to this day.

Later that afternoon, we met our boat, went back across to Peleliu, and congregated at the Storyboard Resort. Those days we didn't have cellphones, but I was able to call home—the time difference between Alabama and Peleliu is something I still haven't figured out—when, for my parents, it was in the early morning hours of the previous day. When my father came on the line, I told him excitedly that we had found the bunker on Ngesebus.

"That's great, Big Shot," he said groggily.

I told him breathlessly that we had seen it all—the shell hole in the side from the 75s, how it was still charred black around the edges from Womack's flamethrower, and how I knelt in the same spot he had when he looked over the wall and the Japanese machine gunner almost killed him.

"Yeah, boy, that was really something," he said.

I knew that he was proud that I had made the journey, and we had found the bunker, but I also could tell he really just wanted to go back to sleep.

I told him how proud I was to be his son and how proud I was that he had written *With the Old Breed*, and how being out on that island that day made me feel almost as though I was with him when it all happened.

There was a slight pause, and then I heard him through the static half a world away: "Well, I'm proud o' you too, Big Shot, and you were with me—in spirit."

I apologized for waking him up, told him I loved him, and said goodbye.

"I love you too, Big Shot. You boys have fun out there—and be careful."

"We set up our mortars in a large crater near the knocked-out pillbox. We prepared to fire the mission that had been interrupted when I heard the Japanese, and then the ensuing fight. About that time, a combat photographer came by and said he wanted to photograph us. Each of us immediately started grinning and smiling. The photographer told us to pay no attention to the camera because he wanted a natural photograph of us firing the mortars. We turned to and started firing, and he took several photographs, said 'good luck,' and went on his way.

"I never saw or heard of those photographs taken on September 28, 1944, until 1975 when a photo of a Marine 60mm mortar section in a crater on Ngesebus appeared in the book ***Bloodiest Victory: Palaus*** by Dr. Stanley Falk. Although I think I can identify the faces of several men in the picture, the shade makes them too dark to be certain.

"To the everlasting credit of that unknown photographer on Ngesebus, he wanted a realistic photograph.

"Toward late afternoon Johnny Marmet came back from his observation post. He took muster and found that Sam was absent. No one knew where he was or had seen him since the landing. We thought he had been killed and fallen where no one had noticed him, but presently here [came] Sam, trudging along from back toward the battalion CP.

"'Where the hell you been?' demanded Johnny.

"'I had to go back to battalion,' said Sam.

"'What for? Did you take a casualty back? Who gave you permission to go? Why the hell have you been back there all damn day?' Johnny asked, his eyes flashing with anger.

"'Well, the firing pin on my rifle broke, and I had to go back to get it fixed,' whimpered Sam.

"By this time the entire mortar section was all ears. Johnny Marmet tolerated no nonsense—so when a Marine in his mortar section did something he'd better do it right or it was hell to pay.

"We knew trouble was coming, and nobody pitied Sam because of the tragic death of Bill, his foxhole buddy a few nights before. [This was an unfortunate incident where Sam had fallen asleep while he was on watch; a Japanese infiltrator got into their foxhole, and Bill was killed in the ensuing confusion by friendly fire.] Johnny was furious. As he glared at Sam he began to nervously fidget with his Tommy gun and said, 'You left your post in the face of the enemy, you bastard. I ought to shoot you right now.'

"The lieutenant came up and said in a calm voice, 'Now Johnny, you'd spend the rest of your life in Mare Island if you did that.'"

"Johnny glared at Sam and said, 'You've got a yellow streak a foot wide down your back.'

"He spun around and moved off a short distance and sat on the deck. His face looked like a thundercloud. Sam looked relieved and tried to make excuses to the lieutenant. As far as we were concerned Sam was a disgrace. No one spoke to him or had anything to do with him—he was treated like an outcast."

They dug in for the night as bad weather approached. Ominous clouds gathered, and the wind began to blow.

"This was actually the edge of a typhoon that piled one of the LSTs on the reef. As darkness fell, I heard the man who had been ordered to dig in with Sam—no one would do it voluntarily—say, 'Look, you sonofabitch, if you go to sleep on watch tonight like you did with Bill, I'll whip your ass.' There was a mumbled reply, and everyone fell silent."

The next day they were told that an Army unit would finish the job on Ngesebus. As they halted to await orders, they came upon a Japanese heavy machine gun squad that had been killed and their weapon knocked out by other K Company men the day before.[10]

"The heavy gun, weighing about 120 lbs. was undamaged and rested on the tripod which still had the carrying handles, like those of a stretcher, front and rear by which it could be moved and carried

10 E.B. Sledge, *With the Old Breed*, 122.

by two men. There was a metal strip clip still containing 7.7mm cartridges extending from the side of the breech."

The dead gunners were sprawled about. Though my father was tempted to extract some gold teeth, Doc Caswell dissuaded him from doing so—the "germs could deadly," he said—for which my father was forever after grateful. He cut off some collar insignia from one of the dead Japanese soldiers.

"Marines held Navy corpsmen in high regard because they went through thick and thin with us, risking their lives caring for the wounded. These men exhibited skill and knowledge, and I thought Doc knew as much about 'germs' as my dad back home."

As two Marine M4 tanks that had been parked near them cranked up and rumbled back toward the beach, their undercarriages rattling and squealing, my father and his buddies suddenly began taking fire from a Japanese 75mm artillery piece somewhere to their right. This weapon caused a number of casualties before it was knocked out by the tanks that quickly returned to help. This was a horrifying experience for the men who were exposed to the almost point-blank fire.

"Without the quick and effective help of the tanks, I am sure many more Marine infantrymen would have been killed and wounded by that Japanese 75.

"There were thirteen tanks operating with 3/5 on Ngesebus. Sixteen had been scheduled but the engines of three were drowned out on the reef. We thought the tankers should get a lot of credit for Ngesebus, and the tankers said they experienced great coordination from the infantry."

The battle on Peleliu had been raging for two weeks at this point, and the men were exhausted, physically and emotionally. When my father became emotional, a lieutenant, Duke Ellington from Birmingham, Alabama, offered a few words of much needed encouragement.

"What Duke said was neither a dramatic battlefield oration nor a pep talk, but it gave me what I needed and remained exactly in my memory."

The Marines shouldered their gear to head back across to Peleliu when a column of Army troops arrived along with amphibious tractors loaded with supplies.

"The capture of the fighter strip on Ngesebus was to no advantage, because the surface proved so sandy our planes couldn't use it. However, our battalion had accomplished two positive results by eliminating Japanese fire from Ngesebus into the flanks and rear of Marine units fighting on the northern tip of Peleliu, and by depriving the Japanese of a place to land reinforcements coming from the northern islands to Peleliu."

The capture of Ngesebus was an unqualified success, but it was not without cost.

"Among our K Company killed was Sgt. Rigney. He was a fine man who had insisted that some man with relatives take his place on the list of veterans to be sent home before Peleliu. Rigney had been raised in an orphanage, so he had no family to go home to. A Japanese shot him from a cave as Rigney stood in front of it firing his Tommy gun into it. He made no effort to be cautious, and it was as though he didn't want to live, as one man said."

CHAPTER NINE

Back in the Ridges of Northern Peleliu

The 3rd Battalion dug in back on northern Peleliu where the decimated 1st Marines were before they boarded ship in rough seas on September 30 to return to Pavuvu.

"We were able to get some physical rest but had to be on watch for the ever-present infiltrators. I do not recall much regarding our move that day from northern Peleliu to this area near Purple Beach. We probably moved by trucks."

The battle was far from over, and anyone who doubted that had only to listen to the shellfire and other noises of battle from the Umurbrogol. The 5th Regiment was soon to join the 7th Marines, who were already there.

"The following quote from *Time* magazine's Robert Martin on October 16, 1944, describes some of the terrible conditions we encountered on Peleliu: 'For sheer brutality and fatigue, I think it surpasses anything yet seen in the Pacific, certainly from the standpoint of number of troops involved and the time taken to make the island secure.'"[11]

In the early days of October, the Marines launched an attack on the Five Sisters. As the riflemen made several fruitless attacks on this particularly difficult section of peaks and cliffs, the mortarmen had to act as stretcher bearers. This was a task that every Marine, regardless of his specific job within the company, had to do at some point on Peleliu.

---

[11] *Time*. "World Battlefronts: Men at War: Compassionate Confusion." *Time* 44, no. 16 (October 16, 1944): 38.

My father told me that "the Japs opened up on stretcher teams mercilessly. This intensified our already intense hatred of them. We were absolutely terrified that one of us would slip on the rugged coral, and of course our greatest fear was that the poor guy on the stretcher would fall off."

Nobody had any doubts about what the Japanese would do to wounded Marines or soldiers if they got to them. Even the dead were not left behind.

"The only time I knew of K Company dead being left behind was on Ngesebus. There was one body left because he couldn't be moved without further loss of life. This happened as we were in the process of leaving our positions to the Army relief. The Japanese couldn't get to the body to hack him up, so we were ordered to let it remain. We were told that Army troops pushed through the spot the next day and recovered it."

"Some of the veterans who had been with the Division since Guadalcanal told me they never saw such constant intense night activity. I saw many of my comrades killed and wounded in these nightmarish episodes.

"Japanese special close quarter combat units holed up in caves all day long, so when night came they were well rested and out for our blood. The whole company often stayed awake nearly all night warding them off.

"We fired mortar HE and flares, threw grenades, and used other weapons to kill them and keep them out of our foxholes. Sometimes they slipped past us and would get into a previously captured position and snipe on us from the rear."

Another pest presented itself during this battle, one that every Marine or soldier who fought in the Pacific knew well.

"After dark when the Japanese started creeping around, so did the infernal land crabs. Considering all the unburied human corpses lying around, it is obvious why they scuttled all over the place at night. In the dark when these creatures moved over the dried debris, leaves, and other vegetation that had been blasted and pulverized on

the ground, it was impossible to determine whether it was a crab or a man slowly and stealthily creeping about.

"Even the most coolheaded veterans couldn't tell the difference. When a flare went off and illuminated the area, we all peered in the direction and strained our eyes and ears to identify the sound."

Men from noncombat units frequently wandered into or even beyond the front lines looking for souvenirs, such as Japanese flags or sabers. At one point during the fighting in the ridges, a major from the 7th Marines would put these men into the lines with a weapon. While he was opinionated on this subject, I also heard my father say many times that rear echelon troops often volunteered and served as stretcher bearers.

Japanese mortar fire was a constant danger.

"One afternoon while we were in front of the Five Sisters, I was talking to an NCO as a file of weary Marine infantry from a company to our left trudged past us to take up positions in a quiet area. They had had a rough time up on some ridges to our left and were exhausted. Just as they got past us some of them bunched up. I saw in the upper field of my vision three Japanese mortar shells streaking down at an angle.

"Instantly I yelled, 'Mortars!' and the NCO and I threw ourselves toward the deck as I heard that deadly whispering sound. It happened in an instant. The shells didn't appear to me as distinct shells, but as an elongated shape like a big arrow rushing out of the sky. The big 90mm shells went off in rapid succession—three flashes followed by ripping explosions and shrapnel tearing through the air. The first one exploded before we could hit the deck. As I went down, I saw several of the men who had just filed past get struck by shrapnel. One man's knees buckled, and he dropped his rifle and fell backward, another pitched forward, and another sagged as though he were weary.

"Their buddies dove for the deck. I felt the waves of concussion and was stung on my hands and face and through my dungarees by flying chunks of coral. The NCO and I were not hit by shrapnel, but eight of those men filing past us were. Ironically the shells fell closer

to us than to them and exploded before we could hit the deck. That we escaped death was unbelievable.

"Our corpsman helped the casualties, and the retiring troops' officers ordered the other men to get the injured and head out on the double. We jumped into the gun pit and stood by to fire if the Japanese mortar was sighted by our observers, but they had secured their gun and gone back into hiding. They had accomplished their purpose.

"My ears were ringing, and my dungarees had a heavy chemical odor for hours from the blast of those shells.

"One of my buddies in the other K Company mortar gun pit got out and sat on his helmet and smoked a cigarette. He was a Gloucester veteran and a complete fatalist. 'Hey Sledgehammer, you gonna stay in that hole all day? That Nip ain't gonna shell us no more,' he said grinning at me.

"'Ole buddy, I'm gonna stay here until I get orders to get out. I'm not taking any chances on what that Nip is gonna do. I'm not striking to be a hero like you.'

"He grinned again and said, 'Oh well, when your numbers up that's all there is to it, I guess.'"

This man was probably Jim Burke. He may have referred to Burke as "the Fatalist," but in no way was that meant with any disrespect. I remember my father speaking of him several times over the years—always with admiration.

With his usual eye for detail, my father described the differences between US grenades and Japanese grenades.

"The Japanese fragmentation grenade did not have an automatic spring driven hammer to pop the primer cap to ignite the fuse like ours. After you pulled the pin on a U.S. grenade you could hold the spoon or lever, down until you threw it. The spoon flew off which would then pop the cap to start the primer. The bursting charge exploded several seconds later. If you opted not to throw and the spoon was still depressed, you could insert the pin again to hold the spoon down and disarm it. But the Japanese had to strike their grenades on some hard object—usually a rifle stock, helmet or rock to pop the cap."

When he first explained this process to me, I was pretty young, maybe nine or ten. I was puzzled because this was not what I had seen in the movies.

"So you pulled the pin with your fingers?" I asked.

"That's right."

I thought for a second and then said, "Well, how come in that John Wayne movie he pulled the pin with his teeth?" I picked up a pineapple grenade off his bookshelf (disarmed and totally safe, of course) and gingerly bit down on the ring attached to the pin. "There's no way you could pull that thing out with your teeth!"

My father chuckled. "Well, we did our best, but we weren't as tough as the Duke."

"Around October 3, a K Company NCO told me that a total of twenty-one Japanese infiltrators were killed in the company area that morning. It was such a rough night that most of us wouldn't forget it.

"The Japanese who slipped into our lines at night all seemed to know the terrain features in their area perfectly. However, on one occasion we saw a man die a bizarre death because he apparently mistook the opening of a deep, dry well for a foxhole.

"He had gotten into the company line one night and some of the men discovered him next morning and fired at him but missed. He took off at a run across the flat ground with Marines still firing at him. He jumped out of sight into what we assumed was a deep foxhole. Upon checking we could see his crumpled body down at the bottom of a hole. Whether he thought he was jumping into the safety of a foxhole or whether he simply committed hari-kari we never knew."

By October 5, the 7th Marines were almost as decimated as the 1st Marines, and the 5th Marines began to relieve them. But the worst was not over.

"Some of the men of the battered and exhausted 7th Marines were still going to be killed or wounded in actions in some of the draws and valleys on Peleliu. Also, the Japanese continued to infiltrate back into captured positions and snipe at the airfield and other

areas. Finding and destroying these fanatics was euphemistically called 'mopping up,' where a Marine could be killed just as dead as hitting the beach or being hit in a big attack."

On October 7 the Army and the Marines experienced an excellent example of interservice cooperation. The Marine's 3/5 attacked up a draw known as the "Horseshoe." This area of the Umurbrogol was a hornet's nest, rife with Japanese caves and protected gun positions. Rather than receiving armor support from the Marine Corps 1st Tank Battalion, which had been relieved and sent back to Pavuvu on October 1, they were supported by six Army tanks of the 710th Tank Battalion.

The Marine infantry had no ill will toward their tank battalion for being removed from Peleliu while they fought on.

"The miracle of the 1st Tank Battalion is that the men were relieved and sent back to Pavuvu along with the tanks. It's a wonder the tank crews weren't put up on the holding line around the Umurbrogol Pocket like artillerymen, Pioneers, and amtrac drivers. I'm glad they weren't."

After this attack, 3/5 pulled back from the area around the ridges, and the mortarmen took up positions between West Road and the thin line of beach on that side of the island.

In their new position, with their backs to the sea, the mortarmen were firing over the road and onto the ridges. West Road was a major conduit on the western side of the island for men, trucks, armor, and amtracs moving from the area around the airfield to positions in the north. The Japanese placed snipers in the ridge in that area who could then fire at anything moving on the road. The mortar fire from my father and his fellow mortarmen served to clean these snipers out.

"We were told that snipers had killed Col. Hankins along this area of the road while he was trying to straighten out a traffic jam of amtracs and trucks. Most of the Japanese fire was well aimed rifle fire, but I frequently heard a Nambu fire short bursts.

"I had a good friend, an amtrac driver from Mississippi, who brought me up to date [on] things around the island whenever we met. Amtrac drivers at this stage of the battle went all over the

Division area delivering ammunition and evacuating wounded, so he knew what was going on. When I talked to him while we were in this particular position, he told me of a tragic event he had just witnessed. He was furious and seething with hatred for the enemy.

"He said he was carrying six wounded, all stretcher cases, in his tractor along the West Road toward the airfield and the Regimental Aid Station, and when he arrived at his destination every one of those Marines was dead. Japanese snipers had fired down into his tractor and shot every one of them on their stretchers as he raced along the road."

With their backs so close to the water behind them, the mortarmen had to maintain a constant vigil to ensure that no Japanese troops could slip up behind them by wading in.

"We fired the mortars a good bit at night, both HE against the Japanese on the ridges, and flare shells every few minutes. The muzzle flashes from our guns were somewhat screened from the front by the vegetation but could be seen easily from up and down the beach and out in the water."

My father told me this story when I was a teenager. He described how that night, they were firing their mortar, putting up flare shells, "**one about every four to five minutes.**"

His buddy, Jim Burke, was positioned next to him.

"He and his assistant were firing slow harassing fire, traversing across an area in front of our lines with about five shells and then cease firing for about half an hour."

"Ole Jim Burke was totally unflappable. Nothing excited him or got him bent out of shape," my father said to me. "I noticed he was really watching something out in the water; even though it was dark, there was just enough light that you could see silhouettes out in the water—and I remember he just leaned over and whispered, 'Sledgehammer, lemme see your carbine a minute.' And he was so nonchalant the way he said it, so I handed him my carbine. He was sitting there on his helmet, and he aimed it at something out in the water.... It was a Jap sneaking along about thirty or forty yards out trying to come in behind us, and we could just see him in that dim moonlight, and Jim squeezed off two quick shots; we could see the Jap out in the water just disappear, and Jim just flipped the safety back on and handed me back my carbine and said, 'Thanks, Sledgehammer.'"

I remember that my father and I both laughed at how laconic and casual Jim was. "He was just totally unconcerned," he said to me.

"The men around us questioned what we saw. We kept close seaward watch the rest of the night but saw no more of that enemy soldier. He must have been carried away by the water because next morning we saw no remains or evidence of him.

"A little later on Doc Caswell took his turn and helped me fire my mortar, because we were shorthanded in the mortar section due to casualties. We heard some noises in the bush in front of us and Doc pulled out his .45 pistol and I raised my carbine, and we waited and watched nervously. As he held his pistol in readiness to fire, he was nervous (like myself) and I could actually hear the worn pistol rattling as his hand trembled.

"The noise in the brush subsided, so Doc and I figured it was a land crab and relaxed. I whispered to him that even if the Japanese didn't see our mortar's muzzle flashes, they could find us by the rattling of his worn out .45 automatic. He whispered back to me, in his Texas accent, that he thought he would have more success with his pistol if he threw it a Japanese rather than firing the worn-out thing.

"The men in the mortar section kidded Doc about his helping on the mortar; 'Hell Doc, you're violating the Geneva Convention—you're supposed to be a noncombatant,' one buddy said. Doc just grinned at him.

"We were in this position next to the water's edge just a few days. The costly fighting all around the pocket continued. Ambulance jeeps and amtracs with wounded moved continuously along the West Road even within our small sector. There seemed to be no end in sight for us."

When I was six or seven, I got a toy jeep from the local dime store—it was plastic and OD green with a white star on the hood. I played with it and the little plastic soldiers—or 'Army men,' as I called them—that I bought from the same place. I would put it beside my bed at night, and it would be there waiting for me the next morning. In the afternoons my brother and I would watch reruns of *The Rat Patrol*, the late 1960s action television series about four Allied soldiers wreaking havoc and just generally being heroes against Erwin Rommel's Afrika Korps in North Africa. The protagonists sped around the desert in two jeeps, and I would sit on the living room floor and play with my green plastic jeep while we watched.

Naturally I asked my father if he saw many jeeps during the war.

"Yeah, I saw a lot of 'em, but I only ever rode in a jeep one time," he answered.

"Many people got the impression that every American in the armed forces in World War II spent much of his time riding around in a jeep. In Hollywood films even the lowliest private seemed to always have one available for his immediate use and sped around gleefully with the convertible top down. Such was not the reality.

"On October 12 I had my first—and only—jeep ride during my entire enlistment. It was an eventful day."

The mortar section, which had been temporarily detached from the rest of K Company, was to rejoin them. My father, Snafu, and George Sarrett gathered their gear and piled into a jeep. An NCO drove pell-mell up West Road.

"He said we would be let off at a supply dump and to wait there until an NCO came and guided us to the company up in the ridges. Snipers kept all vehicles moving at a fast pace along much of the route, but we soon reached a quiet section of the road.

"All the infantrymen we saw along our route were as scroungy, filthy, and exhausted looking as ourselves. They all plodded wearily along, or when halted, sat listlessly looking at nothing. We all looked like zombies. In striking contrast, we passed some of the troops who had been formed into a holding line around the Umurbrogol Pocket. These artillerymen, Pioneers, and amtrac drivers were certainly doing their part, but you could spot them because their dungarees weren't as filthy, they weren't bearded, and they didn't look beat down and exhausted like the infantry.

"Our jeep ride lasted only a few minutes, and our driver pulled up beside a tarpaulin shelter over several boxes of C rations. We unloaded our gear and sat on the ration boxes under the shade of the tarp, sheltered from the broiling hot sun. The area was open, and there were no troops in the immediate vicinity. Across the road to the east were three Army half-track vehicles, each with an 81mm mortar mounted on it. They were parked in the shadow of a secured part of Bloody Nose and were firing up over the quiet ridge at Japanese positions in the pocket.

"I had never seen 81mm mortars mounted on half-tracks, but it looked like a good idea. At intervals we could hear the Army mortar crews calling fire orders and repeating them, then the muffled 'bump' of the propelling charge as each big shell went on its way, followed by a dull crash as it exploded beyond the ridge in the pocket. The ever-present sound of machine guns rattled up the road and across the ridge. We sat listlessly in the shade enjoying the comparative safety.

"We noticed three Army rear echelon souvenir hunters coming along from the direction of the airfield. They carried no weapons, canteens, or other equipment, wore fatigue caps and clean, neatly pressed dungarees. The men were clean shaven and appeared relaxed. We gaped openmouthed at them walking jauntily along the road talking and laughing loudly. They had a spring in their step like it was all a picnic, and frequently picked up and pocketed shell fragments and other war debris which littered the area all around.

"They didn't see us under the tarp, nor did they notice the half-tracks either. I was thinking some pretty spiteful thoughts about them.

"Just as they were across the road opposite to us the Army mortarmen called out fire orders. Then they fired, and the souvenir hunters panicked at the sound. Combat troops got jittery at the sound of small arms fire and shells but would have immediately recognized the muffled 'bump' of our 81s firing and probably not flinched. It was only after the war when you got home and began to unwind that you jumped when someone slammed a door or dropped a book.

"In action our ears were so acutely tuned to every subtle sound that we reacted only to those that meant danger. But the clean men didn't know the difference. They started rushing around in a circle, each following the other with their arms outstretched and looking wildly about them. Then they started bumping into each other. In their panic they didn't even know enough to hit the deck. We knew that the airfield had been shelled by the Japanese periodically and some rear echelon troops had been killed and wounded, so they apparently thought this was the end. Finally, they hit the deck as the 81s continued firing.

"It all happened very quickly and George, Snafu and I roared with laughter and slapped our knees. It was the best laugh we had had in a long time. It was the only time during the war that I laughed at someone who was afraid, and I still enjoy the mental picture of that panicky threesome."

"When they heard the howls of laughter from us, they stopped, straightened up, looked at the mortars and then at us with relief and then chagrin. We continued to laugh, and they began pointing at each other and accusing each other of causing the panic. They looked at us, the raggedy ass Marines, with a good bit of misgivings as though we might be only slightly less dangerous to them than the Japanese. They turned and hurried back the way they came, casting an occasional sheepish look over their shoulders. It was a good show, and I was sincerely sorry the Army mortarmen had been too busy with their guns to see it. They had provided the sound effects that started it all, and they deserved some of the laughter."

Shortly after this bit of comic relief, they picked up their gear and, along with the other mortarmen of K Company who had joined them, headed back up into the ridges. They hadn't gone far when they saw Johnny Marmet come down toward them. It was obvious something was dreadfully wrong.

"At first I thought we had not carried out orders properly, but then I realized Johnny had never looked like this before."

The sad, awful truth was that Capt. "Ack Ack" Haldane, the beloved and revered commander of K Company, the man who had spoken to my father long ago on Pavuvu as they struggled through the gloom of a late afternoon thunderstorm and made him feel warm inside, had been killed by a Japanese sniper on Hill 140.

"In the process of our battalion moving into the positions of the 2nd Battalion, 5th Marines, the Japanese sniper fire was intense and deadly accurate. This had been in progress while my squad was on our way back to the company from the position near the beach. There were twenty-two casualties, and one of these was Capt. Haldane."

In 1999, I got to see many of the areas where my father fought in 1944. On a trip like that, however, it's never possible to see everything on your list. I wanted to visit Hill 140, but time and logistics conspired against us, and I was not able to.

It was just as well.

I knew in my heart that my father felt an enormous sense of pride that I wanted to travel to the other side of the world and retrace his footsteps. I think it was somehow edifying to him, and even though he didn't want to relive the horror and tragedy of Peleliu, I do believe he enjoyed seeing the pictures I took and hearing about my adventures. Had I visited Hill 140, however, I would not have shown him pictures or even told him about it. Anything that would have evoked the memory of Ack Ack's loss would have been too much.

"Tom Clay, a friend of mine in F Co, 2nd Battalion, 5th Marines, was nearby when Capt. Haldane was killed. Tom told me the captain looked over the ridge, the bullets struck him, and his head went down, and he never moved again."

The men of K Company were all upset about Haldane's death, but they took up their new positions on Hill 140—along the northern end of the Horseshoe.

"Emplaced immediately in front of our mortars was a 75mm pack howitzer. It had been disassembled, hauled up the recently captured Wattie Ridge to our left rear, and then reassembled and emplaced on 140. It was emplaced upon a little ledge behind rocks

and sandbags and was anchored against its recoil by ropes tied to rocks and wooden stakes driven between rocks.

"It reminded me of an 18th century ship's cannon secured with ropes and tackle. This gun fired at Japanese positions in the Horseshoe and the western base of Walt Ridge. Naturally the Japanese were anxious to silence this destructive artillery piece, so the Marine crew had to exercise unusual caution to avoid being hit by enemy rifle and machine gun fire.

"A working party from K Company was sent down to the ridge to our rear to bring up ammo for the artillery piece. I was among them, and it was back breaking work. Each of us shouldered a big heavy 75mm shell, holding it in place with one hand while using the other hand to balance on the steep trail to the top of Hill 140. The incline of that trail must have been 45 degrees in some places. As we inched along, I looked out at the foreboding faces of the shell-blasted coral ridges and waited for snipers to open up. Japanese had infested areas all over the ridge system, but none shot at us as we struggled up the trail and stacked the shells within reach of the artillerymen.

"Johnny Marmet was right next to the 75mm howitzer and was so close to us that he simply shouted the fire orders to us and didn't need the sound-power[ed] phone. Snafu and I crouched by our mortar and looked up at Johnny as he directed us with compass settings to place the aiming stakes. These were propped up with chunks of rocks because nothing could be driven into those solid coral ridges.

"The fighting around Hill 140 was typical of most of what we had seen since our regiment had been in action among the ridges the last two weeks.

"Japanese gunpowder being smokeless like ours, it was usually impossible to spot their weapons among the camouflaged positions in the ridges."

It had become obvious that the American troops on Peleliu weren't going anywhere. Once the high ground around the airfield was captured, the battle degenerated into a guerilla warfare peculiar to the Japanese. They knew they weren't going to win, but they were determined to fight to the death and take as many Americans with them as they could—as had been their plan all along.

"Attempts were made to get them to surrender. Leaflets were dropped from planes and told the Japanese where they could surrender. During one such occasion a Japanese language interpreter with a loudspeaker came into our company area and tried to talk some Japanese out of a cave.

"We crouched on the valley floor off about fifty yards from the cave entrance in a steep ridge and waited while the interpreter urged them to give up and assured them of safety. We waited hopefully and watched. The more Japanese that surrendered the fewer we had to fight. Slowly and cautiously, we saw one emerge from the cave mouth. He was in full uniform but wore a cloth cap in place of a steel helmet.

"He carried no visible weapons and had his hands clasped over his forehead as directed. He was followed by another, and then another. We were ordered to remain absolutely motionless, and not make a sound. Just as the sixth Japanese cleared the cave mouth a burst of BAR fire from my left rear ripped the tense quiet. Bullets kicked up dust and went pinging and whining off the rocks all around the surrendering Japanese.

"They were not hit but spun around and raced back into the blackness of the cave. We looked around and saw one of our BAR men lowering his rifle from his shoulder. One of our surviving company officers went back and gave him a tongue lashing no one could forget. That episode, naturally, ended any chance of those Japanese surrendering. Someone near me remarked that the BAR man should have his can kicked—not for opening fire, but for missing!"

Undoubtedly there were mixed feelings from the men when this happened. At this point, they just wanted it to be over, whether by the Japanese surrendering or their being annihilated.

The battle on Peleliu had been going on for almost a month. The heat, lack of sanitation, proliferation of dead bodies, and bloated flies feeding on the dead all served to create an unimaginable environment. Marine dead were evacuated from the battle area as soon as possible or, at the very least, covered with a poncho until they could be. But the Japanese lay where they fell.

Although the tension grew worse by the hour in the contested area near the Umurbrogol Pocket, it was a different world down near the airfield that they had charged across under murderous fire on the second day.

"From certain positions we were in…while on the ridges we could look down with a clear view of the airfield. It was teeming with aviation personnel and service troops. They lived comfortably in pyramidal tents such as [those] we occupied on Pavuvu, and at one point we could even see men taking showers. We sat among the rocks and cursed them for their cleanliness like the filthy, exhausted outcasts from human decency that we were.

"Japanese were constantly slipping back into positions next to the airfield that had been captured weeks before. They would then snipe at the service personnel, but it was always some exhausted infantry unit that had to go find the snipers and exterminate them.

"We never doubted the expert marksmanship of Japanese snipers, because we constantly saw the destructive results of it.

"I experienced some slight peace of mind during quiet periods in the ridges gazing out at our fleet of ships stretched around Peleliu. From certain positions it was possible to look out over the ocean all around us. The fantastic variety of ships supporting us ranged from tiny patrol craft to huge full-sized battle wagons [battleships]. There was comfort in having the fleet out there.

"'Boy, them swabbies got it made, Sledgehammer. They can go to the galley anytime and get a cup o' joe or a drink a' ice water and then sack out in a clean bunk. Wish to hell I'd had sense enough to join the Navy,' mused a buddy one day as we sat looking out at the ships all around the island.

"I did envy the sailors for their clean-living conditions and clean air to breathe, but I never resented their good luck. Most of my buddies felt pretty much the same way about the sailors. As Marines, and being amphibious assault troops, we felt a closer relationship to the Navy than

the Army. Also, we knew that at any moment while at sea any one of those ships was subject to submarine or aerial attack. A swabbie might be sleeping in a clean rack one minute and suddenly be fighting blazing oil fires if his ship got hit or struggling for his life in the water if his ship sank. So, the easy life of a sailor wasn't as safe as it might appear.

"There was sporadic firing by the Japanese across the crest of the ridge to keep our men on the line from firing at their position. Someone yelled 'corpsman' and four of us were ordered up onto the ridge to bring down a K Company man who had just been hit. I slung my carbine over my shoulder and took off on the double with the other members of the stretcher team. We had to run up a steep rough trail stretching diagonally up to the crest.

"'Who got hit?' I asked an NCO as we arrived where the corpsman was kneeling over the casualty.

"'It's _______, shot right in the head,' he answered. 'Dammit, poor kid, it was his own fault too, everybody knew when we moved in up here that the Nips were covering the crest. Damn it to hell, if he didn't look over the ridge, and just as somebody yelled at him to get down a sniper nailed him. It's a pity, but some people just don't seem to get the word.' The casualty was still conscious and managed a weak smile when I told him he would recover soon. The corpsman put a battle dressing over an ugly red lump oozing blood on the right side of his forehead.

"We placed him on the stretcher and struggled down the steep trail with our dying friend. The men on the lower end of the stretcher held the handles above their heads and I, and another Marine, at the head end held our handles just above the rocks as we slid and stumbled down the trail. We struggled down the ridge and carried him a short distance to the road where we placed him aboard an ambulance jeep. He died shortly thereafter. It was such a needless loss.

"I returned to the gun pit and sat down and took a long drink of tepid water from my canteen. While I panted for breath, I looked over the area surrounding us."

The detritus of heavy combat was everywhere, as were the bloated enemy corpses.

"Nearby there were a couple of rusting discarded U.S. light machine gun barrels—burned out from heavy firing. I didn't see many of our M1 Garand rifles, though."

My father wrote and spoke often of how the most trivial things made an impression on him, and other combat veterans, at the time. So much of what was recorded by historians, valuable though it was, lacked something—maybe it was the authenticity of one who actually experienced the event.

"Near our gun pit was a knocked-out U.S. 37mm anti-tank or field gun. The rubber tires were flattened, and one side of the heavy metal protective shield was torn and bent back at an angle, apparently by the blast of a Japanese mortar or artillery shell. A web ammo bag containing 37mm shells was still slung over the trail of the gun carriage. I wondered if any of the Marine gun crew survived."

He told me once that he did not recall a single time on Peleliu that you didn't hear, at the very least, machine gun fire somewhere on the island.

"Since the ridges were parallel and, in many places, separated by narrow canyons, the use of supporting weapons such as naval gunfire and tanks was sometimes restricted. However, when possible, tanks were used against caves. They were always employed with riflemen as tank infantry teams.

"The most awesome to me were the flamethrowing tanks and amtracs. We saw both used against various parts of the ridges. When the long nozzle was pointed at the cave or pillbox a huge jet of flaming napalm would spurt forth with a 'whoosh' sound. The flaming napalm hit the ridge with a splattering sound and set everything on fire that would burn. The fire used up the oxygen in the caves and suffocated anyone who didn't get roasted alive.

"Sometimes, the splattering napalm from the big jets of flame caught them, and it was gruesome to see enemy soldiers scurrying among the rocks with their uniforms on fire. The machine guns and rifle fire quickly cut them down once they left the protection of their caves.

"Of course, when one cave was under attack, we usually received fire from supporting caves nearby, and this caused casualties in our units. Our 60mm mortars usually fired large numbers of shells at areas to be attacked. The heavy mortars of the battalion 81mm platoon and our artillery joined in to cover the target area with a blanket of explosions that sometimes lasted for hours. The 155mm Long Tom artillery pieces also fired their deadly sky bursts which exploded over the target."

"We often fired white phosphorous shells which threw out flaming bits of phosphorous in addition to steel fragments. These shells also covered the area in dense clouds of white smoke which obscured the view of the Japanese gunners and, aided us in evacuating our casualties under fire. It was difficult to comprehend how the Japanese survived such fire storms, but they simply sat it out in their tunnel systems deep under coral rock, and when we moved forward, opened fire on us.

The Umurbrogol Pocket presented a tactical and strategic conundrum for American forces. The Japanese emplaced in this area were still full of fight, well protected, and adequately supplied with ammunition. It was going to take everything the US Marines and the US Army could bring to bear to crush this last enemy stronghold.

"Our Marine Corsair fighter planes flew many airstrikes against the ridges, firing machine guns, rockets, and dropping bombs, both napalm and high explosive. The napalm bombs made huge columns of thick black smoke and burned off the vegetation. We delighted to see those beautiful, blue, gull-winged Corsairs come to our support. In some locations, we could see them take off from the airfield, circle over, drop their bombs, and return to the airfield."

Lt. Glenn "Bud" Daniel, one of the Corsair pilots in VMF-114, remembered these missions:

> "VMF-114 was settling into days of relatively short, but important combat flights.... pinpoint bombing of the caves of Peleliu. These were very short as time from takeoff to target was as low as fifteen seconds. Marine

> infantry covered the entrances to the caves with a circle of smoke. The center of the circle was the cave's entrance. The outer circle of the smoke signaled the location of friendly Marines. Five hundred and 1000 -pound bombs are powerful. Out of necessity we became very precise."[12]

"'Boy, that'll knock them Nips out,' exclaimed a buddy of mine as we watched the awesome explosions. But he was wrong. There were other air strikes in addition to these when 1,000-pound bombs were dropped on enemy positions in the Umurbrogol Pocket. Prisoners captured later said that the only effect the bombs had was to 'make a big noise.'"

In addition to dropping 1,000 pounders, aviation ordnance crews came up with the idea of dropping belly tanks filled with napalm into the area.

The massive 155mm Long Toms were invaluable during this part of the battle.

"Behind one position we moved into one afternoon there was a 155mm Marine Long Tom artillery piece. This huge cannon was somewhat over a hundred yards directly behind us firing flat trajectory fire at caves out to our front.

"Each time the 155mm Long Tom fired we felt the pressure waves, and our ears ached from the thunderous explosion. I saw the dust rise up off the deck all around. The shell would roar over us and almost immediately we could see it explode against the ridge several hundred yards to our front. [Lt.] Duke Ellington went back and talked to the gun crew and observed the effects of their fire through the powerful artillery telescope. When he came back up where we were, he said he watched through the telescope the steel doors open on the cave after each shell exploded. A couple of Japanese would run out of the cave and carefully inspect the doors and the hinges attached to the rock around the mouth of the cave; then they went

---

12 Daniel, *Cowboy Down.*

back in, slammed the doors, and awaited the next shell. The big shells only chipped coral off the ridge peak around the cave.

"The only way a knockout of the cave could be accomplished was by a direct hit on the doors. The Long Tom fired several times, much to the distress of our ears, and secured just before dark without making a direct hit."

The only way to eliminate some of the Japanese cave positions was to have a single Marine, a demolitions man, go up to the mouth of the cave and throw in an explosive charge.

"One of our demolitions men was a fellow Alabamian named Lambert. He had been in K Company a long time and was a great favorite with the officers and enlisted men alike. Lambert was a big, strapping, good natured fellow and, like most demolitions men, always had the stump of a big cigar in his mouth which he used to light the fuse on the explosive charges he threw into the caves.

"As soon as a demolitions man hurled his satchel charge, whether behind the line or during an attack, he yelled, 'Fire-in-the-hole!' Troops all around took it up and passed the word.

"He would then light his fuse with his cigar, and lower the satchel charge in front of the cave's mouth and swing it into the cave on a rope. It would disappear into the dark cave and explode with the usual terrific blast.

There was pressure from above to speed things up. Col. Harold "Bucky" Harris, the 5th Marines commander, recognized that his troops would have no breakthrough in the Umurbrogol; this did not meet with approval at the division level.

"Late one afternoon, another mortarman and I were detailed to carry instructions to an NCO in charge of a detail stringing barbed wire along the lower slope of a ridge. It was one of the few times we had the use of barbed wire on Peleliu. The sector was fairly quiet by day, though a hellish arena of raids and infiltration by night.

"We took the orders to the NCO and exchanged remarks with him on the virtues of having wire out front.

"The detail was stringing 'concertina'— barbed wire formed into rolls about three feet in diameter and having wire handles which would, when pulled apart by two men, separated the roll into a coil of bristling barbed wire extending along the ground. The NCO turned and looked up the ridge in the gathering twilight and said, 'Now who the hell is that joker pulling that wire too high up the ridge instead of along the company front?'

"We followed his gaze and saw a figure with his back to us tugging the wire away from the K Company line. We couldn't recognize him, but his uniform seemed to have an unfamiliar aspect to it even in the late afternoon twilight.

"The NCO shouted at the man who immediately huddled over, keeping his back to us. The realization dawned on several of us instantly.

"'That's a goddamn Nip!' yelled a Marine, and several opened fire on the mysterious figure. To our chagrin he escaped amid the rocks. The men all around cursed a blue streak.

"We were in a particularly bloodthirsty mood that day, too, because of Capt. Haldane having been killed on this very hill that morning."

In the rocky terrain around this area of Hill 140, the simple act of firing the mortar could be complicated.

"I usually dropped the shells into the tube with my left hand and ducked my head down away from the muzzle blast. However, at this position I had to drop the shells into the tube with my right hand and reach back with my left to hold the mortar's base plate against the rock from the recoil. Even with Snafu holding the bipod feet and me holding the base plate with one hand, the gun jumped out of alignment on the hard rock each time we fired."

"Great care and skill had to be exercised by mortarmen because not only would the shells miss the target if the gun was fired after jumping out of sighting alignment, but sometimes short rounds could be dropped on our own troops."

At Georgia Cottage, Mobile, AL, 1942. Left to right: Dr. Edward S. Sledge, Mary Frank Sledge, Eugene Sledge, Edward Sledge, Octavia Wynn. Deacon is at bottom center.

Platoon 984, San Diego, 1943. Sledge is seated on the front row, third from left.

On Peleliu, after the fighting. Sledge is back row, center.

Sledge, back on Pavuvu, after Peleliu, 1944.

Sledge (L) and George Sarrett, Okinawa, 1945.

Eugene B. Sledge, Auburn, 1948.

Dr. Eugene B. Sledge, Montevallo, AL, 1962. Photograph taken by Don Hughes.

An early book signing for *With the Old Breed*, sometime in 1981. In the background, in the center of the photo is Dr. Philip Beasley, friend, colleague, and former FBI agent.

Montevallo, 1987. Left to right: John Sledge, Eugene Sledge, the author.

Eugene Sledge sitting for an interview with a Japanese production company, Montevallo, sometime in the early 1990s.

A warm spring morning, Mobile, AL, March 7, 2001.

A Marine First Sergeant presents Sledgehammer's flag to Mrs. Eugene Sledge. Seated at right, the author, Andrea Sledge, Elena Sledge.

CHAPTER TEN

The End at Peleliu

At long last, it appeared that the Marines would be relieved by Army troops. On October 15, men of the 321st Infantry, 81st Infantry Division, moved into their area, which meant that the Marines would move to a defense zone on the northern part of Peleliu.

"No one thought there was much danger of a Japanese counter landing but in the predawn hours of Jan 18, 1945, long after both the 1st Marine Division and the 81st Infantry Division had left Peleliu, the Japanese did land on the island. The U.S. occupation troops killed 71 and captured 2."

In mid-October, my father's fear was that they would be called back into the line to address a critical situation. They had pushed their luck far enough, and no one felt that they had much left.

With the filth, waste, rotted rations, and dead, bloated bodies of the enemy lying everywhere on the island, the fly population had exploded. My father described to me, "I would literally have to keep one hand free to swipe away those huge flies—they were so huge because they had so much to feed on between the dead and all the other filth on Peleliu—and I remember trying to drink a canteen cup with coffee in it, and those flies would just be all over the rim of it, and sometimes some of them would fall off into our coffee."

"Some of the men found a large Japanese mosquito net and erected it on poles. It was big enough for several men to stand erect in and was a great place to escape from the flies while eating rations.

It was easy to swat what few flies got in, so it worked quite well as an escape from the pests."

Even though K Company was now in what was supposedly a rest area, the danger of infiltrators wasn't over.

"One moonlit night just after my watch ended, I woke Snafu, told him all seemed quiet, handed him the Tommy gun, and lay back in the gun pit. I dropped off to sleep. I soon woke with a start as Snafu yelled, 'Halt! Who goes there? What's the password?'

"I grabbed my carbine. I sat up as Snafu fired a long burst from the Thompson. A jet of flame, and the sound of the .45 caliber shells shattered the quiet. The empty shell casings bounced and tinkled over the rocks. I looked out into the road in the direction he was firing and saw two dark forms against the white coral road surface. One was down and the other staggered and fell. All the men around us began to stir and were on the alert whispering inquiries about what Snafu had seen.

"He said he had seen two people along the road in the moonlight in our direction, and when he challenged them, they did not respond but froze and began jabbering, so he fired, apparently hitting both of them. Very soon we began to hear the groaning of someone in agony. The groans were interspersed with babbling in Japanese. One of the wounded men had crawled somewhere into the shadows at the edge of the mangroves, and his comrade lay still on the road."

"'Throw a grenade out there and shut that poor bastard up,' someone said.

"'He's getting on my nerves,' said another Marine.

"So, for several hours until just before daylight was ushered in by the hum of flies, we listened to the agonized cries until the Japanese died. In the hot moonlit night with machine guns throbbing in the distance, it was like some forlorn plea against the brutality of it all. At daylight we found his wounded comrade who pleaded for mercy, bowed his head and held his hands, palms together. His conduct was unlike the defiant attitude of every other wounded Japanese I ever saw.

"An officer came up and called a corpsman to attend the enemy soldier and sent word back to battalion for an interpreter to question him. As the corpsman bandaged the wounded Japanese the interpreter arrived. The Japanese had been hit several times in the abdominal region by Snafu's bullets but was not bleeding very much internally. The interpreter, a neat and clean-shaven Marine lieutenant, was quite a contrast to the dirty, bearded ragged ass K Company survivors who watched sullenly as he coaxed information from the prisoner with cigarettes and chocolate bars.

"Finally, the officer and a couple of Marines put the wounded Japanese in a jeep and drove off. We heard that he died shortly afterwards but never knew what intelligence, if any, he had supplied.

"Both the Japanese that Snafu had shot had apparently been separated from their outfit. Neither wore helmets or carried the usual weapons and field equipment. One carried a canvas haversack containing several Japanese grenades, and the other had a burned out American light machine gun barrel as a club. After the lieutenant left with the prisoner, Hank Boyes said that the other Japanese had to be buried. He said the body couldn't be left there in our area to rot.

"We all looked around with quizzical glances to see [to] whom he was addressing these remarks. No one made a move, and Hank said, 'Snafu, you shot him, so bury him.'

"Snafu indignantly stated that he didn't see why he had to bury the Japanese soldier just because he had shot him. Hank said it had to be done so do it. Then Snafu did what very few men would have done—he argued with Hank, who told him to knock it off and follow orders. Snafu looked up defiantly at Hank and said that those Japanese would have gotten into the Company CP if he hadn't stopped them. So if he was ordered to bury the dead one, he vowed that next time he would let them get past him.

"Hank Boyes just glared at him while we all admired Snafu's bantam rooster–like nerve. Another such situation would actually occur later on Okinawa, and Snafu would defiantly remind Hank of this.

"Snafu, being a corporal, ordered another mortarman and me to help him with his burial detail, so we dragged the body across the road into a shallow ditch and scraped up enough coral gravel and rubble to cover it over.

"Amphibious tractors patrolled the reef areas out beyond the mangrove swamp to flush out Japanese stragglers and detect any attempts at reinforcements by enemy forces up in the northern Palau Islands. The amtrac crewmen occasionally fired machine gun bursts into suspicious areas of the swamp. There was one particular machine gunner who fired late each afternoon with his .50 caliber machine gun (mounted on the LVT) in a way we could recognize even though we never saw him or his amtrac across the thick mangroves. He squeezed his trigger so that the burst sounded like 'tat-tat tat, tat tat-tat tat,' and several men would chant, 'shave and a haircut, two bits.' This happened several afternoons, and I often admired the control that the machine gunner on that amtrac had in his trigger finger."

As the month of October came to an end, the men discovered that soon they would board ship and be on their way back to Pavuvu.

"Toward the last day of October the word was passed to 'police up the area.'

"'Awright you guys, pick up all brush, trash, wood and busted coral rock smaller than your fist and pitch it across the road into the swamp.' We started complaining of course, and the NCO yelled, 'Some Army outfit is gonna take over this area and we're leavin' it cleaner than it was when we got here. Marines don't ever leave a fouled-up bivouac area. Knock off your bitchin.'

"'Well, there's one thing for sure,' said an old salt, 'we're leaving this island, there's no doubt about it.'

"'How do you know?' I asked.

"'It's easy, when they start them crap details, like cleaning the brush and certain size rocks off a battlefield you can be sure the fighting is over. No officer or NCO is gonna give an order like that

to guys he is gonna have to move up on the lines with. We are headed back to Pavuvu I'll betcha.'

"He was right. We moved to another area of the island—I do not remember whether it was via trucks or on foot."

As it turned out, this was the last time they moved before they left Peleliu for good.

"Whenever we moved into a bivouac area with our jungle hammocks there was a scramble among the men to claim two trees just the right distance apart on which to string one's hammock. Luck was with me, and I found two battered palms just the right distance apart with a small crater about two feet deep between them. I staked them out as my territory. I slung my hammock between the palms and arranged my pack and other gear in the shallow crater beneath the hammock.

"We went for a swim in the sea and went along the beach and did some grenade fishing. This consisted of tossing a grenade out into the water and then collecting the fish that were killed by the concussion. We got numerous strange looking fish of a species I had never seen before. These we cleaned, scaled, and tried to fry using a U.S. helmet with the liner removed for a frying pan and tropical butter for shortening.

"They tasted good to us—but our digestive tracts were pretty insensitive."

At long last they were finally able to clean themselves up.

"We were a stinking, crummy looking lot after over thirty days of Peleliu's filthy conditions."

My father was finally able to use the writing paper and ink he had been carrying around in his combat pack. He wrote his first letter home to my grandparents in over a month. I still have this letter, and on the envelope, worn, faded, and duly stamped by all the proper postal authorities and the censor, my grandmother wrote, "1st letter off island after invasion—32 days in the same clothes."

The letter itself, written on US Marine Corps stationary, is dated October 18, 1944, and it reads:

"Dear Mother Dear and Pop,

Well, I came through without a scratch. God certainly watched over me and cared for me. It was your and my prayers and I am really thankful and say so in my daily prayers.

I have gotten a lot of mail from you both and Sid too. He really boosted my morale. Your letters I read over and over. Also got the pictures and thanks. We have our hammocks and are camped along the beach in a palm grove. It is one of the few places on the island not ripped apart by shells. The flies here run you insane. In the middle of every word I stop and brush them off. Today I bathed, shaved, and put on clean clothes for the first time in 32 days. It will take much scrubbing to remove the dirt, my beard was about 1 inch and red. I shaved it off with only minor lacerations.

Give thanks to God for protecting me. I'll write whenever I can.

Your devoted,

Gene

Excuse dirty envelope but I've carried it 32 days just to write this letter—I'm OK."

Twelve days later, on October 30, they squared away their packs and gear and filed down to the beach to board a landing craft and head out to the *Sea Runner*, the troopship that would take them back to Pavuvu.

"I have no memory of whether we put out to sea in amtracs (probably so because Higgins boats couldn't cross the reef).... I think we must have been in a Higgins boat and not an amtrac, but anyway, we bounced up and down and banged against the side of the ship for some time before my turn came to climb onto the net.

"[W]e were surely glad to get up that cargo net and onto the deck of the ship. It made me realize fully how physically drained I was after Peleliu."

The long climb up that cargo net, burdened by all their gear, was symbolic to my father—he exulted that they were crawling up out of the abyss of Peleliu.

He stowed his gear below decks and went topside to enjoy the clean air and begin the emotional healing process that all the survivors would have to go through. Even then, it was no secret to the troops that Peleliu was of dubious strategic necessity.

"If Peleliu was unnecessary, it was not the fault of the Marine Corps that it was assaulted."

The Marines, my father included, were always quick to blame MacArthur, which is perfectly understandable, but in fairness it must be pointed out that Admiral Nimitz made the critical decision not to bypass the island. Though MacArthur was presented with the plan and did not object, the final decision lay with Nimitz.[13]

"One of my most vivid wartime memories is of myself, with a couple of other mortarmen, leaning against the ship's rail and silently looking across the water at Peleliu. We could see an occasional puff of smoke as a shell exploded on the ridges, and hear the muffled bang of the explosion, and as always, the distant rattle of machine guns.

"Always that on Peleliu."

---

13 Frank, email message to author.

CHAPTER ELEVEN

Back to Pavuvu on the *Sea Runner*

"An LST was moored alongside the *Sea Runner* and several of us were assigned to a working party to unload regimental gear from it onto the *Sea Runner*. The sea was so rough that the two ships rose and fell and bumped hard against the thick rope fenders hanging over the sides of each to prevent damage to the steel plates. We climbed into a cargo net with the four corners attached to a big steel hook on a cable, and a winch then cranked up the cable, and the boom on one side of the *Sea Runner*'s masts swung us out and over the LST.

"The swabbie operating the boom gently lowered us on to the topside of the smaller ship, which was heaving up and down. We worked some time to load the cargo net, but all the gear tumbled around, and we stumbled so much because of the rough seas that the work was finally called off. Some of the gear had to be left behind and shipped to Pavuvu later.

"Darkness fell while we were working aboard the LST, and to my amazement an electric light was used to illuminate the deck so we could work. I thought this was risky, because we were subject to Japanese naval and air attack from the northern Palaus. All ships I had been on always maintained 'darkened ship' topside in the Pacific during the war. We were so weary we were glad when the loading operations were ordered secured. We rode the cargo net back aboard the *Sea Runner*.

"We went to chow, the usual dehydrated fare served aboard troopships, but it was better that anything I had tasted in weeks.

While I was on the chow line a big hulking Marine with a ruddy friendly face came along asking, 'Any of you guys from K Company?'

"'I am,' I answered.

"He rushed over to me and with an anxious smile on his face said, 'Say do you know Sgt. Teskevich? Is he OK?'

"He was referring to the sergeant with whom I had had the long talk along with Hillbilly on the edge of the airfield one night.

"'I knew him real well, but I hate to tell you he was killed,' I answered. The big Marine threw his hands up and grasped his head with widespread fingers, and look[ed] at the overhead and sobbed, 'Oh Jesus, no! He was my buddy. We was in school together.' He turned and stumbled off along the chow line forming in the companionway, sobbing as he went.

"Everybody around me looked gloomy and stared at the deck or blankly at the overhead.

"The 5th Marines had come to Peleliu aboard several troop transports and LSTs, but the survivors of the entire regiment were now returning to Pavuvu aboard the *Sea Runner*.

"After chow I went below to my rack to get some sleep. Many men were doing the same thing and were quiet or talking in subdued voices. A troop compartment of a ship had little about it to evoke admiration, but it seemed so quiet and far removed from the battlefield that it gave me a cozy sensation.

"As I was unlacing my battered boondockers to hit the sack, a fellow K Company man sleeping a couple of racks over from mine let out a bloodcurdling shriek and started screaming "Tank attack! Tank attack!' All the poor men who had been asleep sprang out of their racks and instinctively started groping for their weapons.

"Someone yelled, 'It's Hurricane, he's having a nightmare, it's OK you guys.' My heart was pounding even though I had been awake.

"'Hey, Herk, wake up ole buddy, we're aboard ship, it's OK,' said a man near the troubled sleeper. Wisely he did not touch or shake his sleeping comrade. To touch, even gently, a sleeping infantryman after he had been in combat in the Pacific was to cause him to react violently and to come up thrashing out and fighting for his life before he was fully awake.

"Hurricane was an old timer and a respected NCO in K Company and need not have felt any embarrassment over his nightmare. The reliving of the horrors of combat in hellish nightmares was a torturous legacy most of us would have to suffer for years after the war. In no mood for sleep after being unnerved by this, I was afraid the same sort of thing would tear me from sleep—I relaced my boondockers and slowly went up the ladder topside. Few men were on the darkened deck. Over on Peleliu the occasional glow of a flare or star shell and the flash of shells with the stuttering of machine guns made me feel sorry for the unfortunate soldiers who had relieved us. I leaned wearily on the ship's rail and was staring blankly at that crucible of suffering and waste.

"'Now hear this, now hear this! Condition red. Condition red. All troops lay below,' yelled a voice over the squawk box.

"'Condition red. This is not an aerial attack. This is a surface attack. This is a surface attack,' continued the squawk box. I always dreaded being below decks on a burning or sinking ship, so I scurried over beneath a Higgins boat set up on low blocks and hid under it. A couple of guards came by and told some of the men still on deck to lay below, but they did not see me.

"The officer on the squawk box kept us informed as best he could on what was going on. He reported that a Japanese surface vessel was in the vicinity and that U.S. Navy ships had gone out to intercept it.

"Shortly after I saw streams of machine gun tracers and what appeared to be 20mm automatic cannon tracers out in the blackness across the water a long distance away. It was all over very soon. Apparently, a Japanese torpedo boat had tried to slip in on our convoy but had been detected. A destroyer went after it but a heavily armed LCI got there first and sank the Japanese boat with 20mm gun fire. The Japanese boat was said to have fired several torpedoes which luckily hit nothing. I slept the rest of the night topside on the steel deck under the Higgins boat."

The *Sea Runner* got underway the next day for Pavuvu in the Russell Islands. One of the stated reasons for invading Peleliu was to neutralize its airfield and secure MacArthur's right flank as he advanced on the Philippines. However, MacArthur hit Leyte on October 20, 1944. As I heard my father say more than once, "MacArthur walked ashore upright with cameras grinding, and Peleliu wasn't even secured yet, and wouldn't be for several more weeks. It made a lot of us ask ourselves, 'What the hell are we doing here?'"

I would say to my father, if he were still around, that Peleliu was not without value. Yes, it could have been bypassed, but while the island was never exploited as a land base for US forces, it was an active and necessary air base until the end of the war. On many occasions, R4D transport planes, carrying wounded Americans home from the Philippines, would stop there. And the search plane that discovered the survivors from the sinking of *USS Indianapolis* flew from Peleliu.

The *Sea Runner* dropped anchor in Macquitti Bay, and the survivors of the 5th Marines shouldered their gear and walked down the gangway. It was vastly different from the island they had come from, and the incongruous appearance of tables set up on the beach where a neatly starched Red Cross girl served them fruit juice in paper cups was baffling.

I remember my father describing to me how he stared at her—not out of any sense of sexual predation, just amazement.

"I moved through the line and got my cup of juice from this Red Cross girl, and I guess I wasn't moving fast enough, because there was this second lieutenant standing there to tell us which truck to get on," my father told me, "and he was obviously fresh out of the States and hadn't seen a lick of combat, and I remember as I passed by him he said, 'OK, Sonny, let's move it out.' And I just remember that I stopped and stared at him, because I was just not prepared to be called 'Sonny,' and I wasn't being insubordinate, but he knew then what he had done because he just looked away."

"I looked like some dumb beast who had just emerged from a horror chamber.

"If he had been a seasoned officer his manner would have been totally different. However, he was new to the Division, and I guess he had to impress the Red Cross lady with his authority. As we climbed aboard a ten-wheeler one of my buddies said, 'Sledgehammer, did you hear what that damned boot lieutenant called you? I'd like to kick his can."

After returning to the familiar camp area of the 3rd Battalion, 5th Marines, my father and his fellow survivors stowed their gear and settled into their tents. While the latest batch of new replacements was sent out on work details, they relaxed and began making the rounds of the other units in the division area.

"Visiting other units throughout the Division to inquire about the fate of friends occupied a great deal of time during the coming days. The men in other units were always cordial and offered us what hospitality, cigarettes, candy, jungle juice, coffee or whatever they could share with us on these visits, because we were asking about men who had been their friends.

"One of the first units I went to visit was F Company, 2nd Battalion, 5th Marines, to ask about Tom Clay, a Mobile man who Sid Phillips had introduced me to when I got to Pavuvu. Big Tom, a rifleman, had survived Peleliu unscathed (he was already a veteran of Guadalcanal and Cape Gloucester) and gave me a broad grin as we shook hands.

"'Well now, how do you feel that you've got one under your belt?' he chuckled.

"I smiled and must have made some comment about being overwhelmed by it all, because Tom instantly got serious.

"'Well, I'll tell you, I have never been as scared as I was on Peleliu!' he said gravely.

"Tom went home with the next group of veterans rotating back to the states. Before he left Pavuvu he had promised to go by and visit my folks when he got back to Mobile, but he did not do so. Years later he told me why. He had gone to visit my father but while he thought of what he would tell him about my general welfare, Tom began to think about how slim the chances were of my ever getting

home unhurt. He had paced back and forth in front of my father's office dreading how he could lie enough to make it appear that it would just be a matter of time before I returned home safely. Finally, considering what the 1st Marine Division had suffered through on Peleliu and what probably lay ahead of it in the next battle, Tom gave up the idea of visiting my father.

"'I just didn't have the nerve to go in there and lie to him and make him believe he didn't have anything to worry about. So, I left and didn't go back to see him.'

"I told Tom I probably would have done the same thing.

"It was not until November 27 that all Japanese resistance was overcome on Peleliu. Elements of the 81st Infantry Division saw it through to the bitter end. The soldiers, after weeks of exhausting attrition, made a final attack through the Umurbrogol Pocket which they had constricted by their attacks since we had left the island. They met no Japanese fire on November 27."

Final Thoughts on Peleliu

"I thought of Capt. Haldane and 1st Lt. Hillbilly Jones, and others too....

"I believe that only the finest troops America had could overcome that 2x6 mile piece of hell. Less dedicated or less disciplined troops would certainly have failed. My everlasting admiration for the Marines I served with is matched only by my undiminished awe of the horror and hardships we suffered.

"I look back with nostalgia and cherish their comradeship, but time has not deceived me about the fighting on Peleliu. The 'field of glory' and other fine phrases used in past wars do not apply to Peleliu, because it was waste, shock, agony, and terror from beginning to end. Peleliu was one of the hardest of them all."

My father wrote those words in the late 1970s, and I do not believe he had any idea then how his memoir would alter that dynamic. Peleliu may never be a household name like Iwo Jima or Normandy, but it will never be a forgotten battle.

CHAPTER TWELVE

Back on Pavuvu—Rest and Rehabilitation

Reacclimating to Pavuvu meant not just visiting and inquiring after old friends but sorting through piles of care packages sent from back home.

"We all received many packages from home after we returned from Peleliu. Most contained cookies, cakes, and candy. Some packages had been aboard ship so long coming from the U.S. that the contents were dried out and hard. A civilian would have thought these things unfit for rats.

"After each mail call during this period there were piles of unclaimed packages that were addressed to our comrades who had been killed or wounded back on Peleliu. These were divided among us by the Gunny. I had some misgivings at first about enjoying cookies and candy intended for some pal now dead or in the hospital, but it was the only thing to do because the packages would have been thrown away. The personal belongings of our casualties were sent to next-of-kin, and GI equipment reissued where needed, but packages of food were best divided among a man's surviving buddies."

One evening, after a week or so on Pavuvu, my father was on his cot in his tent. It was twilight, and one of his tentmates was snoring softly.

"[O]ne of the men, a Gloucester veteran who had been wounded on Peleliu, said in steady measured tones. 'You know something Sledgehammer?'

"'What?' I answered.

"'I kinda had my doubts about you,' he continued, 'and how you'd act when we got into combat, and the stuff hit the fan. I mean, your ole man bein' a doctor and you havin' been to college and bein' sort of a rich kid compared to some guys. But I kept my eye on you on Peleliu, and by God, you did OK; you did OK.'

"'Thanks, ole buddy,' I replied, nearly bursting with pride. Many men were decorated with medals they richly earned for their brave actions in combat, medals to wear on their blouses for everyone to see. I was never awarded an individual decoration, but the simple, sincere personal remarks of approval by my veteran comrade that night after Peleliu were like a medal to me. I have carried them in my heart with great pride and satisfaction ever since."[14]

"The man who had addressed me went on with the company to Okinawa where he did outstanding service under fire, and fortunately survived the war."

I heard similar remarks from R.V. Burgin when I visited him in Texas in the summer of 2006. He said, "Henry, I gotta tell you, one of the things I always admired about Sledgehammer, I knew he came from a well-to-do family, and he probably could have gotten out of volunteering for the Marine Corps if he had wanted to, but he didn't do that: He signed up for it; he did his job, I never heard him question an order; he always did everything he was asked or told to do, and he was a damn good Marine."

"We had been told many times that it was forbidden for us to keep diaries because they might fall into enemy hands. [Some men did have them, though.] It was at this time in 1944, however, that I bought a little notebook at the PX [probably on Banika, but possibly on Pavuvu] and began recording times and dates in it."

This was in addition to the notes he had scribbled on bits of paper kept in the New Testament that he carried in his breast pocket.

One of my father's best friends was Howard Nease. My father described him in glowing terms and described fondly how, on New Year's

---

[14] Sledge, *With the Old Breed*, 166–67.

Eve 1944, Howard staged a diversion with a flaming bucket of gasoline outside near the mess hall—a tent, really—so that he and another man could pilfer, or moonlight requisition in the vernacular, a couple of turkeys, which they then took back to their tent and carved up for their buddies.

"The mess hall and attached galley were made of light wooden framework covered with canvas screening and would have gone up like paper if the fire had reached those buildings."

Sharing those turkeys, carved by Howard with his Ka-Bar in a tent under Pavuvu's palm trees, lit by the warm glow of a flambeau, and singing, joking, and laughing with their buddies was the greatest New Year's celebration my father ever had. Sadly, Howard was later killed on Okinawa.

"He, like so many others I knew, would have made a solid citizen after the war, I have no doubt. His life was snuffed out in the full vigor of youth—part of the terrible cost of war.

"Next morning, the mess sergeant was 'blowing [his] stack,' predicting harsh discipline and punishment to the culprit who stole the turkeys, but he never found out what happened. We enjoyed another turkey feast at noon chow—but this time with official blessing and in the mess hall."

And thus did the Marines on Pavuvu usher in 1945.

"One day not long after we returned to Pavuvu, Sam showed up for a visit in the company area. At some point after the death of his foxhole mate on Peleliu, Sam was transferred out of K Company and, I think, into the division military police. I have no doubt his transfer was made because there was so much bitterness against him, and the company officers thought Sam might meet with a 'fatal accident' sooner or later. The men had as little to do with him as possible after the death of Bill on Peleliu, and then particularly after he went to the rear during the Ngesebus fighting. But when Sam came into our tent everybody just glared at him.

"He sat on a cot and began talking to us, and no one would answer. I must admit I felt sorry for him, but we felt that he had caused the death of a man who trusted him, by sleeping on watch. He then compounded his crime by leaving the outfit a few days later while under fire without permission on Ngesebus."

My father and I were having a conversation once when I was a younger man about the importance of doing what was expected of you, not letting people down who depended on you, and earning the respect of your peers. He told me Sam's story. He said that, at one point, Sam sat near him and tried to engage in idle conversation.

I asked my father if he spoke to him.

"It was very uncomfortable," my father said. "I'm not going to say I didn't feel bad for him, but I knew that if talked to him I'd lose the respect of the other guys, and I wasn't about to do that."

"Sam finally got up and went out into the company street where he [was] met with the same cold stare of hatred from every man who came by. Finally, looking thoroughly humiliated and disgraced, he slowly walked off toward Division headquarters, and I never saw him again.

"It was a terrible thing to witness a man scorned and treated with such contempt by his peers. From down the company street came the twang of a guitar and a melancholy voice singing, 'When I was a boy and Shep was a pup, over the fields and the meadows we'd roam.'

"As I went to join in the chorus, I contemplated the indispensability of mutual trust and respect among us all."

"In one of the letters from my folks at this time was a newspaper clipping about a lady back in the States who had written to her congressman complaining about the harsh and brutal treatment her son, and Army draftee, was receiving from his drill sergeant in basic training. It seemed that the drill sergeant had on occasion halted his platoon of trainees so that they faced the sun. The new draftee had complained to his mother about this 'terrible treatment, and she demanded of her congressman that something be done to stop such inhuman training procedures.'

"I remember how Cpl. Doherty in boot camp had routinely faced us into the sun whenever possible, and I recalled the sun on Peleliu. There, on many occasions, we were pinned down by enemy fire which forced us to lie on our backs for long periods facing the blistering sun with temperatures around 115 degrees. I had realized on Peleliu that he had been preparing us to cope with just this kind of reality in combat.

"When I read the newspaper account about the Army trainee to my tent mates they howled with laughter and made derisive comments about the poor mother's darling being mistreated by the mean sergeant. The men in the next tent asked what all the laughing was about, so I read them the short account. They too, greeted the story with howls of laughter and mock sympathy.

"The word was passed from tent to tent and finally Marines all along my side of the company street were sitting on their bunks and laughing over the story—particularly the irony of it when recalling the hardships of Peleliu."

Howard Nease did more for K/3/5 that just appropriate turkeys via moonlight requisition.

"Howard Nease had his barber shop in a vacant tent down the company street from my tent. He had built an elaborate barber's chair out of ration and ammo boxes. If I remember, the price of haircuts was 'two bits' [twenty-five cents]. Howard picked up a good bit of change serving as K Company barber on Pavuvu.

"It was amusing to see a suntanned Marine, clad only in khaki shorts and boondockers, climb into the barber chair, and Nease, clad likewise, adjust the camouflaged poncho around the customer's neck and greet him with all the professional finesse of an exclusive civilian barber back in the States. In a semicircle around the chair were boxes which served as chairs for those waiting their turn, or, more often, those men who were there just shooting the breeze or swapping sea stories. It was much like a small-town barber shop back home where everyone knew everyone else, but the setting and subject

of conversation differed. Nease was a lively conversationalist, and there was never a dull moment in that 'K Company Barber Shop' on Pavuvu."

The barbershop in Montevallo in the 1970s was named Bean's Barber Shop, and it was owned and run by Ottis Bean. Inside the shop, on a dusty shelf above the customer seats, sat a model (still in its faded box) of the *USS Wisconsin*. Ottis had been a barber on the *Wisconsin* and therefore was an expert in his profession. His partner was Raymond Bearden.

When I was a young fellow my father and I would walk into downtown Montevallo on Saturday mornings for our haircuts at Bean's Barber Shop. When we would open the door and walk in, the bell over the door would tinkle merrily, and I would step into what was a world of classic manhood to my five-year-old mind—a world that does not exist anymore, one of dim, overhead fluorescent lighting; a wall lined with mirrors behind the barber chairs; the smell of witch hazel, hair tonic, cigarette smoke, and Pinaud aftershave; the hum of electric clippers; and the endless array of hair products in their classic bottles used by the barbers to ply their trade.

Ottis and Raymond would greet my father with "Hey Doc, how are you?" or words to that effect. Many people in town back then would call my father "Doc" because they knew he was a professor of biology at the local university and had a PhD. Along the opposite wall would sit the customers—local businessmen and farmers from the outlying areas, the latter with their overalls, co-op hats, and flannel shirts. Most would nod and smile at my father and me as we walked in and took our seats. It was just like Floyd's Barbershop in Mayberry.

When my turn came, I would walk up to the chair, and Ottis or Raymond would help me up into the booster seat they would put there for me. After fastening around my neck a sheet that cloaked me, the barber would strop his razor and set to work. As he snipped away with his scissors and clippers, I would listen to the conversation between him and my father as they discussed the pressing issues of the day—Watergate, President Nixon, the energy crisis, Vietnam.

When my haircut was done, they would brush my neck clean and powder it, then I would hop down and my father and I would walk up to Cunningham's Union 76 gas station, buy a twenty-five-cent Coca-Cola, and head home. With his typical humor, my father always referred to Bean's Barber Shop as the "Alabama Center for Advanced Political Analysis." Those will always be some of my most cherished memories.

Not long after the First Division got back to Pavuvu, certain Marines, those deemed worthy, were asked to interview for possible selection for OCS back in the States. Although pleased that he was asked to interview—not many men were—my father had no interest in being an officer. It would have meant leaving K Company. It also would have meant doing something he had no desire to do—order fellow Marines into harm's way.

Despite his conviction, certain aspects of being an officer appealed to him.

"The privileges of rank, out of combat, did look good to me.

"Snafu was less complimentary about junior officers when he often said, 'Them second lieutenants is as useless as tits on a boar hog...the NCOs run the outfit.'"

My father made it clear in his interview, when asked, that he could not send men into situations where they could be killed. It was important that he felt sufficiently comfortable in his own skin to assert that, and it settled the matter.

"I never heard anything from the interview and gave it no more thought at the time. From what I was told on Pavuvu at the time, only one other man in K Company was chosen for an interview. He was an outstanding NCO we called Dutch; he was certainly officer material. After his interview Dutch told me he was scheduled to go to OCS. However, there was some delay in his orders, or a replacement for him was unavailable, so Dutch went to Okinawa with us.

"Unfortunately, he was badly wounded in the leg during the fighting there, and some of the men speculated he might be crippled.

I never knew whether he got to OCS or not, but he would have made a good officer.

"Jay De L'Eau and I spent many pleasant evenings discussing the books we were reading or had read. He wrote home for a copy of Rudyard Kipling's *Department Ditties and Barrack Room Ballads* which he presented to me. I derived many hours of pleasure reading Jay's gift on Pavuvu. During the Okinawa campaign I stowed it safely in my seabag. The faded red volume made the trip to China with me and now occupies a place on my bookshelf."

My father's love of reading continued throughout his entire life. He inculcated that appreciation in both my brother and me very early in our lives. He always told me as I was growing up that Pop, my grandfather, advised him to keep his mind occupied by reading good books when he came home from the Pacific after the war. My father always felt that reading helped him deal with his demons. He read to me often when I was a child.

"There was an extremely disturbing occurrence at this time that made us feel we were still within reach of Japanese infiltrators at night. I heard a man in a neighboring tent let out a yell one night, and everyone was on the alert. The man supposedly awakened to see a figure looming over his sack, slitting his mosquito netting with a knife.

"Speculation was that the prowler was a Marine who had cracked up and was insane from the horror of Peleliu, or possibly, a Japanese who had slipped ashore on Pavuvu from a submarine.

"It was an unknown and mysterious thing, making the troops jittery while they were trying to recuperate from Peleliu. I slept lightly and with my Ka-Bar (my foxhole companion) clutched in my right hand for several nights. Most of my comrades did the same thing. It was unnerving having to contend with fear again—we were supposed to be in rest camp. Finally, after a few days, it all subsided to our relief."

When I was about nine or ten years old, I had a plastic Tommy gun that I had bought from the dime store in downtown Montevallo. One night after supper, I got the bright idea to hide in the pantry in our kitchen—it was a large cabinet-like affair that I could fit inside comfortably—and jump out at my father as he walked into the kitchen. I heard him coming down the hall from his study, humming to himself, which he frequently did. I jumped into the pantry and closed the door softly, clutching my trusty plastic Tommy gun with my finger on the trigger. The trap was set!

My father rounded the corner and came into the room. At that moment I pushed open the door of the pantry cabinet and jumped out as I squeezed the little trigger on my toy Tommy gun. I will never forget the look on his face as he spun around and faced me. I immediately realized that I had grievously miscalculated his reaction to my prank; he was not amused, I had screwed up, and I was about to be severely punished. In the next moments of my sheer terror, he grabbed me by the shirt collar and, if I remember correctly, lifted me off the ground. He was not a large man—five-foot-nine, or maybe an inch more—but at that moment it did not matter. I don't remember if he marched me into the bedroom or not; I just remember his belt coming off rapidly and giving a spirited thrashing.

He did not lose his temper; he was not raving; in fact, I don't believe he said a word through the entire event. It was a controlled, calculated, and instantaneous response to a foolish error on my part. That night I learned to never unnecessarily startle a combat veteran. He also took away my plastic Tommy gun.

"After Peleliu I got a great deal of satisfaction out of replying to the statement by prewar Marines bragging about long years of service who used to say, 'I've worn out more sea bags than you have socks,' by asking with a grin, 'How much action have you seen?'

"If they were fresh from the States, they shut up immediately, and if they were combat veterans they no longer tried to 'pull their time' on any of us who had fought on bloody Peleliu."

Replacements were arriving to fill out their ranks and make good the losses from Peleliu. They also began training for their next operation.

The war was far from over, and everyone knew it. They engaged in weapons training and practiced amphibious landings.

In late January 1945, they, along with other rifle companies, boarded LCI's and headed down to Guadalcanal for maneuvers. In late February, the 3rd, 4th, and 5th Marine Divisions invaded Iwo Jima. My father and his buddies felt more than sympathetic interest in what was happening there. They knew the island came at a terrible cost in blood and treasure, and to some it had to seem like a larger version of Peleliu.

"But Iwo proved valuable beyond any doubt as a stopping place for the big B-29 bombers raiding Japan. It also became a well-known battle to the American public and symbolized Marine bravery and dedication. The survivors of Iwo could take some comfort in knowing that they captured an island of value, and America knew it.

"We received letters on Pavuvu from buddies who had returned home after Peleliu. Some wrote bitterly that they encountered almost no one Stateside who had ever heard of the 1st Marine Division's terrible fight on Peleliu, or the few who knew of it thought the battle had been unnecessary. Such news from home was discouraging."

A new man came into the company: Tex Barrow, a relative of the infamous Clyde Barrow.

"Red was another replacement, a draftee. He had flaming red hair. Red had a prodigious capacity to imbibe jungle juice with little apparent effect on him.

"'Sledgehammer, that damn hillbilly can drink more jungle juice than anybody I ever saw, and it don't seem to make him drunk. Hell, he's drinkin' up all our supply,' one man told me. Red and I became great friends. Although our drinking habits were vastly different, as were our educational backgrounds, we had a lot in common because we both loved the outdoors."

My father always had a great ability to make friends with a variety of people. He instilled in me, from an early age, the belief that regardless of a person's background and education level, you could probably learn something from him.

"One night when all my tent mates were out, Red walked quietly into my tent and sat on my sack while I leaned over my little desk writing a letter by the light of a flambeau. In an embarrassed voice he asked me if I would read a letter for him. I said I'd be glad to, and he handed it to me. He made some excuse about the poor handwriting or something and looked ill at ease. The letter was from some of his family, a sister I think, and written in a clear, legible hand.

"I watched Red out of the corner of my eye as he sat beside me with his chin in his hands listening intently to every word. When I finished, Red confided in me that he could neither read nor write. He asked me if I would answer the letter for him if he told me 'what to write down.' I readily agreed, and with Red dictating I wrote his answer. This became regular practice with us.

"Red was nobody's fool; he had plenty of common sense and confidence. He told me he was the youngest child in his family, and his parents made moonshine whiskey.

"While his older brothers and sisters were in school, Red said he was forced to help his father tend the whiskey still cleverly hidden in the woods. Consequently, he didn't get enough schooling to learn to read and write.

"New replacements for the company included several new officers, because only two survived Peleliu unhurt. Stumpy, the 1st lieutenant who was former company executive officer, became the company commander. Duke Ellington, the other surviving officer and our mortar section commander, transferred to Battalion."

CHAPTER THIRTEEN

Prelude to the Invasion of Okinawa

The 1st Marine Division packed their gear and headed to Guadalcanal for maneuvers. They were ashore for a few weeks, occupying the same area that had been the bivouac camp of the 3rd Marine Division, who were at that very time on Iwo Jima.

Their training continued, with one boot lieutenant lecturing these hardened veterans on water discipline. This officer's nickname was One Grease Ball.

"A buddy growled, 'What a bunch of crap—I bet he ain't never been thirsty in his life.' I agreed with my friend that there wasn't much a boot lieutenant could teach about water discipline to those of us who had fought on Peleliu for a month.

"To sharpen our communication skills, we were ordered to stand in the inky darkness strung out in a long column in a coconut grove passing orders back and forth for about four hours in the pouring rain before being marched back to the bivouac area.

"Most of us strung our jungle hammocks between trees. Whenever we would get all settled in our hammocks, the inevitable tropical downpour would commence, and you would hear a dull snap as a cord snapped on a hammock.

"The snap was always followed by a fervent, profane oath as Marine, hammock, rifle, and all hit the deck with a thud, and much swearing and laughing.

"After several cords on my hammock broke, I laid it flat on the deck, staked up the roof, ditched around the hammock for proper drainage and used it as a snug, dry pup tent.

"One day when I came out of the shower, I discovered that someone had taken my boondockers. Upon reporting my problem to the company Gunny Sergeant, he ordered me to remain in the bivouac area until a new pair could be obtained from the quartermaster.

"Gunny ordered me to stand by for light working parties in the area until my new boondockers arrived. This suited me fine, because I missed having to plod through muggy heat over miles and miles of Guadalcanal's hills, kunai grass fields, and jungle trails on field problems.

"Being an experienced old Pavuvu hand at doping off from working parties, I could sense one coming. The poor, unsuspecting new men got all the working parties, and I logged in many happy hours reading a good historical novel about the American Revolution in a quiet spot where no one could see me. My new boondockers finally arrived the day before we broke camp and moved out."

Even though my father had not taken part in the epic fighting for Guadalcanal, he ruminated on the significance of that battle.

"Few Americans probably realize now how dangerously that six-month long jungle campaign teetered in the balance between turning the tide against the Japanese or becoming another Bataan-like defeat for the U.S.

"As we looked over rusting Japanese landing barges, found skulls in the underbrush, and empty cartridge cases, I really appreciated what a long, lonely ordeal the men had endured.

"Some of us had an experience during those Guadalcanal maneuvers that nearly ended in tragedy."

Since the 3rd Battalion, Fifth Marines, had been in the assault waves at Peleliu, it was determined that for the Okinawa landing they would be in regimental reserve. This meant that instead of riding to Okinawa in LSTs, they would be aboard a transport ship—the *USS McCracken*. It was late one afternoon, following a full day of intensive field training on

Guadalcanal, and the tired and thirsty men of K Company were waiting on the beach for a Higgins boat to pick them up and take them back out to the *McCracken*, which was among the fleet of ships and other vessels standing offshore in Sealark Channel.

The beach was crowded with Marines from other units who were also being picked up and ferried back out to their ships, and as the sun slowly sank lower in the west, my father and his buddies could see that the ships out in the channel were beginning to form up and move past them in the gathering twilight, headed away from the island. Just as they were starting to think that they would have to spend the night on the beach (all the other troops had been picked up), an LCVP came roaring towards them through the salt spray. The Marines clambered aboard after he lowered the bow ramp.

"The coxswain was a decent fellow and said it was all his fault. He told us he was late because he simply got confused as to where we were to be picked up, and he had been up and down the beach searching for us for hours. As tired and exasperated as we were, no one could grumble at him, because of his forthright honesty about it all."

Pounding through the water in the twilight, it was almost dark, and they were chasing the transport. Heavily loaded down with all their gear and weapons, they were shipping water and started to slow down. Unless they could catch the transport and offload the Marines, there was a real danger of the Higgins boat sinking.

However, they finally did catch the last transport in the column—it was not the *McCracken*—and were given permission to offload the Marines. It was just in time because, as cables were hooked on to hooks in the floor of the LCVP, and the men were climbing a cargo net that was lowered for them, the LCVP was starting to sink from the water it had taken on.

"As for the boat itself, sailors hoisted it up and pumped it out. We were instructed to go to chow and told that we could reembark in the landing craft and put out for the *McCracken* when we arrived where the fleet was anchored for the night. I talked to some of the ship's crew, and they said they had just come from the European theater of war where they had transported Army infantry and had participated

in landing them during some of the amphibious operations in the Mediterranean. They seemed to have great respect for the German Stuka dive bombers."

They got back aboard the *USS McCracken* when they reached the fleet anchorage area.

On March 15, 1945, the convoy sailed from the Russell Islands to Ulithi atoll. There they anchored on March 21 and would remain until March 27. The massive invasion fleet that would be bound for Okinawa would stage from Ulithi.

"A regiment of the 81st Infantry Division had taken Ulithi, abandoned by the Japanese, without the loss of a man while we were fighting on Peleliu. So ironic that so much blood was shed for Peleliu, pointlessly we thought, yet Ulithi was taken at no loss of life and became a valuable and much used naval base."

Their officers briefed them on what to expect at Okinawa, and they were not encouraged by the news that casualties on the beach during the landing were expected to be 80 to 85 percent. As always, they were constantly reminded of being in harm's way.

"There were several 'condition red' alerts at night, because of Japanese reconnaissance planes while we were at Ulithi. You could always recognize the characteristic throb of their engines compared to ours. I managed to hide in the shadows under a Higgins boat, because I didn't want to get trapped below if the ship was hit.

"I would check my life belt as the ship's crew quickly donned life jackets, steel helmets and manned battle stations. On these occasions, however, the Japanese planes were not bombing but were probably gathering intelligence about the fleet."

When they weighed anchor on March 27, the huge armada of various vessels got underway to Okinawa. It was mostly uneventful, and the men began to notice the cooler temperatures, especially at night, as they steamed from the south and central Pacific into the northern Pacific.

"One day while some of us were watching a huge aircraft carrier not far off, we saw a destroyer in action. The men around me watched

tensely and in admiration as one of these sleek, swift vessels came across the stern of our ship, passed us like a shark knifing through the big waves, and positioned itself between our line of advance and the carrier. We could hear the warning signal on the destroyer sounding as the fast ship went into action. We could see its crewmen running to various battle stations topside. The destroyer discharged several depth charges (ash cans) which threw up huge geysers of water when they exploded. As our ship moved past, the destroyer circled the area where the depth charges blew up and then quickly resumed its position in the convoy. Apparently radar had picked up a suspicious signal indicating a Japanese submarine in the area, but everything settled down shortly."

Only 350 miles from the home islands of Japan, Okinawa was the emperor's doorstep. It was many times larger than Peleliu: sixty miles long and, at its narrowest point, only two miles wide. It was eighteen miles at its widest.

"The countryside was open cultivated fields, meadows, and thick mixed woods with pine, oak, brush, and vines, steep rocky ridges, and deep rugged gorges and valleys. The soil was clay and loam. A reef surrounded the southern beaches.

"The native Okinawans were basically of Chinese origin. Although they had been dominated by the Japanese for centuries, these people retained their own language and a cultural tradition akin to China."

The island was defended by the Japanese 32nd Army, approximately 110,000 troops under the command of Lt. Gen. Mitsuru Ushijima. Although comprising the usual experienced and fiercely determined troops, the veteran 9th Division (the best in the garrison, according to Richard Frank) had been sent from Okinawa to Formosa (what is now Taiwan), since the Japanese feared that that was the next step for the Americans. Had this not been the case, the cost of Okinawa would have been even higher, so in at least one respect the Americans who fought for this island got one major break.

"There were probably some Okinawan men incorporated into the Japanese defense force. But their number was never determined.

"Japanese defense organization was basically similar to that which Americans had faced on Saipan, Peleliu, and Iwo Jima."

Where the terrain was conducive, the enemy had constructed the usual assortment of mutually supporting gun positions, caves, and interconnected tunnels. Both forward and reverse slopes of hills were fortified, and caves were emplaced with automatic weapons, mortars, and artillery. As for American forces, the overall commander of all US ground forces, Lt. Gen. Simon B. Buckner, had considerable assets in men and materiel at his disposal, yet the Japanese had a distinct advantage in the terrain, and the defense-in-depth strategy that had been so costly to US forces at Peleliu would be practiced to an even higher degree at Okinawa.

The campaign's early stages called for Marines and Army forces to come ashore at the midsection of Okinawa's west coast. Two Marine Divisions from General Geiger's reorganized III Amphibious Corps, the 1st and 6th, and two Army divisions, the 7th and 96th of the XXIV Corps, would advance east across the island until they cut the island in two, at which point the Marines would turn left and move north, and the Army divisions would turn right and move south. A third Army division, the 27th Infantry Division, would be held in floating reserve until needed; backing up the XXIV Corps was the highly regarded 77th Infantry Division.

"There was a large amount of artillery and heavy guns emplaced on Okinawa because the shipment of them had been diverted from the Philippines when the situation there became hopeless. The Japanese had the usual large numbers of mortars; 50mm (knee mortars), 81mm and 90mm, and cannons; 70mm howitzers, 75mm, 120mm, and 150mm. They also had some of the huge 320mm spigot mortars throwing a massive 675 lb shell. These had first been encountered on Iwo Jima.

"The magnitude of the Okinawa landing, consisting of four divisions and supporting troops, was a tremendous undertaking. It required a 6,000-mile-long supply line stretching across the Pacific."

For this operation, the 1st Marine Division would land the 7th Marines on the division left and the 5th Marines on the division right. The 1st Marines that had been so chewed up in the early stages of Peleliu were to be in reserve—in stark contrast to the battle on Peleliu.

"To have an entire regiment in Division reserve was a luxury in stark contrast to the inadequate reserve consisting of a single battalion we had on D Day at Peleliu. The inadequate size of our reserve was the most serious failure of American command at Peleliu."

In 1945, April Fool's Day fell on Easter Sunday. This was the day they were scheduled to land. Many years later—my best estimation is around 1975—I remember a beautiful, sunny Easter morning. I noticed my father was in an unusually lugubrious mood. This was contrary to his nature, and it concerned me. Later in the afternoon I went into his study to talk to him. He was sitting in his chair staring out the window.

I asked him if he was OK.

"Yeah, sure, Big Shot, just thinking...today is the day we hit Okinawa in 1945."

At the time of the invasion, the fact that April Fool's fell on Easter Sunday and marked the beginning of the battle drew much conversation, "**both profane and profound.**"

"[T]he Army high command said that the day of the attack was to be called L Day, or, in the phonetic alphabet used by the communications people—Love Day. All I Marines I knew scoffed loudly at this as 'Army Talk,' and consistently referred to the day as D Day.

"As our convoy neared our objective, we began to hear Japanese propaganda messages in English over the loudspeaker in the galley. There were threats that Kamikaze aircraft would cripple our fleet. There would also be massive attacks against our ships by suicide torpedo boats. Knowing the Japanese, we didn't take the threats lightly—although we acted as though we did. On D-1, or the day before D Day, the 77th Infantry Division invaded a group of small islands offshore from Okinawa and captured and destroyed three hundred and fifty Japanese suicide boats which were scheduled to attack our transports loaded with troops and supplies as we landed on D Day. The soldiers surprised the Japanese on these islands and, by destroying those suicide boats, erased a major threat to our invasion fleet."

CHAPTER FOURTEEN

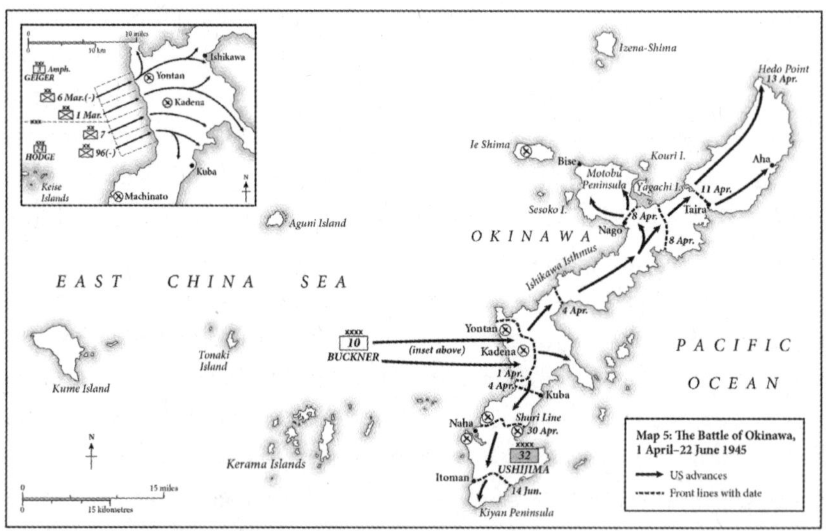

D Day, Okinawa, April 1, 1945, Easter Sunday

The night before D Day, final orders were issued. Even though 3/5 was in regimental reserve for this landing, they were told to expect heavy casualties both heading into the beach and upon landing. Before the first rays of the sun peeped over the horizon on Sunday, April 1, the *McCracken* and the other vessels in the massive invasion fleet were humming with activity.[15]

---

15 E.B. Sledge, *With the Old Breed*, 182.

"We had been assigned quarters in the forwardmost troop compartment in the bow on the upper deck for our voyage to Okinawa. The hatchways led right out onto the main deck, which I liked."

"On the deck above our compartment were several 40mm antiaircraft gun tubs [circular steel enclosures three or four feet high around the doubly paired 40mm guns to give the gunners protection.]

"The guns were fully automatic and fired the big shells rapidly as the sailors placed them in the breech in clips of five shells each. I had watched the 40mms fire many times with their characteristic 'tum-tum-tum,' and the barrels recoiling back and forth. However, I had never considered where all the empty brass shell cases went. On D Day morning, I found out with a jolt."

After chow the men made their way back to their compartments. The first light of dawn was showing. The sailors were at battle stations because of the threat of Japanese air attack. The cruisers and battleships had begun their pre-assault bombardment.

With all his gear squared away, my father went to the head for one last visit, much as he had aboard LST-661 the morning they hit Peleliu. He was the last one in the head, since the other Marines were already moving out on deck. As he settled himself on a seat, he noticed an iron mesh chute that came from the overhead (near one of the 40mm gun tubs above it on deck) and extending down through the deck below the head.

"Between the head compartment and the guns above there was only a thin layer of insulation material on the overhead. Suddenly, like a rumble of thunder, the guns directly above me began to fire. I hoped the gunners hit the Japanese plane they were firing at. I had never been in the compartment below the 40mms when they were firing and was astonished at how deafening the sound was."

My father was chagrined at how it startled him.

"Sid Phillips told me after the war that he was just as startled aboard ship by an identical experience just before H-hour on Cape Gloucester. A simple example of the fact that combat troops shared many similar experiences during the war."

My father joined his buddies on deck. Each man stuck close to his buddy as they waited. Since K/3/5 was not in the assault wave as they had been at Peleliu, they would ride the LCVPs to a rendezvous point where they would then transfer to the amphibious tractors that had already delivered the assault waves across the reef and onto the Hagushi beaches, and that now would take them in.

As the preinvasion bombardment grew in intensity, the familiar cacophony grew with the addition of the AA guns' increased fire, a result of Japanese planes appearing over the fleet. Because of this added threat, the Marines were ordered to lay below to minimize casualties from strafing enemy planes. As the Marines crowded into the compartments, loaded down with all their battle gear, the sailors dogged down the hatches per their orders. The electrically operated blowers were shut down because the electricity was needed to operate the 40mm gun mounts. The air quickly grew foul, and breathing became difficult.

"Whether our air supply was dangerously low I do not know, but it was certainly a desperate sensation, and we felt that we would suffocate in there."

After much yelling and cursing at the sailors who kept the hatches dogged down (there were only two of them), the Marines were finally able to force open the hatches through their combined efforts. They spilled out into the cool clean air on deck. As they hit the deck, a khaki-clad Navy ensign yelled at them to return to their quarters. My father and his fellow Marines could not help but notice the contrast between this pompous officer (with a web pistol belt containing a .45) and themselves, dressed in green dungarees and loaded down with their gear. At that particular moment, there were no Marine officers present.

"All were either getting their gear on in officers' quarters or attending last minute briefings. About that time several of us noticed that the metal on the handle of the ensign's .45 automatic protruding from his holster was covered with a film of rust!

"'Jesus,' whispered a Marine, 'his .45 is rusty!'

"This was whispered among us. This fact alone put that officer in the same category as some civilian or clerk. We were so indoctrinated

to keep our weapons in the best of condition that it was a shock to see a new rusty pistol."

My father never stopped preaching to me about the necessity of cleaning and oiling a firearm after shooting it. When I was growing up, I was around firearms pretty frequently, either my Marlin .22 rifle or, later, the actual .45 pistol that my father carried on Okinawa. He would always say, "If you even touch the metal or anything other than the stock, make sure you wipe it off with an oily cloth."

Fighter planes and dive-bombers rumbled overhead to plaster the beach. The men were tense, expecting another heavily opposed landing.

"This terrific bombardment was provided by ten battleships, nine cruisers, 23 destroyers, and 177 gunboats. We fully expected the Japanese to have the beach under heavy fire all day, as they had done at Peleliu."

They clambered down the cargo nets to the Higgins boat pitching in the swell below them, its engine idling. Although far from a luxurious vessel, the *McCracken* had been a safe home for them, and they hated to leave it.

It was 0830 and loaded Higgins boats were shoving off from the *McCracken*'s side and other ships. They ploughed through the water some distance from the ship, where they circled with other Higgins boats and waited for amtracs returning from the beach.

"The fleet and planes began lifting their bombardment inland, and we could see big shells, rockets, and bombs exploding inland where the island sloped upward from the beach.

"We were all wondering how the assault waves were making out. Soon we saw amtracs churning through the water toward our Higgins boats. We spotted the number on the tractor we were to board to go in on, and our coxswain headed toward it. A sailor on our boat and a Marine on the tractor got ready with wooden poles with hooked ends to bring the two craft together. The Marine on the amtrac was laughing and yelling something. We didn't know what he was saying,

because of the noise of the bombardment and engines. As the boat and the amtrac came together the coxswain slowed his engine, and the Marine yelled, 'The landing is unopposed!' We looked at him in amazement as we picked up our gear and climbed from the Higgins boat to the amtrac. We couldn't believe it.

"The empty Higgins boat headed off for the ship, and our amtrac moved into line abreast of others as our wave formed up to move to the beach. According to a note jotted down on the flyleaf of my pocket New Testament, I was in the ninth wave ashore at Okinawa. The amtrac crewman and his driver filled us in on what they had seen—there was practically no Japanese opposition! When we overcame our astonishment, everybody started laughing and joking."

Several of the men, including my father, began singing "Little Brown Jug" as they headed toward the beaches. He always said that finding out that the landing was unopposed was the most pleasant surprise of the war.

"We passed very close to a huge battleship that was firing its massive 16-inch guns inland. A full-sized battle wagon in action was something so awesome you didn't take it for granted like some of the smaller vessels. Someone said this particular ship was the *Tennessee*, but I am not certain."

The only enemy fire seen was a couple of desultory mortar rounds landing out in the water. It may have been April Fool's Day, but no one was fooled. My father later told me that the Japanese lack of response came across as sinister. "We knew the Japs were up to something," he said. "There were thousands of them there, and we knew they weren't going to give that island up cheap."

They were in an LVT-4 with a tailgate, and when it emerged from the water and crawled up on the beach, the tailgate came down with a bang. They picked up their gear and walked out onto the beach. Down a short distance to their right was the mouth of the Bishi Gawa, or Bishi River. This small river was the boundary separating the US Army's XXIV Corps on the right, or south, of the river, and the III Amphibious Corps—consisting of the 1st Marine Division and the 6th Marine

Division—on the left, or north, of the river. Near the mouth of the river was a promontory extending out into the sea, and they could see the remains of a large-caliber Japanese gun that they had been warned about and the rubble of a sea wall.

"The sea wall had also concerned us greatly during our training on Pavuvu."

They began moving inland. Some of the replacements joked with the veterans that amphibious landings didn't seem so tough after all.

"3/5 moved up behind other troops of the 5th Marines. I saw our battalion CO, Major John A. Gustafson, and his radioman with some other men move forward to check positions in the early afternoon. About an hour later we heard some Japanese rifles, and the word was passed that a group of Japanese had fired on Gus and his group. He was wounded and evacuated. Scuttlebutt said the major and one enlisted man were the only casualties our battalion suffered that day. Incredible to lose only two men out of a battalion of about 950 Marines in a landing predicted to be the bloodiest of the war. Most of the other battalions of our division also suffered little or no loss."

Units of the 2nd Marine Division, aiming to fool the Japanese, had approached the southeastern beaches.

"It was apparently effective in this, but Kamikaze planes crashed into a troop transport and an LST causing considerable losses before the troop-laden amtracs turned back from the beach, and the ships took them up and departed.

"Why [did] the Japanese not defend the Hagushi beaches and try to stop us on D Day at Okinawa? It was known that they had learned from past U.S. invasions, from Tarawa to Iwo Jima, that we could not be stopped at the beach because of our devastating naval and aerial bombardment, and the efficiency of our amphibious assault techniques. The Japanese were also relying on their kamikaze attacks to cripple or knock out our fleet, then fight a decisive land battle of attrition against us on southern Okinawa."

As late afternoon gave way to early evening, my father's squad halted in a field that showed signs of a recent harvest. They dug in for the night and immediately appreciated how the clay-like soil compared to the coral of Peleliu. It didn't take long before K Company's three mortars were set up in their gun pits. They fired a couple of rounds of HE into possible target areas out to their front, then prepared for their first night on Okinawa.

"I put plenty of flare shells, HE shells, and phosphorous shells within easy reach, and the ammo carriers fixed their ammo where they could get it to me as fast as possible."

These tasks done, they scouted out a nearby farmhouse.

"We had been ordered repeatedly in our briefings that we were not to molest civilians or their property—no looting. Therefore, we did not take anything we found (a practice that soon changed later on) but we just looked around. I was struck with how clean the house was, but also so totally different from anything I had ever seen."

As they returned to their position in the field, they heard the characteristic sound of a Japanese aircraft engine. It was a Zero fighter at high altitude headed out to sea.

"It was unnerving to watch a plane slowly circle over the fleet looking for a likely target, and then to see it go into a screaming suicide dive with no intent of pulling out. We watched silently. A buddy said thoughtfully, 'By God, there's one thing for sure, them Nips got plenty a' guts.'

"This dramatized that deep devotion to duty characteristic of the Japanese in World War II. It was called fanatical, but it was incredible bravery. No matter how much we hated the Japanese, we certainly did respect their bravery and devotion to their country. Kamikazes reaffirmed our belief that Japan would never surrender, and that their military forces and many civilians as well, would have to be killed to the last man before the war could end."

That first night, every Marine and soldier who had experienced the enervating heat of earlier campaigns like Guadalcanal, Cape Gloucester, Bougainville, and Peleliu delighted in the cooler weather.

"Temperatures in the sixties seemed cold to [those of] us who had been in the tropics for months and months. Several men commented that they really felt pity for the army infantrymen fighting in cold weather in Europe. We realized that regardless of how hot it was (with the possible exception of Peleliu's 115-degree temperatures) living conditions would be even more miserable in colder climates. The field jacket felt mighty good."

I was always fascinated by the Thompson submachine gun (Tommy gun) from an early age, and my father would describe how he and Snafu shared one. It wasn't often that he watched war movies, but he would always chuckle at the image of John Wayne firing a Tommy gun in long bursts that had to be at least a hundred rounds—with no recoil!

" My father would chuckle, "Shucks, those Tommy guns had serious recoil. I never fired more than three round bursts." Any more than that and the recoil would pull up and to the left. As he explained this to me, he would mimic the motion with his arms.

"In our company, mortar gunners as well as assistant gunners had both been issued .45 automatic pistols in place of the carbine for the assistant, after Peleliu. But we always managed to hang on to our Thompson submachine gun in our squad."

CHAPTER FIFTEEN

Heading Across the Island

The 1st Marine Division continued to push across the island, with their objective the eastern shore. They had yet to encounter serious Japanese resistance. They did, however, begin to see a larger number of civilians. This was something that had not been seen at all on Peleliu. Never one to be oblivious of suffering, animal or human, my father took note of these people and the shock and bewilderment on their faces when they saw the Marines.

"They filed past us and, when on a narrow trail or roadway, each always bowed from the waist in the Japanese fashion as he or she encountered each Marine. Most of my buddies looked at them sympathetically and did not respond. However, the first time an Okinawan bowed to me, he was a stooped old man, I returned the bow, out of pure curiosity. The effect was incredible. The old man's face had amazement and disbelief written all over it.

"He had bowed obsequiously to one of the helmeted conquerors who had invaded his quiet island home in the wake of a storm of explosions and steel, and that barbarian, which is what the Japanese told them we were, had courteously returned the bow. The old man looked intensely at me with his dark eyes, and I thought he was going to weep, but he bowed again. I bowed again, and so did he, and then I did again. When we had each bowed five times an interpreter yelled at the old man to move out—he was holding up the people behind him.

"The old fellow took off with a spring in his step grinning like he wasn't afraid anymore. The woman behind him bowed to me, and I went through the same routine with her. Then our column moved out. 'Sledgehammer, you are gonna give all these people a backache if you don't cut out all that bowing stuff,' laughed a buddy behind me. From then on, every time an Okinawan bowed to me I returned the bow. The effect was always the same, first disbelief, followed by relief. It was the only way I could assure those pitiful people we weren't going to harm them, and they seemed to understand."

This was always one of my mother's favorite stories of my father's WWII experience.

As they moved toward the eastern shore, they were able to get a sense of the terrain. When they saw areas of steep ridges and gullies, they were glad that there were no Japanese in the vicinity, but they also wondered what lay ahead.

At one point, K Company was crossing a small valley and happened upon a little horse that was trapped in a flooded ditch. They were able to calm the animal and rescue it by slipping cartridge belts under its belly and lifting it up out of the ditch.

"Once during the procedure, a Marine Corsair circled over, the pilot apparently trying to figure out how he could help us."

They reached the east coast on April 4, K Company arriving in an area of marshes near freshwater reservoirs. They were near Chimu-wan, or Chimu Bay.

"One of my friends shot a chicken near an Okinawan house and proposed to cook it. However, being from a large city, he didn't know how to pluck and clean the bird. I agreed to do it for him in return for some fresh cooked chicken. This he agreed to, so we set down our gear at the edge of a large freshwater pond, or reservoir, with a concrete spillway.

"During our four day move across the island the 1st Marine Division had killed 79 Japanese, captured 2, and sent 500-600 civilians to the rear. It was too easy to last."

Near the village of Hizaonna, north of K/3/5's location, K/3/7 was ambushed by Japanese troops.

"A rescue column helped the company withdraw during the morning of April 4. The men of K/3/7 gave a good account of themselves, because tank patrols next day counted 126 dead Japanese in the area."

Around this time, K/3/5 headed inland, away from the shore of Chimu-wan, and to the north. The terrain consisted of valleys and steep ridges.

"The little valley where K Company was located, like most valleys on Okinawa, had several burial vaults on some of the sloping hillsides too steep to farm. The Japanese used the vaults as strongpoints and machine gun emplacements. The valley had been tilled by the Okinawans and most of the surrounding areas were potato fields. Our transport packs were brought up by jeep trailers."

A bivouac was established with two-man pup tents, and it rained for the first time since landing on the island.

"We were already settled in the bivouac area when the rain started. The Japanese began their first series of extensive air attacks against our fleet and land troops ashore. Yontan airfield, which we could see in the distance, was to the west of us. These attacks were part of the first massed aerial offensive launched from Japan against our invasion.

"The radio picked up constant messages from U.S. fighter pilots reporting on the presence of enemy planes and damage caused by kamikaze pilots to ships of the fleet. On one message we heard an officer on a destroyer report that they were under heavy air attack and that a bogey had crashed into the ship and the engine of the plane was stuck in the metal plating of the ship's side just at the waterline."

"Many of the Japanese air raids lasted a long portion of the night. Big searchlights around Yontan would pick out and follow a plane with giant silver beams against the dark sky. The antiaircraft guns fired streams of tracers at the plane, and it was hard to see how

any escaped being knocked down. The tracers from the numerous antiaircraft guns were so thick it was difficult to describe. It looked like luminous hail.

"Everyone cheered loudly when a Japanese plane got hit. We were far enough removed from it all not to be endangered unless a Japanese headed toward our area after his attack run on Yontan.

"However, when we saw a Japanese plane head our way and the big searchlight beams brilliantly shining against its aluminum surface, the men yelled and cursed the enemy pilot to go the other way. We scattered and hugged the sides of the ridges and cursed our own antiaircraft gunners. The worst of it for us came from the big 90mm guns, because their shrapnel whined and growled down through the air after the big shells went off near the plane.

"The American metal would smack and thud against the deck all over the place around us. There was little we could do but hug the dirt, pray, and curse. I found one of several niches dug in the ridgeside by Okinawans to seek shelter from U.S. air attacks before D Day. This gave good overhead protection from our own AA fire; but there was one serious disadvantage—fleas. After the first trip to the hideaway, I almost would have rather risked the shrapnel—which we kept telling ourselves was spent and wouldn't really do anything but cause a bruise.

"Many of my buddies sought shelter in similar niches along the ridges and eventually we all had a heavy infestation of fleas. I never realized they could bite so painfully. During the day you often saw Marines sitting around naked to the waist picking fleas out of their dungaree jackets. To me, it made us look like [those] pictures of Americans in France in World War I picking lice out of their uniforms. Our dungarees had been impregnated with DDT prior to the campaign, but it didn't seem to deter the fleas."

Growing up, my family always had dogs—living without one or more dogs wasn't an option for my father given how much he loved them. When one was sitting in his lap, which was most of the time, he was almost always looking them over to make sure they didn't have fleas. To me he almost seemed obsessed with that. I didn't understand it until I was older and had conversations with him about his experience in Okinawa.

At this point, daily patrols were sent out to probe for the enemy. Because the Japanese had yet to be found in large numbers, mortars were not needed, so my father and his fellow mortarmen served as riflemen.

"Certain Okinawans were helping the Japanese and had to be stopped. Some men from each rifle platoon, machine gun platoon, and the mortar section were always left in the bivouac area as security. Those of us assigned to make a patrol drew extra ammo, rations, and filled our canteens from a water tank trailer before we headed out each morning."

His first patrol was commanded by Mac, the new mortar section lieutenant.

"There were about a dozen of us enlisted men armed with M1 rifles, carbines, Tommy guns, pistols, and grenades. Molestation of civilians or their property would not be tolerated. Japanese had been encountered in the area where we were to patrol so we were not to notify them of our presence by unnecessary firing. Our mission was to check out our assigned area for possible signs of enemy activity."

April's lack of action had begun to lull even the hardened veterans into a false sense of security. But things were about to change.

"The security of April [would] cause the events of May 1 to plunge us all into a state of near shock. The road inclined to higher elevation, and we passed some rugged, steep ridges perpendicular to our road with little cultivated valleys between them. But the road was easy going. We had become rested after our rapid four day move across the island, and the weather was invigorating.

"It was nice that day that I did not know that come May 1 our nostrils would be saturated with the smell of death for seven full weeks—for the few of us who stayed on our feet that long.

"We came to a village on the high ground overlooking the east coast. The village appeared to be deserted. We prepared to spread out and check it for hiding Japanese. An elderly Okinawan man came

down the dirt street in full view, holding his right hand up in a gesture of friendship. He wore a tall silk hat, formal black evening coat with tails, a stiff white formal shirt, no tie, formal evening trousers, and was barefoot."

"He came up to us, apprehensive, bowed gravely, and with gestures and a few badly pronounced English words managed to tell us he was the head man, or mayor, of Hizaonna. He tried to convey to us his friendship for Americans and hatred for Japanese, and he was surrendering his village to us. We gave him some cigarettes and indicated our desire not to harm anyone or anything.

"We nicknamed him 'His Honor of Hizaonna.' From then on, we always referred to that village and surrounding area as 'His Honor.'"

Despite the evidence of the recent firefight involving K/3/7 when they were ambushed in this area, my father took notice of the bucolic setting.

"I looked over the scene in the bright, clear cool morning air by that village. Over next to a farmhouse. there was a worn path, used by generations of Okinawans in their peaceful everyday existence.

"As we moved away from Hizaonna on that first patrol we encountered a couple of old Okinawans and several children. The old ones gave us the 'No Nippon' routine, and we shared our K rations with them. One bright faced little girl indicated she wanted to learn to count in English. So, we sat around and ate our rations and after she learned 1-10 pretty well, counting on her fingers, she decided to teach me the same thing in Japanese. We went through it several times, and as I was catching on, we heard firing in the distance. Our patrol was not alarmed because it was the unmistakable muted sound of .50 cal aircraft machine guns at high altitude."

The memories I have of my father describing what happened in this town are as vivid as if he and I talked about it yesterday. It was always one of my favorite stories, not just because of my love for all World War II airplanes but because the F4U Corsair was my favorite. When I was about five or six, my brother built a model of a Corsair—probably one-thirty-second scale, but I don't remember—and it had a little pilot figure in the cockpit and a sliding canopy. It was my favorite toy for a long time, and I wouldn't let it out of my sight.

"We looked up just as eight Japanese Zero fighters and about as many Marine Corsairs broke their respective formations and tangled in a swirling dogfight. I had been told many times about dogfights by the Guadalcanal veterans, but, as we had aerial superiority at Peleliu, I had never seen any. We watched in awe as the planes climbed, turned, and dove at each other with thudding gunfire and whining straining, engines. This lasted probably about fifteen minutes.

"The Marine pilots shot down all eight Zeros one right after the other. Each time a Zero went down we Marines cheered. I started counting them in English, and Japanese for the Okinawans, and it was obvious they did not appreciate my keeping tally for them. They might have been 'No Nippon' but, by the looks on their faces it was obvious where their sympathies lay. Only one Corsair went down. It suddenly began to trail a plume of thick black smoke after a Zero made a pass at it with a muffled rattle of machine guns."

"The Corsair started into a long slanting dive and suddenly we saw the tiny figure of the pilot jump out of his cockpit. We cheered as his parachute opened out like a big white umbrella. He floated down and landed behind some trees far away but within American territory. That was the only Corsair that we could distinctly see hit by Japanese gunfire.

"Others may have been hit but they did not appear damaged or crippled. However, when most of the Zeros were hit by Corsair gunfire it was obvious. We saw one Zero explode like a firecracker. Another broke in half, and another lost a wing which went fluttering down like a tiny leaf as the plane went spinning down in a whining dive. All the others caught fire and trailed thick black smoke when hit, and they went into dives and crashed far from us. We saw no Japanese pilots escape from their Zeros. I had even greater admiration for our fighter pilots after seeing them in action that day. That dogfight was the subject of conversation among us for a long time. We

returned without incident to our bivouac in the little valley before dark that afternoon."

As I recall, my father told me there were eight Japanese Zeros and five Marine Corsairs.

The veterans continued to be amazed at the lack of Japanese resistance. It was around this time that several of them, my father included, had a close encounter with a Japanese Zero fighter. Just like the story of the dogfight between the Zeros and the Corsairs, this incident was one of my favorite stories from my father.

"It was a bizarre and astonishing experience, although it might strike the reader as only passing interest. But it was that leer on the pilot's face!"

As he described to me, that morning was cool and clear, and after their breakfast, several of the Marines had walked up the side of a ridge that bordered their valley to get a better view of an ongoing air raid over to their left on Yontan airfield. Since they weren't on an official patrol, they carried no weapons—foolishly, as it turned out.

"With the delicious smell of coffee and pine needles in my nostrils, I watched the raid with detached interest from the top of the razor-backed ridge. You could hear the rattle of their bombs as they dropped them on Americans stationed on and around Yontan.

"Several U.S. fighter planes were circling outside of the flak barrage to attack the bombers."

My father told me, "We heard an airplane engine to our right, and as we looked in that direction down this big valley that our ridge overlooked, we saw this airplane just droning along. It was a Jap Zero, and he had his engine throttled back, you know, just cruising along looking for trouble. He was flying parallel with the ridge we were standing on and right at eye level with us. We couldn't believe how slowly he was moving. He came right by us, and he couldn't have been more than thirty or forty yards away. He was going so slow that we could see every detail—the pilot [was] in the cockpit, his canopy was closed, and he had on one of those fur-lined leather flight helmets with goggles pushed up on his forehead and a scarf and a flying jacket. He turned and looked right at us as he cruised by at eye level, and right when he saw us his face broke into this fiendish grin, because he knew he had us. We were exposed out there on that ridge, and he could see we didn't have any weapons. Well, he passed by going from right to left, and when he got past us, he banked and started turning to gain altitude. He went out of sight around another ridge, and we knew he was going to come back and strafe us.

"Well, we were scrambling around out there in the open trying to figure out what to do, and then we heard a plane engine again, only this time it was at full throttle—the Jap Zero came screaming by us going back down the valley in the opposite direction, still low, only this time he had a Marine Corsair on his tail, boring right in on him, both going full throttle. The Corsair chased that Zero on out of sight over the ridge tops."

"We cheered the Corsair and cursed the Japanese. He had surprised us like a bunch of new recruits, and we had no weapons. The thought of missing our chance to fire at a slow-moving enemy plane going past us at eye level made us furious.

"Needless to say, it was hard convincing our buddies in the bivouac area what we had just experienced, even though many of them had heard the aircraft engines. All the men with previous combat experience had developed [a] state of mind which always expected the unexpected. However, our account of a low flying Zero and the grinning pilot was a bit more than some could accept, and they passed it off as a good sea story."

As K/3/5 moved across the Okinawan landscape, they came across many little farms. All were deserted by their owners, of course, but in many cases the animals on these farms had been left behind—pigs, goats, and horses, all in many cases still penned up, desperately hungry, and in need of attention.

"We released all of the goats as well as the pigs. A K Company man had found a can of green paint, and as each goat was let out of this pen, it was painted with distinctive identification marks. I often wondered what the Okinawans, and for that matter some Americans who didn't know, thought of all those happy goats gamboling all over

the fields wagging their tails and displaying in large, bold green letters, 'K Co' on one side and '5th' on their other side.

"During my boyhood I had had two fine pet goats, Tom and Jerry, trained to pull a wagon, so the Okinawan goats really appealed to me. It amazed some of my buddies to see how eagerly the goats ate cigarettes I fed them. They got a laugh out of my story about the time when I narrowly missed a hard whipping from my father because he caught me feeding some of his good Lucky Strike cigarettes to Tom and Jerry.

"We also took a liking to the shaggy little Okinawan horses. On several occasions we used these gentle creatures to carry part of our load of weapons and ammunition. I personally never saw or heard of a Marine mistreating any of these animals, and the men were very careful not to overload them with our heavy gear."

On Friday, April 13 (April 12 back in the States), the news about the death of President Roosevelt was released.

"Word came in by various radio messages from ships and planes. Some historians would imply that all men in uniform felt a deep bond of devotion and grieved for the president. This was not necessarily so."

As my father told me in conversations through the years, the most prevalent emotion among the Marines was speculation on the man who would take his place.

"The men from Missouri were proud that our new president was from their home state. When asked who Harry Truman was, however, they didn't know any more about him than I did. Politics was not our area of greatest erudition."

Happy Landings—The Eastern Islands

Shortly after learning of the president's death, they were back on the move, this time to take part in a shore-to-shore amphibious operation to hit one of the eastern islands—Takabanare. No Japanese were expected there.

"Marine reconnaissance personnel had landed on Takabanare and other eastern islands during early April and had found only 200 civilians. We had to occupy the islands to prevent the Japanese from moving on to them from Okinawa."

They boarded amphibious tractors on the east coast of Okinawa and headed out into Chimu-wan to make the short trip to Takabanare. Other companies from the 3rd Battalion would hit other islands of the group.

"3/5 occupied the eastern islands April 17-23. The landing was quiet, not preceded by any pre-assault bombardment."

They moved rapidly across the island, confirmed there were no Japanese, then pulled back to the beach to set up a defensive perimeter.

"Our move back to the beach was unhurried, so when I came across an old Okinawan woman trying to catch several of her goats, I stopped to help her. The animals had gotten out of their little corral which was apparently damaged during an American air strike on the island—probably weeks ago. The house was badly smashed up, and I felt sorry for her.

"We finally got the goats herded into the corral and the fence fixed. That done, she turned to me, shook her finger, and pointed at her ruined home. She then gave me a thorough tongue lashing in Japanese or Okinawan, I couldn't tell the difference, while gesticulating wildly toward her house. Using sign language and making a noise like an aircraft I got the idea across to her that planes had smashed her house and not infantrymen. I felt some pangs of guilt about laying the blame on those fine Marine and Navy pilots who supported us so well in combat.

"'Move out!' came the order, much to my relief. I left the woman glaring at me and then up at the sky."

The Advance Continues—Back on Okinawa

"One of the last patrols we made was through some of the most beautiful countryside on the island. We moved out at dawn, a small group of us under the command of Mac. We soon came to a series of steep, rolling hills covered with knee high amber grass. The air

was brisk and clear, and the sunrise was spectacular. The wind made waves and troughs on the surface of the sea of amber grass and was so strong that my heavy steel helmet once blew off my head, and I had to chase it down a slope. This all reminded me of a beautiful spring day back home in Alabama, where I felt so close to nature watching the wind playing on a hillside of wild broom sage.

"About midday we climbed a high hill, and 'took ten' for lunch. I explored a small, demolished house on the little round top of this hill. It stood alone on the windswept peak with a large, gnarled pine tree whose graceful branches gave us shade.

"The ruins and the scattered personal belongings—clothing, a few photographs, indicated a nice-looking young man and his pretty wife had lived there. The simplicity of their life could be seen from the surroundings. Leaning against the pine was a thick wooden work bench containing some primitive farm tools. A broken-down pen and a coop revealed that the only livestock kept there had been a couple of goats and chickens, all gone now. The open stone hearth was small, just big enough for two, and a steep stone path led down the hill to a well.

"It was pathetic and forlorn under the open sky with shattered mud-wattle walls tumbled down around it and the remains of charred roof thatch. The wind sighed and the grass swayed gracefully on the hill side. The simplicity of this tiny homestead was poetic but tragic, because it was destroyed—by the technology of war."

This poignant scene reminds me of the compassion and sorrow my father felt for the Okinawans and what they had to endure because of the war. We often spoke of the peaceful simplicity of their agrarian life and how it was destroyed around them. No civilians had been on Peleliu, or what few were had been moved to the islands to the north before the United States invaded. But Okinawa was wholesale suffering writ large, and it amplified the senselessness of the war.

"We heard the inevitable 'OK you guys, let's move out.' We shouldered our weapons and moved on down the hill in dispersed order. A short while later we came upon a well-made, low bunker

with several firing ports. We cautiously approached and heard low voices inside.

"We took no offensive action, because we had no desire to injure civilians unless they were belligerent. These people had taken refuge in this bunker. We cautiously called to them in the few Japanese words we knew to not be afraid, and to come out. We could hear men and women inside.

"Jim Dandridge and I were standing in a depression by the bunker entrance. He said, 'Hand me a smoke grenade, somebody.' A man above us handed Jim a grenade, but it wasn't a smoke grenade; it was a white phosphorous grenade, which threw out vicious chunks of burning phosphorous as well as releasing a thick cloud of dense white smoke."

"It was a thick metal cylinder, larger and much heavier than the true smoke can, so why Jim didn't realize this, I do not know.

"Jim grabbed it without looking and yelled, 'Look boys, just like Hollywood!' as he pulled at the ring with his teeth.

I yelled to Jim, 'Look out, that's phosphorous!' He didn't catch what I said but was chagrined because the pin only jerked Jim's head to the side instead of releasing.

"He grabbed the ring with his left hand, jerked it free and threw the grenade at the entrance.

"'Phosphorous!' I yelled and jumped up to ground level. Jim staggered back and the others hit the deck. It exploded with a muffled 'thump', and sprayed burning chunks all around, and a cloud of thick smoke erupted. Miraculously no one was injured. That Jim and I were not terribly burned was unbelievable.

"Jim began bawling out whoever it was that handed him a white phosphorus grenade instead of a smoke grenade.

"After this the frightened civilians weren't coming out, and I didn't blame them. Word was sent back to send a patrol to collect them later. It was a long time before we quit kidding Jim about 'Look boys, just like Hollywood.'

"We came to a small building built against a cliff with an overhanging porch. We investigated and found no signs of Japanese in the area. When I came back out in front of the house onto the pathway there, I saw an old Okinawan man in peasant's attire walking toward us.

"Facetiously I spoke to him, 'Hey old man, you know where there are any pretty geisha girls?' He stopped and looked thoughtfully for a moment then said, in impeccable English with an American accent, 'No, indeed I do not. There may be some dancing girls in the city of Naha to the south, but I am sure there are none near here.'

"My face flushed as my buddies all around stopped in their tracks and looked toward the old man and me. We were all surprised, but some character spoke up and said, 'Hey Sledgehammer, you really speak the language, don't you?'

"Someone else said, 'Sledgehammer, G-2 could use you as an interpreter.' The Okinawan smiled.

"Ignoring my buddies, I struck up a conversation with the Okinawan. We all asked him many questions. His opinion about the Japanese on the island was that they would fight to the death—not that we had any doubts about that fact.

"During the first month of the campaign it was easy to determine which Okinawan children had been in contact with American troops. The moment you saw these children they would smile, wave, and always say, 'Hey Joe, Tojo eat crap. Roosevelt good man.'

"We were always amused by the little speech, and it usually brought forth ration candy, so the children performed it willingly. They seemed to enjoy the idea that all Americans answered to the name Joe."

Around the middle of April, the 1st Division's artillery regiment, the 11th Marines, moved down south where things were heating up to assist the Army.

When thirty US Army tanks, along with the 27th Division, attacked one of the main Japanese defensive lines on southern Okinawa, Kakazu Ridge, they suffered extremely heavy losses. As the tanks separated from the infantry, twenty-two were destroyed. Cleverly coordinated Japanese tactics involving anti-tank guns, suicide tank destroyer teams, mines, and satchel charges caused this separation, and the tanks kept advancing even after being cut off from their infantry support.

"The remaining eight tanks managed to withdraw to their own lines. We heard rumors about all this, but it was hard to believe. From our experience, tanks and infantry always attacked or withdrew together. Tanks without infantry were extremely vulnerable."

This would turn out to directly affect the 1st Marine Division.

It became necessary to commit the 1st Marine Tank Battalion to assist the Army's 27th Infantry Division. Naturally, this invited sardonic comments from Marine infantrymen who did not want to see their fellow tankers employed piecemeal after the disastrous losses at Kakazu Ridge. Both the overall force commander, General Geiger, and the ground force commander, General Buckner, believed that Marine tanks and infantry should be deployed intact, so the entire 1st Marine Division was to relieve the 27th Infantry Division.

"At least this meant our division would fight as a unit and not as a battalion put into the Army line here or there."

The 1st Marine Division marched in to relieve the beleaguered 27th on the right, or west, of the American lines, just north of Machinato Airfield, around May 1. The stay of execution was over.

"It drew us into the abyss."

CHAPTER SIXTEEN

Back into Action

As April gave way to May and the Marines moved south to assist the army, it was hard not to see that the dismal cycle of every Pacific battle fought against the Japanese thus far was about to repeat itself in the ridges and mud fields of southern Okinawa: fighting strongly emplaced Japanese troops and rooting them out in attritional fighting. Rain and mud made it worse.

But the rain hadn't yet started as they boarded trucks and headed south over dusty roads. My father observed that the men who had seen heavy action prior to this were grim faced and tense as they got closer to the sounds of shellfire, but men like Lieutenant Mac, who had not been in heavy combat, seemed unfazed.

"Mac seemed to be the only person who wasn't nervous as we got closer and closer to the rumbling of artillery fire."

My father told me about Mac and his bravado. He and the other men who had survived Peleliu knew that tough talk wouldn't get you very far in this war. Mac wasn't indecent, but he was an obtuse and pugnacious man brimming with false bravado, and this engendered no small amount of resentment.

"Mac had been spouting off manfully about what he was going to do to the Japanese with his Ka-Bar and his .45 the first time one of our men got hit, and we got so sick of it that we began to move away from him."

The combat veterans also noticed the number of brass large-caliber shell casings around the artillery emplacements in the area, and the shell craters they saw everywhere. That meant only one thing—counterbattery fire.

"At some place, the location of which I do not remember, we detrucked."

My father clearly recalled moving along a road bordered by shell-pocked potato fields toward the all too familiar sounds of battle. Soon they saw soldiers from the 106th Infantry, 27th Infantry Division, marching single file on the opposite side of the road. These were the men they were relieving.

"You could spot them as Army troops by their bare steel helmets, big pocket dungaree trousers, and combat boots [a very practical boondocker with a wraparound leather ankle top held in place by two buckles]."

Their facial expressions said everything that needed to be said about what lay ahead for the Marines. They approached a low, sloping ridge where K Company would go into the line. They could see shell bursts up ahead. The volume of Japanese fire increased as they raced for cover.

"Upon entering the frightful abyss, our feelings of dread were shared throughout the Division."

It was a jolting shock for my father to dive back into that maelstrom, but the feeling of being totally overwhelmed, as he had been at first at Peleliu six months earlier, was now gone. Terrified though he was, my father knew, because of his experience, that he could control his fear.

"I reacted differently to it than any shelling I had endured on Peleliu. I found that I could immediately identify almost every type of Japanese shell by their whining and roaring as they came in and by the sound of their explosions when they struck the deck. One of the new men digging in near me began asking me the same kinds of questions about the shelling that I had asked Snafu that first day at Peleliu. My answers seemed to help him.

"It was bad enough for the veterans, but the new men seemed to be even more stunned by it all. When we got to the place where the mortar section was supposed to be positioned, we began to dig in."

As my father and Snafu dug their gun pit, they received the sad news that among the casualties of K Company were Cpl. Howard Nease and Private Westbrook. Nease was fondly remembered by the surviving K Company men as the affable, smiling comrade who ran the barbershop on Pavuvu and who, in the glowing light of the flambeau in his tent that night under the palm trees of Pavuvu, carved the stolen turkey and said, "Happy New Year, Sledgehammer!"

"The road we had been on earlier continued on through the ridge via a roadcut. When Nease and Westbrook were in this area they were killed by machine gun fire that came through the roadcut.

"Most of the Japanese guns had secured, and the shelling had subsided into knee mortar and 75mm artillery rounds going into that area. Men were still getting hit though. I saw one man jump out of a foxhole after a 75mm shell hit close by and run to another hole. A 75mm shell then exploded near that hole.

"'He better stay put for a while,' someone commented.

"The man jumped out of the second foxhole and headed a short distance to what he presumed was a safer third foxhole. Just before he jumped in, a 75 exploded very close, and the blast knocked him into that foxhole. Two men crawled out to him with a stretcher and carried him back to where he had been.

"Next day I talked to a corpsman who said that even if he survived, he would probably lose both legs and one arm."

The 1st Marine Division relieved the Army's 27th Division on the right of the American lines on May 1. This Army division had been in action since April 15. They had taken a beating on April 19 around Kakazu Ridge, Machinato Airfield, and other nearby areas.

"I never knew the name of that low ridge we occupied on May 1. 3/5 went into position on an east west line somewhere in the area stretching between the villages of Awacha on the east and Miyagusuku on the west.

"This was as far south as the Army units had pushed after costly fighting during the last two weeks of April. Kakazu Ridge was the first of the three parallel east-west defense lines along key ridge systems.

The second and strongest was in the area north of Shuri Castle, and the third ran east from the town of Itoman to include Kunishi Ridge and the large escarpments Yuza-Dake and then Yaeju-Dake across the island.

"The Japanese fiercely defended Kakazu Ridge against Army attacks for several days. Finally, when it was no longer tenable, they withdrew on the night of April 24. The 27th Division then pushed to the area where 3/5 went into the line between Miyagusuku and Awacha.

"After we got settled in, the Japanese shelling subsided into an occasional shell whining over and crashing into the area behind us followed by the 'thump' as a dud hit the ground and ploughed up a furrow. We would remain tense, waiting for an explosion.

"The low ridge K Company was dug in on sloped down to a flat potato field just to our left, then there was about a 50-yard gap to the next ridge in line with ours. Anyone in that low field was vulnerable to Japanese firing down from the ridges out front.

"We saw, on a little mound just at the edge of some bushes, a US Browning .30 cal water-cooled machine gun on its tripod. As we looked back at the gun to our left we wondered who was manning it.

"A youthful Marine wearing no helmet crept along on his belly out of the bushes up to the machine gun. He reached up and adjusted the setting knob for elevation with his right hand and squeezed the trigger with his left. His burst of red tracer fire zipped across the potato field on our left and out past our ridge to the front. Almost immediately a long burst from a Japanese Nambu came zipping across the field from the ridge out front. The slugs kicked up dirt all around the Marine machine gunner.

"Uninjured, he scuttled back down out of sight behind the mound. In a few minutes he cautiously reappeared and fired another burst from his Browning. Instantly the Nambu out front fired a long burst at him that kicked up little chunks of dirt all around the Marine. He again scrambled back for protection.

"The Nambu had the position so thoroughly covered that the Marine assistant gunner who typically attended the ammo belt never

got into position. We requested permission to fire white phosphorous shells out to our left front for a smoke screen to blind the Nambu gunner. Permission was denied because he was not in K Company's sector. So, we sat back and helplessly watched. He got driven back again, but fortunately he was not hit.

"Finally, the machine gunner crawled forward and flipped off the latch that held the gun on the tripod. He jerked the gun up, cradled it in his arms and rolled back out of sight. Then a hand reached out and slowly pulled the heavy tripod back down behind the mound. The Nambu gunner had won the duel, but fortunately had not hit the Marine."

In the predawn hours of May 1, they were told to get ready for a push all along the line.

"It was bound to be bloody. Weapons were checked and extra ammo was issued to all hands. We were to fire our mortars along the company front prior to the attack, then stand by to fire HE on any target of opportunity holding up the riflemen. We stacked plenty of 60mm white phosphorous shells beside our gun pit in case we needed to lay down a smoke screen if the men should need help getting wounded out. [This paid dividends.] The machine guns were to provide covering fire. When the rifle squads advanced a certain distance forward, the reserve rifle platoon, mortars, and machine guns would move forward into new positions of support."

The Asa Gawa stream lay about 1,500 yards to the south. At that point it emptied out along the Hagushi beaches and stretched inland, eastward, to the area near Dakeshi.

"It took our Division several days to push as far as Asa Gawa at a cost of hundreds of casualties. We prepared for the immediate night. We fired flare shells at intervals of a few minutes and on call from the different platoons. We had a sound power telephone line running to us from each platoon. There were several fire fights along the line, but it was not too bad for our company that night.

"I quickly developed a hatred for the Japanese 150mm shells. A drizzle of rain began during the evening and was greeted with curses and grumbling.

"The rain increased into a downpour by daylight. It was chilly and clammy. The rain not only added to our misery but would hamper support from our planes the next day.

"Though our mortar ammo was packed in waterproof containers, we carefully protected the increments between the tail fins of our 60mm shells from the rain.

"At dusk the password was sent along to remain alert as usual. Mac, having dug in as thoroughly as he could, began to assert his authority again, but now he was much subdued.

"My father had always taught me to 'let sleeping dogs lie,' but here it seemed a shame to let Mac so soon forget the absurdity that was his former bravado. Particularly in view of the loss of our friends like Nease and Westbrook. So, in the gathering darkness and miserable dampness, I called over to his foxhole to ask him some simple, unnecessary questions about his orders.

"'Lieutenant, Lieutenant!' I said in a loud, excited voice.

"'Knock it off! Knock it off!' came his nervous reply. 'Don't call me by my rank, use my code name!' Mac said in a desperate voice.

"'Yes sir,' I said with feigned ignorance.

"'Don't say that either!' came Mac's voice with greater excitement.

"Someone near me snorted softly with laughter. Mac's obvious nervousness having satisfied my spite, I said no more. Had Mac been a veteran officer, or anybody other than a new man who had bragged so much I wouldn't have desired to pull that trick. We all knew that no one was to be addressed by rank, particularly at night—we always addressed our officers by their code, or nicknames. Anyway, it had the desired effect.

"Our officers didn't wear bright rank insignia in combat either.

"The Japanese, however, did wear small red felt tabs on their collars, or shoulders, to show their rank. These were popular souvenirs with us."

Indeed, I have several of the tabs my father collected. When I asked him how he got them, he said simply, "I cut 'em off the collars of dead Japs."

This early May attack on Asa Gawa was heavily opposed, and the driving rain didn't make things any easier. Both Marine and Army units took casualties.

"The attack demonstrated that the Japanese could smother us with artillery, mortars, and small arms fire from their protected positions. It also demonstrated that all American units had to move forward in a big, coordinated push or those getting ahead suffered flanking fire from Japanese in front of our units that moved too slowly."

Dawn finally broke, weak and gloomy. The rain was pelting down. My father and his buddies ate what rations they could and heated up some coffee in their canteen cups. As 0900 approached, their artillery and naval gunfire increased in tempo. Japanese shells began screaming back in response. At last, the order came to open up with their mortars out toward K Company's front.

"Snafu aimed on one of our prepositioned aiming stakes, and we fired HE shells. He yelled 'Fire' after turning two turns on the crank of the gun's traversing screw and levelling the sight bubbles."

The rate of fire increased as it got closer to the time of the attack's start.

"Someone made the usual comment, 'They're throwin' everything at 'em but the kitchen stove.' Our mortars fired several short missions."

As K Company troops began the attack, heavy Japanese fire forced them back. The mortars fired white phosphorous rounds to shield their withdrawal with smoke. A Marine running toward them yelled that a stretcher team was needed.

"I was wearing my .45 on my belt, so all I had to do was buckle my helmet chin strap. I jumped out of the gun pit, and we four took off on the double after the messenger. Another man in my squad jumped into the gun pit to take my place as assistant gunner."

The stretcher team ran along below the crest of the ridge, where Nease and Westbrook had been killed the day before. As usual the enemy had absolutely no mercy on medical corpsmen, stretcher bearers, or wounded Marines.

"My mountaineer friend, Red, came dashing through the cut. He was holding his M1 at high port, and one of his hands was bloody from where he had been slightly wounded. Red saw me and came over panting as I greeted him and asked him if he was badly hit. He began yelling at me in a loud accusatory voice saying, 'By God, Sledgehammer, there couldn't have been no place on Peleliu no hotter [from Japanese fire] than this here place! I don't care what ya say—by God I don't!'

"I agreed with him that this was as 'hot' as we had seen. I tried to calm Red and explain to him that he had asked me questions about combat when he came into the company as a replacement, and I had answered them honestly and without exaggeration. Red was so wild with fear and excitement that he stumbled off to his foxhole mumbling and grumbling that Peleliu couldn't have been worse."

As it turned out, at the roadcut they did not have to go out to retrieve wounded because most of the casualties had been taken out further down. They returned to their posts in the pouring rain.

"Across the muddy fields we could see our soaked comrades crouching forlornly in their holes, ducking like us each time a shell came whining or roaring over."

"Little did we realize on May 2 that we would spend about ten days and nights in one position in the shell torn, muddy, stinking morass in front of Shuri where decomposing corpses lay all around us like dead animals in some large garbage dump.

"I had thought rain on Peleliu had transformed everything into incredible forlornness and misery, but there we were usually among rocks, and the rain drained rapidly away—there was no mud. On Okinawa the clay soil quickly became mud, and our holes held water like buckets—and the rainy season was just beginning on Okinawa. The Gloucester veterans hated mud as much as I did."

My father never hesitated to express his distaste for mud when I was growing up.

"We were surprised at the number of Japanese shells that were duds—more than on Peleliu. We speculated that these shells had detonators on

the nose that didn't function if the projectile struck the soft clay. Others suggested that it was because the Japanese ammo was stored in damp caves in the clay ridges. And some thought that the Japanese were using time fuses set to explode when we might get out of our holes.

"It was an eerie sensation when a shell came whining or roaring over, expecting the thunderclap to jolt your world, or end it, and then hearing a dull thump; to see dirt and mud kicked up like a big stone was striking and ploughing up the ground—instead of a flash and explosion.

"I saw it many times on Okinawa, and also saw shells ricochet off the ground up into the sky and out of sight. However, the sight of one particular 150mm shell on May 2 was seared into my memory.

"Our mortars were dug in behind the low end of the ridge just below the crest. A Japanese 150mm howitzer battery was firing at our area. Several of the big shells came roaring over simultaneously and exploded with a terrible 'kaboom' when they hit. We crouched in terror. The massive shells exploded back in the pines behind and in front of us.

"Two of them exploded to our left in the field.

"Then I heard the third shell coming—the roar grew louder, then a swishing sound followed by a terrific thump. I was facing the ridge and at the thump glanced up and saw a shower of mud spew up directly in front of us where the dud struck the ground. I saw the big shell ricochet up into the air and followed it as it arced low directly over us.

"It seemed to float through the air and slowly fishtailed from side to side as I watched it in disbelief. To my horror, the big shell came down on its side and flopped onto the muddy ground with a splash. We peered at it from our holes. Wisps of steam drifted upward from its hot steel surface as it lay there, and the rain fell on it. My heart was pounding, and I couldn't swallow. We just stared at it. Finally, someone said, 'Look at that damn thing; it's as big as a Higgins boat.'

"'Jesus, you reckon it's gonna go off?' someone else asked.

"We finally began joking about the big dud. There was some discussion about how far the shell was from us. Naturally it evolved into the inevitable argument. There were some suspicious glances thrown

at that 150 by my buddies next day when we picked up our gear and moved through the sticky mud to another position.

"I think that shell hit the ridge about 20 yards in front of us and landed no more than 40 yards behind us. It was never out of my sight once it hit out front. We all had many narrow escapes from death or wounding that were 'closer calls,' but none scared me more than that."

The word came down that K Company would push again the next day—May 3.

"Extra ammo was brought into position from an ammo dump. It was unloaded from an amtrac to our rear. Mortar shells, grenades, and rifle ammo [were] issued to the proper platoons. The green metal boxes, about a foot long and a foot high, with .30 cal machine gun cartridges, were issued to the machine gun squads. These boxes were to become popular tools with civilians for years after the war."

We always had several of these olive drab-colored metal boxes filled with targets and shooting supplies sitting around in my childhood home.

"They had a folding metal handle on the hinged top which seemed to make a harmless enough little clatter when handled on occasions like this. But I had seen the time during perilous nights on Peleliu when Marines cursed such clinking and clattering of metal boxes because it could reveal their positions to Japanese infiltrators. K rations were brought up and each man stuffed two or three boxes into his combat pack."

They faced strong opposition and were only able to advance two hundred to three hundred yards in the May 3 attack.

"After the attack we passed right by several US Army Sherman tanks that had been knocked out during the earlier fighting before we came into the line to relieve the 27th Infantry Division. Each of these tanks had several dead Japanese around it. From the location of these tanks, the appearance of the bloated, rotting corpses, and the rust on the tank treads we surmised that these vehicles had been among the 22 lost by the Army around mid-April.

"The Japanese dead that we saw were obviously members of special suicide tank destroyer teams. We saw several unexploded mines

that they threw against the side of tanks. I had seen similar mines strapped to Japanese dead who rushed our lines near the airfield on Peleliu."

"We also saw numerous decomposed enemy dead apparently killed in past counterattacks on Army positions. I noticed one in particular, the first of six or eight strung in a line near an old Army machine gun pit. He was sprawled on his back with the handle of an Army fighting knife protruding from the middle of his chest. The knife was in up to the hilt, and we wondered why the soldier hadn't recovered his knife and whether he had been killed.

"All the Japanese dead wore the split-toed rubber sole canvas tabi shoes we had seen at Peleliu, and the usual wrap leggings. They had a newer model rifle than the Japanese had on Peleliu where, except for a few short carbines, I saw the long Type 38, 6.5mm (.25 cal) Arisaka rifle. On Okinawa most Japanese rifles I saw were shorter Type 99, 7.7mm (.303 cal) Arisakas. Both models were bolt action and held a five-round clip.

"We were told to dig in around the battalion aid station to form a line. As we watched, casualty after casualty was carried into the aid station which was in a large tent behind a ridge nearby to our left.

"The mortarmen were positioned on a low mound about thirty feet long and situated in a small sugar cane field. To our immediate front was an open area where trampled cane allowed a clear view to a ridge some 100 yards or more ahead. Marines of the other companies of 3/5 occupied that ridge. To our right flank and front was a line of pines and bushes extending up toward the front line. The aid station was to the left front, screened by a ridge and pines.

"We stayed in this area for several days. The other K Company men were tied in with us.

"The sun and wind had dried out the ground from the previous rains. There were some foxholes already dug in along the mound we were on. They were "standing foxholes" that offered protection to a man standing erect. We occupied the existing holes and dug others if needed.

"Before dark we cleaned our weapons and ate some K rations. A canteen cup of hot bouillon or coffee always made a man feel better. We could hear occasional firing up on the line to our front and stretcher teams periodically brought back wounded to the aid station tent.

"I saw two somber looking men emerge from the aid station, bring out a stretcher with a poncho covered form and quietly lay it on the deck to our left. Some mother's son would never go home. Jim Dandridge went over and lifted the poncho covering the face of the dead Marine, and I saw him wince. He came back and told us who the dead Marine was—we had all known and liked him.

"There was a concealed light in the aid station tent, so the care of the wounded went on day and night. Before dark other stretchers were placed alongside the first, and before we left several days later there were two or three rows that had grown tragically in length. Many had been good friends and had already survived a lot of combat.

"I knew we had to defeat the Japanese and the Nazis—we had to fight, although none of us liked it. I was fiercely proud of my outfit, but I could never accept the death of comrades as anything but tragic, abominable waste.

"The more fortunate casualties who survived were carried out of the aid station on stretchers which were placed on jeeps. I think each jeep carried about four stretchers. The luckiest of all the casualties—the walking wounded or the ones with the million-dollar wound—were helped aboard the jeeps. The little vehicles then sped to the rear and were then evacuated to hospital ships or various field hospitals set up on the island.

"The Japanese commanders chose to launch a large offensive. Their plan called for a series of mass kamikaze and conventional aerial attacks against the US Navy support fleet offshore, and the supply and communication areas on the island behind the front lines, to begin during the night of May 3 in coordination with the counterattack on land. The Japanese ground attack was to be no suicidal banzai.

"They had ample support to crush the 1st Marine Division; the Japanese 44th Independent Mixed Brigade had heavy support of tanks, artillery, and anti-tank elements. The US soldiers on the American left (eastern) flank discovered the Japanese landings behind their lines and slaughtered several hundred of the enemy."

The Japanese landing on the western coast in the Marines' sector was also discovered, and three hundred to four hundred Japanese were killed both in the water and on the beach.

"When the 1st Marine Division attacked on May 4 these Japanese fought with incredible ferocity, determined to hold and not lose any ground in guarding the approaches to Shuri after the failure of their offensive. In hindsight, I realize that we were in a more dangerous situation the night of May 3–4 than any of us realized.

"During the remainder of the Okinawa campaign, the Japanese resorted to skillful, ferocious defense tactics just like at Peleliu. They made only local, limited counterattacks to delay us and extract maximum losses, and they succeeded in this respect.

"On May 4, or it may have been the next day, I saw one of the strangest things I ever witnessed in combat. Three or four Sherman tanks of an Army unit were parked near us. I went over and struck up a conversation with one of the men on a tank parked to the right near our fox holes. I sat on my helmet near the rear of the tank. He put aside his helmet and stripped to the waist. As he stood behind the turret we talked while he began various maintenance chores on his tank. He was friendly and said they had just come back from where they had been supporting the Marines. He said the Japanese opposition up there was as rough as ever. His tanks now had orders to leave and return to support an Army division.

"'I guess you'll be glad of that,' I said.

"'Why? No, I won't,' he said.

"'Well, don't Marines have a bad reputation for being too aggressive and trying to push too hard on an attack?'

"The soldier stopped his work, straightened up, looked at me and said, 'Buddy, you guys got a great outfit, I like working with

Marines. When things get rough with you guys and anybody has to haul ass, everybody hauls ass together. It ain't none of this crap of infantry and tanks getting separated and every man for himself.'

"Just then a Marine Corsair fighter flew over low and circled very slowly over us. We waved at the pilot, and he waved back to us. Our pilots often did this, and it gave us a real feeling of comradeship for them, although I never had the opportunity of talking with a Corsair pilot but once during the war.

"Just as the plane made a second circle, I saw with astonishment that the auxiliary fuel drop tank under the fuselage was becoming unfastened. The fuel tank came loose from the plane and tumbled down end over end. I was terrified, because I had seen similar fuel tanks loaded with napalm dropped on Bloody Nose Ridge on Peleliu, and I had seen the fire and devastation caused to everything but coral rock.

"I yelled and dove away from the tank. The aircraft fuel tank tumbled down and fell directly onto the rear of the Sherman. It landed on a grill covering part of the engine; it split open, gasoline spilled out, and caught the Sherman on fire. The army tanker I had been talking to didn't flinch. He yelled to a fellow crewman through the turret hatch, and I saw an arm thrust a fire extinguisher out to him. He sprayed the chemical on the fire and put it out quickly.

"Luckily the Corsair drop tank had been nearly empty; if it had been full, the tank's crewmen and I would have been caught in a flash fire. The man I had been talking to was nonchalant about it all. His surprised buddy emerged from the hatch, and they inspected their machine for damage. They told me the fire had been extinguished before anything but some waste grease and oil ignited. It was a close call, and the Sherman tanker's quick thinking saved his vehicle.

"The amazed Corsair pilot, probably attracted by the smoke, circled back a couple of times to see what had happened. He may not have even realized that his fuel tank had broken loose. Previous damage from Japanese gunfire could have caused this to happen. While the Sherman crewmen and I were commenting on the freak accident and how lucky we were, they got orders over their radio to move out. We exchanged mutual wishes for good luck as their tank engine roared to life, and they went rumbling on their way.

"Most of the next day K Company remained near the battalion aid station. We would be back up on the line soon enough. As usual, the men passed the time cleaning weapons, writing letters, playing cards, or sitting in their fox holes talking with friends. Up ahead the fighting rattled and rumbled, and casualties came by us to the aid station. The immediate area seemed quiet to us, but it was not without its hazards.

"Mac was over at the CP and several of us were using his walkie-talkie to listen in on conversations between officers up on the line. Two officers were calmly discussing the proper size bomb to be dropped by an airstrike on some Japanese positions out in front of 3/5. They sounded more like civil engineers discussing the routine removal of rock from a construction site than two combat officers deciding what size bomb was most likely to blast an enemy emplacement into dust.

"When they agreed on what to use, I got up and walked over to the edge of our mound to try to see the planes make their bombing runs. I stood on the back edge of a deep foxhole. Just in front of this the mound dropped off vertically about six feet to the level cane field surrounding the area.

"Behind me four mortarmen were sitting around an old ammo box playing a spirited game of cribbage with a pack of dirty, greasy cards. Another mortarman had taken his entrenching tool and some toilet paper a little way out into the field behind the mound. We felt secure.

"As I looked out beyond our front lines, I saw a Japanese 90mm mortar shell explode about two hundred yards away in the field between us and the front line. There were no Marines in this area. The Japanese rarely fired their mortars and artillery during daylight unless they had a definite target, so this seemed unusual.

"The next shell exploded closer, in a direct line between us and the first shell, but still at a safe distance. This would have made sense at night as harassing fire, but not in broad daylight. That gun crew was trying to zero in on something, but what?

"I watched with the professional interest of a mortarman wondering how many turns on the gun's elevation crank the Japanese mortar gunner was making between shells.

"Their third round struck closer still, and in line with the first two. This indicated the enemy gunner was searching toward us.... Then a fourth shell, and my interest changed to concern as I turned to my cribbage playing buddies and said, 'Hey, you guys, there's a Jap 90 walking 'em right down the valley this way.'

"They had paid no attention so far to the shells, and a couple of characters answered without even looking up, 'Screw the bastard, he ain't firing at us.'

"The next big shell exploded with a flash and a deafening crash directly in front of me. It was no more than a few yards out in the field. The concussion knocked me feet first right into the deep fox hole on the edge of the mound. I sank to the bottom of the hole with my ears ringing and my heart pounding. Stunned as I was, there was not a scratch on me. The steel fragments coming in my direction had been absorbed by the vertical face of the mound at my feet.

"Another crash behind followed the one in front of us. Someone yelled for a corpsman. I looked back at my buddies I had just warned. They were dazed and stunned, but they were all getting up. Hudson was gripping his bleeding upper arm and grimacing with pain where a large fragment had made a nasty wound. Another man was wounded less seriously in the back.

"'Where is Newt?' someone asked, referring to the man who had gone down to the field behind us to relieve himself.

"'God, he must have been blown to pieces!' another man groaned. Just then Newt came wobbling up looking dazed and sheepish. The shell that struck behind us exploded not far from him in the cane field while he was relieving himself. That he was unhurt from those big fragments was incredible. The corpsman tended to Hudson and the other man, and they made the short walk to the battalion aid station.

"Those of us from the mortar section on that mound that day were very lucky. Every one of them but me would become a casualty before the campaign on Okinawa dragged out to its bloody end. I was told by a man in the aid station that another shell in the same barrage fell further behind us and landed directly in the middle of a jeep carrying three Marines, one of whom was an officer.

"All three were killed and terribly mangled. It was freakish for a mortar shell to land directly on a moving vehicle while we had only two wounded, but in combat the freakish and unlikely were often everyday occurrences."

Back to the Front Line

Heavy rain started May 6 and went on continuously until May 8. The 1st Marine Division had reached the Asato Gawa with many casualties. My father remembered that when they went into the line there was a railroad track on their right running south. It was a visual landmark for the rest of the month of May. The 5th Marines began to encounter well-developed Japanese positions around Dakeshi and the area called the Awacha Pocket.

On May 8, Nazi Germany surrendered unconditionally. I remember my father telling me that all that concerned them in the mud and rain on Okinawa through the rest of the month of May was just surviving. "Nazi Germany might as well have been on the moon," he said to me. "Most of the guys didn't give a damn. We had our hands full where we were."

"At some point not long after this we moved out for the front line again."

The 6th Marine Division moved into the line on the right of the 1st Division, which shifted them to the left and put them in the center of the American advance. While the war ending in Europe meant nothing to them at the time, the arrival of another Marine division to help shoulder the load was a boost to their morale.

The heart of Japanese defenses on Okinawa was the Shuri line, and they were getting close. But first they had to contend with Awacha and Dakeshi. Their battalion dug in in front of Awacha. Ammunition was brought up as close as possible, but the horrible mud caused it to be dumped on the other side of a draw about fifty yards behind them. Because of this, work parties had to carry the ammo and supplies from the dump and across the draw to the various K Company positions.

As my father told me many times, carrying ammo and rations was something all the veterans had done many times. Depending on the circumstances, it didn't matter what a Marine's specialty was; if the situation called for it, he carried ammo. My father, for example, was an assistant gunner on a 60mm mortar, not an ammo carrier, but it was a task he performed many times when the situation demanded it, as did many other Marines.

"Our 60mm mortar ammo was hard to handle unless partially unpacked. Each shell was in a tarred waterproof cardboard canister with metal ends. Six mortar shells were packed per canister. Each of these contained a range card."

My father probably used some of these range cards to keep notes on, then tucked them into his Bible.

"Three of the large canisters of six shells each were held together by two clover-shaped pieces of black metal, one at each end, and held together with a long bolt and nut. This cloverleaf of shells, eighteen shells in all, was then enclosed in a heavy wooden crate."

When I was on Peleliu in 1999, I saw many of these metal "cloverleafs" all over the island. Whenever we were exploring an area where K Company had been known to operate during the battle, I would pick up each one I saw and wonder if it had once been in my father's hands.

"Two pieces of wire about ¼ inch in diameter were tightened around the crate for extra strength. This wire gave us trouble. Before Peleliu, Dad had sent me a heavy knife with a blade like a tapered meat cleaver, and our mortar section found this invaluable for breaking open crates of ammo.

"On Okinawa for the first time we received some 60mm HE shells packed not in a heavy, bulky cloverleaf, but in handy metal boxes with a handle. There were about eight or nine shells per box.

These boxes were heavy, but you could carry one in each hand. You simply twisted the handle to open the box and get to the shells.

"The empty boxes were put to a very practical use at times. We often filled them with soil and stacked them around the gun pit as a parapet to protect the crew against Japanese shrapnel."

While they were near Awacha, they made trips back and forth across the muddy draw to bring back ammo. On one such occasion, suddenly, from their left, a Japanese Nambu opened up on them.

"There was a knoll to the left of our mortar section area, and we moved out into the draw from behind this to the supplies situated in the protection of another knoll across the draw."

When the enemy machine gunner began firing, my father just happened to be about midway out in the draw. The Japanese slugs were snapping and cracking around him as he sprinted in the mud toward the ammo dump.

"We didn't know whether the front lines curved back on our left and this Japanese was firing from out in front of them, as often happened, or whether he had infiltrated the lines, or had been bypassed."

It was a tough situation; if they kept exposing themselves in the draw, eventually the Nambu would start picking them off, but they had to get the ammo back to their positions.

"We picked up loads of ammo but hesitated before trying to return across the draw. The Japanese Nambu was a fine weapon with a rapid rate of fire, and we dreaded it."

Across the draw, near the mortar section, they saw John Redifer begin throwing out phosphorous grenades to screen them with the smoke. They heard the distinct bump of each grenade, then saw the flashes and the billows of murky white smoke. They gritted their teeth and dashed back across amid the vicious Nambu slugs zipping around them. They made it without anyone getting hit.

When they dropped their loads of ammo boxes, one commented on the fire discipline of the Nambu gunner. It was hard not to admire the well-timed bursts, each precisely two to three rounds.

"'Yeah, that way the bastard don't heat up his barrel and waste his ammo—he's bound to hit some of us sooner or later,' came another comment.

"'He's not going to cease firing until he gets knocked out,' I said."

Help came in the form of an M4 Sherman tank. They heard its engine across the draw, and John Redifer ran out to make contact with its crew near the knoll where the ammo was located. The tank crew agreed to act as a shield for them. So with my father and the other men crouched in the lee of the Sherman, it moved back and forth across the draw, its engine roaring and spewing exhaust fumes that added to the already misty, murky air. After several trips with the tank, they got all the ammo they needed.

"As we moved along beside the tank backing slowly across the draw for our first trip with it, I looked toward the ammo dump, and saw a familiar figure approaching from the battalion rear. It was our friend Captain Paul Douglas. He shook hands and greeted us like old friends. He said he remembered the time he helped some of us Peleliu veterans unload an amtrac under mortar fire in front of Bloody Nose Ridge. We were delighted to see him, and the fact that this brave, brilliant compassionate man remembered me gave my morale a tremendous boost. He affected my comrades the same way.

"After greeting us Captain Douglas said, 'You boys look like you could use some help with this ammo.'

"We told him we surely could. He said he would 'turn to and bear a hand,' and help us finish that working party in short order. And that's just what we did with his generous help and that of the tankers. The Nambu kept firing down that draw until night fell.

"After we finished carrying all the ammo and rations across the draw we thanked the tankers and they moved on to support the impending attack. Captain Douglas stayed and rested with us a while, and we talked about the battle and about Captain Haldane and all the good Marines we lost on Peleliu. Finally, Douglas said he was going to shove off, and so we said goodbye to him. He was wounded a couple of hours later, and I did not see him again until

years after the war when he was a well-known US Senator on a lecture tour through Mobile.

"In addition to the Sherman tanks—with 75mm guns, there were other armored vehicles that supported us on Okinawa. The flamethrower tanks we had first seen in use at Peleliu were used extensively on Okinawa against Japanese emplacements. More heavily armored than flamethrower amtracs, these tanks were less vulnerable to Japanese guns.

"The M-7 self-propelled howitzer became a familiar [sight] to us. This weapon consisted of a tank chassis that mounted a 105mm howitzer and an air-cooled .50 cal. machine gun, had a crew of seven men, and could go 26 miles an hour. It had been developed to allow a howitzer to keep up with rapidly advancing ground troops and was very successful.

"For several days an M-7 self-propelled howitzer stayed with K Company, and we got to know the Marine crewmen quite well. Like the tankers and amtrac crewmen, they were a friendly bunch. The M-7 crew generously shared their extra 10 in 1 rations with us when we were in quiet areas and could build a fire and cook the delicious, canned bacon and other goodies they contained. It was a treat for us compared to our constant diet of C rations and K rations.

"This M-7 was kept parked behind a protected position until it was called on to move out and fire its big 105 into some Japanese cave or pillbox. We always hated to see it go because, being an open tank chassis with no turret, the crew had limited protection from Japanese snipers as they worked their 105. Our friends on the crew consistently suffered casualties, mainly from snipers. New replacements came up to fill out the crew so that before the M-7 was ordered to move to another area, only one man of the original seven crewmen remained. The M-7 might have been very successful as far as fast moving, mobile heavy artillery, but its lack of protection was a problem.

CHAPTER SEVENTEEN

Attack on Awacha

An attack on Awacha was planned for May 9. Men squared away their gear, naval guns out at sea fired periodic fire missions during the morning, and Sherman tanks stood by with engines idling and their crewmen waiting in open hatches. Above all, my father noticed how many replacements there were—new, untested men. He felt sorry for them. They looked bewildered and confused.

The storm of steel commenced, and the artillery fire blended with the naval gunfire, as well as that of the Corsairs and torpedo bombers overhead.

The call came down the line for the mortar section to stand by.

"One of my buddies who was dug in near the gun pit had a sound-power field telephone with a line laid along the ground up to the Observation Post (OP). An NCO in the OP would specify how many rounds for us to fire, and whether it was fire for effect on a specific place or search and traverse fire to cover a larger area.

"Once we began firing, I was oblivious to all else around me. Snafu set the sights on the mortar, yelled out the range and how many of the four increments I was to leave on the base of each shell and yelled, 'Fire One.' After I set the increments, pulled the safety wire, and dropped the shell into the muzzle, we both ducked down to protect our eyes and ears from the muzzle blast. After each round fired Snafu leveled the elevation and windage bubbles on the sight and yelled, 'Fire two.' This kept up until we fired the number of rounds specified by our observer or received further orders.

"When the May rains turned the whole area around Shuri into a morass, we often could not have the protection of a gun pit. Fox holes and gun pits caved in or filled with water so that it was impossible to work the gun.

"Then we sought what shelter we could find behind some nearby knoll or contour and set the gun on the surface of the ground with no protection from enemy shelling, and proceeded to fire as fast we could while Snafu cursed, and I gritted my teeth and prayed that we didn't get blown to bits by Japanese shells. How their observers always spotted us I never knew, but they did.

"When we were in open rolling terrain, we often had opportunities to fire HE on Japanese troops in defilade, ravines, behind ridges, and even in the open during their local counterattacks or withdrawals. They responded in these situations with counter battery fire that inflicted casualties, and it was remarkable that our whole mortar section wasn't wiped out."

On May 9 against Awacha this was the case, and K Company suffered heavy losses. The battle on Okinawa became a bloodbath as the Americans fought their way south through Awacha, Dakeshi Ridge, Dakeshi Village, Wana Ridge, Wana Village, and Wana Draw. Beyond lay the main defense line of Shuri itself.

"After the costly attack of May 9 on Awacha, 3/5 moved off the line. Our battalion was assigned to protect the rear of the 7th Marines during its attack on Dakeshi Ridge."

The 7th Marines were to the right of the 5th Marines. When they dug in, the K Company mortar section was to act as riflemen.

"Our battalion was ordered to keep on the alert for any enemy movement trying to flank us and get in the rear of the 7th Marines. My mortar squad was dug in, two men to a hole which were five yards apart, along the base of an embankment about eight or ten feet in height."

As they sat in the drizzling rain, chilled and soaked to the bone, they got rations, water, and mail. My father sat on his helmet in the mud and read in a letter from my grandfather that Deacon, his beloved spaniel, had been hit by a car and had died.

"Deacon had been given to me several years earlier by my aunt, Octavia Wynn, who raised thoroughbred Cocker Spaniels in Selma, Alabama. Because of some broken fence or unlatched gate, a male Springer Spaniel had been able to get into the pen where Deacon's mother was kept. The result was that Deacon was a mixture—half Cocker and half Springer."

"He was a beautiful black, white and tan spaniel, with a tan spot over each eye. Deacon was one of the most intelligent dogs I ever had. I trained him to do many tricks, and he would even respond to signals such as the movement of my eyes."

My grandfather never met a dog he didn't want. My father told me that friends of theirs in Mobile, who hunted and owned dogs, would sometimes become displeased with these animals and how they handled themselves on a hunt. On one occasion, a particular individual complained loudly about what he was going to do with a certain dog who had not done as he was told. My grandfather intervened, gave the man a severe dressing down laced with some expletives, and said, "Don't you dare hurt that dog. Give him to me, I'll take him." And he did.

"A buddy nearby looked at me and asked if I had received bad news from home. When I told him what the letter said that weary, muddy, grizzled veteran was as sympathetic as though I had lost a member of my immediate family. He understood, because he had a favorite dog back home himself.

"A damp darkness settled on us. Not long after dark I heard the roar of a Japanese 150mm howitzer shell coming our way from somewhere above and beyond the embankment. Fear gripped me as the shell roared closer and closer. It hit the deck with a thud above us and between the other two mortar squads. The big dud ploughed a furrow through the ground like a giant mole between the two lines of foxholes. It then came out of the face of the embankment directly above my hole and threw a shower of mud and dirt onto my

buddy and me as it went whirring off through the darkness into the valley beyond.

"'God, that was close!' my friend groaned.

"'It sounded big enough to blow us all up if it had exploded,' I stammered."

As the night wore on, they could hear the battle near Dakeshi rumbling. The Japanese were trying to push the 7th Marines off the ridge.

"During the wee hours of the morning the word was passed—stand by to move back up into the line. Readying our gear was as easy for us in total darkness as in broad daylight. Even though we were off the lines the smoking lamp was always out because of the ever-present threat of Japanese infiltrators. The sound of firing rose and fell to our left front as we waited."

At last, the order to move out came in the gray light of early dawn. The air hung heavy with mist.

"My squad had to climb up the embankment to take our place in the company column to move out. I got a good look at the furrow made by the Japanese 150mm dud shell between the mortar squads up there. The men said they thought it was the end for them when that big shell tore right through the ground between the lines of fox holes. I still had mud on me from the shower it threw over us below when it tore out through the crest of the embankment.

"Mud contributed greatly to our fatigue, and nothing caused us more irritation and exasperation."

My father once told me the story of Snafu slipping in the mud one especially wet day. He was carrying the 45-lb baseplate of the 60mm mortar. Although it didn't fall into the mud when he slipped, he was so exhausted and enraged that he shouted, "Goddamn!" as he threw the baseplate down into the muck as hard as he could. It landed with a splat and, of course, became completely covered in mud. Snafu then had to pull it up and thoroughly clean it. The moral of the story, as my father related to me, was to practice self-control and, even under trying circumstances, to never lose your temper.

"Frequently an order was passed by word of mouth from front to rear along the column during these night moves. I must admit that those of us who had experienced that exercise to 'sharpen our attention to the correct relay of orders' during maneuvers on Guadalcanal made sure the word was repeated correctly."

When they got to where they were headed back into the line that early morning of May 10, the situation had been contained, and it was determined that 3/5 was no longer needed at that location. As they prepared to file out, they looked around and saw evidence of a tough fight.

"The Marines who had been under attack were assessing the damage they had done to the Japanese and caring for their own wounded. I counted the enemy dead. Just within the restricted area, with smoke hanging low in the air, I counted about forty bodies strewn out on the muddy slope to the front."

It was at this time that the men of K Company heard that their skipper, Stumpy Stanley, was very sick with malaria and would have to be evacuated. Stumpy had taken over K Company after Capt. Ack Ack Haldane had been killed on Hill 140 at Peleliu. Though a different kind of leader, he was nonetheless popular and well respected.

"He had a sort of substantial calm about him that inspired confidence and respect. He was a good officer, but sometimes distant and preoccupied. He didn't give off the warm, friendly feeling to the men in the ranks the way Ack Ack did.

"Stumpy was simply a different type from Capt. Haldane. As one of my buddies summed it up: 'Stumpy don't say much to ya, but he's a damn good joe.'

"He was about medium height and had slightly curly hair. I never really got to know him, and I doubt if he even knew my name. We were glad when he was back with the company after only a couple of days."

My father got to know Stumpy very well in later years as he was writing *With the Old Breed.* They had many late-night phone calls discussing their time together in K Company. I remember one warm sunny day when I was in the garage working out. My parents were out of town for a few days, and I had the house to myself. I don't recall if I was in high school or college. The phone rang, and I ran inside to answer it. I heard a gravelly voice on the other end say, "Is Sledgehammer there?"

"No, sir, he and my mother are out of town," I answered.

"Tell him Stumpy Stanley called," the gravelly voice said.

"Yessir, I will," I said. And that was my one conversation with Lt. Thomas J. Stanley. Brief though it was, it is a treasured memory, and another example of how the lore of K/3/5 shaped my youth.

Another Respite

"In June we were pulled off the lines and marched to some showers that had been set up beneath some big pine trees. They were built up on a wooden platform off the deck, and everything around was coral surfaced. What a fine sensation it was to scrub away the grime, filth, and mud. I scrubbed my filthy, muddy dungarees in the shower, wrung them out and put them back on wet—but clean!

"A bath, clean dungarees and clean socks made me feel human again. All my buddies felt the same way. From May 1 when we went into the front lines on southern Okinawa until the end on June 21, we were taken to a field shower on two occasions—this being the first. Those were the most delightful refreshments of my overseas duty.

"During one period while we were off the front lines and in reserve, several K Company men and I were detailed to a working party to load boxes of supplies on a truck."

"We carried only carbines and pistols and followed an NCO a long distance over coral roads down to the beach. The weather had cleared temporarily, and it was pleasant. It was almost like the old Pavuvu working parties with the men cracking jokes and kidding each other.

"On this occasion we were muddy, bearded, hollow-eyed creatures who had come slithering out of the muck and filth. As we approached the beach we were impressed with the huge piles of equipment and supplies that we passed.

"'God where did all this stuff come from?' one man asked.

"We arrived at the beach and went to an LCT that had just unloaded supplies from one of the cargo ships lying offshore. There were some Marines stacking the last boxes from the LCT when we came up. While our NCO went over and talked to the sergeant in charge of them, we struck up a conversation with some of these men.

"They wore Marine dungarees, helmets and boondockers but no cartridge belts, leggings, or other field equipment. They probably had rifles stacked somewhere, but I didn't see them. We asked them what unit they were from, and they said they were Supply and Beach Party.

"We had heard of the amazing work the Beach Party men had done on Peleliu after we had pushed inland. They had kept the supplies moving up to us during the early days of the battle when the Japanese had the beach under heavy fire.

"'What outfit you guys from?' asked a Beach Party man, noticing our bearded, filthy appearance.

"'Fifth Marines,' we answered.

"The Supply man looked duly impressed at the mention of our famous regiment and said, 'Hey, you guys from a line company then...bet you seen plenty of action ain't you?' He looked at us with honest, unconcealed admiration.

"'Enough,' answered a K Company man with resignation in his tone.

"'We've had a bunch of air raids with Kamikazes coming over after them ships,' said one of the Beach Party men.

"'Yeah, things are rough all over,' said a friend of mine sarcastically.

"Each of these Beach Party men had a bright red spot about 2 inches in diameter painted onto the back of the helmet, on the shoulder, and on the hip pocket. I had never seen this, so I said, 'What are the bright spots? Doesn't look like good camouflage?'

"'Oh, that means we're specialists at handling supplies, so nobody can order us up to the front lines.'

"I simply said, 'Oh, I see,' and was prepared to let it drop.

"However, a K Company buddy took exception to this and began arguing with the Beach Party man about the idea of a Marine who couldn't take his turn on the front lines. Things were starting to heat up when an NCO came over and ordered everyone to get the stuff on the truck.

"In retrospect, I sympathize with the Beach Party man; he was only doing the job he was assigned to do just like we were in the rifle companies. But in the context of that time, we envied and resented anybody who didn't have to be exposed to the constant dangers, terror and filth—and worst of all the sight of bleeding, mangled friends suffering and dying—which was our existence as infantrymen.

"We loaded the supplies on a small truck and rode back to the area where 3/5 was resting.

"Snafu somehow got some real coffee, far superior to the dehydrated type in C and K rations.

"We would boil a helmet full of water and then carefully pour in a measured amount of the good coffee, stir it, and let the grounds settle out.

"'That's as good a cup of joe as you can get anywhere,' Snafu would proclaim with pride in his thick Louisiana accent. He was right. It did smell delicious but was black as ink, and so strong that two cups of it would give you the shakes. Anything hot was a treat in those chilly May rains, but this coffee was special.

"The aroma attracted K Company buddies from surrounding areas like honey draws flies. Snafu would solemnly pour out just the right amount into the canteen cups of only a chosen few. The only reason I got my share was because I always built the fire. If the wood was wet, and it usually was, I had difficulty with the fire, and Snafu would grumble mightily. Finally, he agreed to take turns with me building the fire and brewing the coffee.

"The coffee I brewed caused Snafu to shout with fury when he tasted it. 'Damn, Sledgehammer, you went and wasted that coffee! That's the worst joe I ever tasted!'

"'It tastes just as good as yours,' I insisted. He demoted me back to fire builder for a while. Eventually, I had another try at brewing his precious coffee. This time, he exclaimed in amazement when he tasted it, 'By God, Sledgehammer, you finally learned how to make joe!'

"I answered, 'Hell, it's just like all the rest.' However, he insisted that he possessed a subtle sensitivity of taste (which he didn't express in those words) that I didn't have, because I was too dumb to know the difference. Anyway, we enjoyed the real coffee during our reliefs. Snafu kept it carefully stowed in a waterproof bag in his pack. He hoarded it like gold, but it finally ran out."

Dakeshi Ridge was finally secured by the 7th Marines by May 13. K/3/5 moved into Dakeshi Village, or what was left of it.

Mud continued to cause problems, especially for the mortar crews.

"I remember one occasion while our company was on the line during the fighting around Dakeshi. The K Company riflemen and machine gunners were dug in on a low ridge, and our mortar positions were about 50 yards back. We dug the gun pits in muddy ground on the side of a little rise, but the whole area was so flat we could look straight up past our line to the dominant high ground out front.

"Out there the Japanese were emplaced in caves and had unobstructed observation of our entire battalion sector. It was a hot spot. We were in this position for about a day and a night, firing our guns frequently out beyond our lines.

"Every time we began firing our 60s the Japanese immediately responded with counter battery fire—81mm or 90mm mortars and 75mm artillery. Finally the bottom of the gun pit got so mucky that we couldn't work the gun and had to cease firing to reset it.

"Just as we were tugging on the gun to pull the base plate up out of the mud, a frantic voice came over the sound power phone,'Why the hell did you cease firing?'

"The ammo carrier dug in next to us was taking the fire orders via the phone, and he told the observer that we had to reset the mortar because of the mud.

"'Screw the goddamn mud!' shouted our mortar NCO who was observing. 'Get that damn gun outa' that gun pit and commence firing on the double! There's Nips running all around out front of us and hiding in ditches, and small arms fire can't get at 'em! Forget the gun pit!'

"The ammo carrier told us exactly what the observer said, and he looked dismayed as he did so.

"'Orders is orders,' Snafu said in a resigned tone. We dreaded being out on bare ground during the counter battery fire, but we quickly got the gun up out of the muddy pit, realigned it, reset the aiming stakes and commenced firing.

"'That's better,' the observer said, 'keep it up! We're tearing their asses up in them ditches!'

"We crouched as low as we could to avoid the counter battery fire. The ammo carriers in our squad passed the ammo to me from their holes and we kept up rapid fire for effect. Snafu and I lay down and hugged the mud as best we could while still working the gun. Japanese shells crashed and exploded—hurling deadly steel fragments around. We were terrified, but our discipline and training kept us from panicking.

"The Japanese shells flung geysers of mud into the air, and it splattered down on everybody. There were some K Company men in reserve dug in near us. Doc Caswell was in a large hole not far from my gun. Men began to get hit by the shelling. It finally subsided and our order came to secure.

"We scrambled back into our gun pit. Doc had a regular dressing station in his foxhole, and there were wounded in the hole with him and lying around it. With his usual cool efficiency, he administered aid, tagged them, and sent them to the rear as quickly as possible.

"After a couple of more harrowing episodes of lying above ground and firing the mortar during counter battery fire we managed to build a footing of boxes and ammo cartons to support the base plate of the mortar in the gun pit. It was a relief to get that done.

"Toward dusk it began to rain. The Japanese shelling began again, but we were not firing our own guns, so we crouched in the gun pit. The shelling was not heavy, but it caused casualties around us. I looked over and saw Doc tending to more wounded in his fox hole. Suddenly, I felt something humming in my ear. It was only a mosquito, but it was annoying. I slapped my ear to get rid of him. My hands were caked with mud of course, so some of that mud stopped up my ear canal with the mosquito still inside. I wiped mud off my hand, cleaned my finger, and then poked it into my ear to try deal with it, but this only drove the mud and the mosquito deeper.

"'Hey Doc,' I yelled, 'I've got a mosquito stuck in my ear. Can you get it out?' Doc looked up from bandaging a bloody arm and calmly told me to come on over and he would get to me as soon as he could. My foxhole mate, a Gloucester veteran, looked at me with amazement.

"'Sledgehammer, have you cracked up? With all that shellin' you're thinking about a damn mosquito!'

"'This thing's about to drive me nuts buzzing in my ear!' I said.

"'Hell, you're already nuts if you're gonna get out of this hole during this shelling!'

"I jumped out of our hole and, crouching low, ran over to Doc and flopped down in the mud beside him. Shells were shrieking and wining and exploding all around us. Doc had five or six casualties with him. Most of them were replacements who had been in the company such a short time I didn't even know their names.

"Doc tended to them and then said, 'OK Sledgehammer.' I slid into the hole among the wounded. Doc took a cotton swab from his canvas pouch and after considerable cleaning solved my problem.

"The shelling stopped shortly, and I headed back to my own fox hole where my Texas buddy told me I was crazy as hell. I told him he couldn't imagine the sensation of an insect being caught in his ear.

"It was the sort of ridiculous episode that no one who had ever been shelled would ever believe—but it happened."

CHAPTER EIGHTEEN

Stalemate at Shuri

After bitter and costly fighting, Awacha and Dakeshi fell to the 1st Division. The next fortified Japanese defense system was called Wana Draw.

"The stream called the Asato Gawa meandered through Wana Draw across the northern approaches to Shuri and emptied out to the sea on our right, in the 6th Marine Division's zone."[16]

The plan was for a coordinated tank/infantry attack on Wana Draw by the 5th Marines. The tanks received so much Japanese shellfire that they had to withdraw along with the infantry. After they got clear, American artillery and naval gunfire began to pound the area, and carrier planes launched an air strike. It quickly became obvious that Wana Ridge and Wana Draw would be costly, and all available firepower would be needed.

Around the middle of May, Doc Caswell was hit by Japanese shellfire. Several Marines ran to where Doc was lying on his back in a muddy hole and being tended to by another corpsman. My father leaned over him and spoke to him. He saw that when Doc tried to answer him, blood trickled out from between his lips. He had been wounded by a shell fragment in the neck. In that moment it didn't look as though Doc Caswell would survive, and my father and his buddies tried not to show their grief.

---

16 E.B. Sledge, *With the Old Breed*, 239.

"A buddy mused that he'd bet Doc Caswell had saved the life of many a Marine at Peleliu and Okinawa. So true. Doc Caswell was greatly missed by us all. He was universally admired and respected by everyone I knew."

Fortunately, Gerald K. Caswell survived the neck wound he received that day near Wana Draw.

"He returned to his native Texas, and he has been one of my most faithful old 3/5 buddies; we exchange cards every Christmas.

"Darkness soon settled on us, and we were shelled off and on during the night. Our own artillery kept up heavy barrages on the Japanese positions in Wana Draw, and on Wana Ridge to our left where the 7th Marines was having a terrible fight."

At this point, around May 19 or May 20, Wana Ridge was to their left and Wana Draw was in front. Both areas were receiving a massive amount of American mortar, artillery, naval gunfire, and aerial bombardment. At least thirty tanks, four equipped with flamethrowers, blasted and burned the draw.

These barrages went on for hours, and there was plenty of Japanese return fire. My father said to me more than once that they had seen plenty of heavy stuff at Peleliu, but it was nothing compared to what they saw at Okinawa. He said he would get headaches that lasted for days.

"A headache was certainly of no consequence with all the suffering and dying going on all around us, but it showed the sheer magnitude of the noise of countless heavy explosions. All this massive heavy weapons support was to augment our infantry on Okinawa, and the sheer volume of it for hours on end day after day tended to fray our overtaxed nerves."

The time came to cross Wana Draw itself. This they did in dispersed order at the direction of an NCO. My father was going to go across with three other Marines. They were supposed to get across the mouth of the draw as fast as possible behind some troops from 2/5. They were told to drop anything heavy and haul ass. My father didn't carry his mortar ammo bag, just his Tommy gun slung over his shoulder. They slid down a ten-foot embankment to the sloped floor of the draw to start their dash across.

"I ran as fast as I could and was glad I was not carrying my heavy mortar ammo bag, but only my Tommy, pistol, and my combat pack—which I always kept as light as possible."

They made contact with some men from 2nd Battalion, and my father was asked to help out with a wounded Marine who was nearby. They found this young man dazed and bloody, taking cover beneath a bush. They called for a stretcher. My father asked the man where he was hit and unhooked his cartridge belt and adjusted the man's dungarees so the corpsman could get to the wound, which was from a shell fragment rather than a bullet.

"I did not put my battle dressing over the wound for fear of increasing the chances of infection and because the corpsmen were close by, and the external bleeding was minor."

It didn't take long for them to get to the casualty, and he was placed on a stretcher and moved from harm's way down the ridge to a deep ravine where several other corpsmen were tending wounded.

"I never knew a Marine who didn't feel the same admiration I did for the bravery and efficiency of the Navy Corpsmen who served alongside us."

My father and the men he went across the draw with split up and took positions along the slope to await orders. He occupied a larger two-man foxhole that had been used by the Japanese earlier. This provided a good view of the draw.

"About the time I got settled in the hole, just watching an occasional Japanese shell burst out behind our lines in the draw I had crossed, my old friend Jay came along. He joined me in the hole.

"Jay was pretty nervous. The extreme stress and strain of his third campaign was wearing his nerves badly. Okinawa was my second, and my nerves were frayed, but many Gloucester veterans who survived Peleliu now felt that their luck was running out on Okinawa. A new replacement might come into the company and get

hit immediately—I had seen it happen often—but the third battle just seemed to be pushing a man's luck too far.

"Jay confided in me about this. I tried to cheer him up. He had helped me through Peleliu, and now I was trying to do the same for him, but the truth was his luck was pretty thin by now.

"He would go home if he survived Okinawa, but for those of us who came in for Peleliu, the inevitable invasion of Japan would be our third blitz. That was a dismal prospect and I knew my luck would run out. Despite all that, I think my words helped Jay for the moment.

"We looked back across the draw, toward our battalion rear at the point where I had slid down the embankment to come across, and we saw an armored bulldozer—it had a protected cab for the driver that was high profile and angular, not like a Sherman's turret.

"This machine approached the crest of the embankment, dropped its blade, and began digging a slanting road cut to the draw. Immediately, Japanese 90mm mortar shells began to explode all around it.

"'If one of those hits close enough it'll sure knock out that dozer,' I said to Jay.

"The driver, buttoned up in his thin armor-plated cab, worked furiously with his blade to finish the road cut. The big shells erupted thickly around his machine with orange flashes and dirty smoke as it trundled back and forth to finish the job. We were impressed with the expert way the dozer driver made the cut in a few minutes under such perilous conditions. He finished, spun around, and went bouncing out of sight to the rear in a cloud of exhaust smoke. The mortar fire then ceased.

"Several Sherman tanks then came speeding into view across the field and down into the draw via the newly made cut.

"Across the draw well to our right beyond the road cut, we saw a platoon of three Marine 37mm antitank guns in a trench on the side of the ridge with an earth parapet. They were firing slowly and deliberately at targets way up the draw to our right.

"They secured after a few rounds and the gun crews lounged around their weapons, apparently awaiting further orders. Then, all hell broke loose for them. Japanese 90mm mortar shells began exploding along the parapet and in the trench itself. I could see Marines get hit, pitch forward, sprawl over backwards or sag down out of sight. The uninjured dove for cover. It was pathetic—the Japanese mortarmen were right on target, and their big shells erupted in a line right along the trench.

"When the smoke cleared, we could see the survivors scurrying around aiding their casualties. Then a storm of Japanese machine gun bullets came snapping and popping around our heads as we flopped down below the edge of our hole.

"'You OK Sledgehammer?' asked Jay.

"'Yeah, are you?'

"'Yeah,' he replied shakily.

"A Japanese heavy machine gunner had sighted in directly over our heads as we stood in that hole looking back across the valley. This was not random harassing fire—he had us in his sights. Had he not fired a little too high these words would not be written.

"After a period of quiet we slowly raised our heads to see if we needed to move out with our buddies. Another burst of heavy machine gun fire sent us to the bottom of the hole again as the 7.7mm bullets cracked overhead.

"'He's got us pinned in here, Jay. How the hell are we gonna get outa here?' I said.

"'Lord I don't know, but keep down.' The Japanese fired another long burst. This time he corrected and lowered his elevation just enough so that the slugs grazed just over the edge of the hole and kicked up dirt in the embankment at our backs. But tracers didn't penetrate the soil the way the lead-filled, copper-jacketed bullets did. After hitting the bank at the back edge of the foxhole many of the tracers came rolling down into the hole—white hot, sputtering and hissing as they burned.

"The machine gun kept firing at brief intervals, so we had a wild time of it, keeping our heads down and dodging tracers.

"I thought of that day so long ago on New Caledonia when Big Red, the Marine raider, had put several of us green recruits in a hole and fired hundreds of rounds of Japanese machine gun ammo over us. I remember that then a few tracers had bounced around after impact, just like I was seeing here.

"Even with as much combat as I had been through since New Caledonia, it seemed each day some new situation confronted me. I always felt that thorough training and strict discipline had prepared me for what to do—if only my luck didn't run out.

"Machine gun fire under any circumstances was terrifying. However, like being shelled, it was worse if you were in the open and on your feet. But Jay and I were in a unique situation there in a foxhole on a recently captured, bare hillside, not a bush or rock within 50 yards, and no other Marines anywhere visible along the slope. The men of 2/5 had moved on over the ridge crest behind us and all our buddies of 3/5 were further to our left around a curve in the ridge. We were isolated. The Japanese gunner stayed registered in right over us—continuing to fire occasional bursts. It was a very personal experience.

"There was no one we could call to for artillery or mortar help, so every time the bullets cracked overhead, grazing over the hole, we continued to thrash around trying to avoid the white-hot tracers that came rolling in like glowing hot coals.

"We decided that the weapon was firing from a cave in the ridge about 400 yards across and up the draw, to our right. The time dragged on. I cursed the enemy machine gunner vehemently.

"We began to think we would be trapped till darkness fell, and we dreaded the idea of trying to move around after dark. Suddenly, we heard artillery fire over to our right. It grew louder, to an incredible intensity. The Japanese machine gunner stopped firing.

"'Listen to that,' I said.

"'Yeah, I wonder what's up?' Jay said. Then we heard a familiar voice from our left yelling, 'Hey Sledgehammer, where the hell are you?'

"We peered out cautiously over the edge of our hole and saw a tremendous area being blanketed with white phosphorous shells from our heavy guns. They were laying it on thick. Smoke was drifting down the draw.

"'Look out, there's a Hotchkiss that's had us pinned down tight,' I yelled back to the K Company Marine coming toward us.

"'Aw, that barrage is bound to have knocked him off or blinded him,' he answered confidently.

"'What's up over there?' Jay asked as we cautiously climbed out of the deep hole.

"'Word is, Nips got in behind a Marine outfit on our left and they called in that phosphorous barrage to hide the guys till a reserve battalion can clean out the bastards,' our buddy said. 'Anyway, the Company is movin' out and the Lieutenant sent me to find you. He's been wantin' to know where you been.'

"'Where have I been?' I responded indignantly. "We've been pinned down tight—can't that...' I didn't finish and just glanced at Jay. He shook his head slowly in disgust. The three of us hoisted our gear and began the trek along the ridge back to K Company."

The weather grew worse around the third week of May. It got chilly, and mud was everywhere. As the 1st Division continued to hammer the Wana positions, the 6th Marine Division to their right fought the terrible battle on Sugar Loaf Hill. This, along with other important terrain like Horseshoe and Half Moon Hill, was a key area that, like the area around Wana, guarded the approaches to Shuri Heights.

"During their defense of the entire area composing these approaches, the Japanese put up a ferocious, skilled battle that drained our strength, and theirs. The Japanese fought nowhere else in WWII with greater bravery, skill, and effectiveness than they did in their defense of Shuri during May 1945."

On May 23, as the boundary between the two Marine divisions shifted west, or right, 3/5 went into the line in what my father would describe as one of the most horrific places he had ever seen on a battlefield. Carrying their weapons and gear they trudged, slipped, and slid along muddy trails through an area that had been heavily fought over, judging from the number of Japanese dead they saw.

They weren't far from Sugar Loaf Hill, and even though that epic ten-day battle was over and the area secured by the 6th Marine Division, there had been so much Japanese artillery and mortar fire that the dead, both enemy and Marine, had not been buried. The sight of Marine dead, who lay where they fell, was profoundly disturbing to even the most hardened veterans. The driving rain, the stench, and swarms of flies made it horrific.

As they moved through an area near the base of a small hill, they saw six dead Marines to their left.

"The poor fellows were all lying face down against a gentle muddy slope where they had apparently hugged the deck to escape Japanese shells."

It was apparent that they had been killed by the same shell, and my father and his buddies gazed at them sadly.

"The first man's left leg was blasted off at the thigh and lay a little way to one side, the green dungaree trousers leg neatly tucked into the legging laced along the calf and over the top of a new boondocker."

He also saw how each body had a rusting M1 Garand rifle clutched in the hand. From the look of their dungarees and weapons, these pathetic figures were probably new replacements.

"They were bunched up close together, and their dungarees, boondockers and 782 gear were all unmistakably new. As we filed past, I noticed on the left hip pocket of each corpse a bright red-painted spot. I recalled the Beach Party man who had told us a bright red spot meant a man couldn't be sent to the front lines because he was a Supply Specialist—I also remembered my buddy reminding him that 'every Marine is basically a rifleman.'"

Half Moon Hill

While heavy caliber gunfire from both sides rumbled overhead in opposing directions, the men of K Company moved into position to occupy the western-most extension of Wana Draw. It was, like everything else they had been seeing, shell torn and muddy.

"The Marines we relieved were hollow-eyed and weary. They wore that expression unique to men who have faced death, terror, and violent shock, almost to the limits of emotional strength, and who have endured physical fatigue to the brink of collapse."

This was Half Moon Hill. K Company was dug in along the ridge of Half Moon Hill, and the mortarmen, in this case about a hundred yards behind the Company front line, dug their gun pits and set up their 60mm guns. Shuri Heights, wreathed in smoke, lay out in front of the Company and to their left. The mortarmen were on a low rise of ground, and around them it was mostly flat. There was a narrow gauge railroad a short distance to their right.

"I saw no live troops to our immediate right on that flat ground."

The area of Wana Draw was like a lake, with bogged-down tanks and amtracs that were rendered immobile and useless.

"A sound-power phone line was laid by Paul Wright, our mortar section communications man, along the muddy ground up to our OP on the ridge. Paul was from New York, and he had come into the company after Peleliu. We were great friends."

He and Snafu registered their gun and stacked ammo for future use, then took stock of their surroundings.

"This was always important in a new position to familiarize myself with the terrain. The sight that met my eyes made me recoil in horror! This was the ghastliest corner of hell I had ever seen. Nothing on Peleliu, or anything I saw later on Okinawa matched it for sheer horror."

To the right of their position, in a defilade, lay twenty Marine corpses. Each was on a stretcher, muddy, and, in a pathetic attempt by their comrades to offer some sense of respect, covered by a poncho.

"Their comrades had been able to make that last feeble but sincere gesture of respect for fellow Marines by shielding them with a poncho. When a man was wearing a Marine uniform there was something special about him, and if he was killed and his body couldn't receive the simple attention of being covered with a poncho until he could be removed to a rear area, we all regretted it extremely. Such was the meaning of esprit de corps."

The moonscape-like, desolate terrain was full of shell craters.

Japanese gunners on Shuri blanketed the area with 75mm shells, and my father and his buddies quickly understood why the Marine dead had been left where they had fallen.

"The Marines who attacked across this area and onto Half Moon Hill had been hit with both small arms and shell fire primarily from Half Moon and Shuri to the front, but also from Sugar Loaf Hill and the Horseshoe Ridge on the right. As soon as the battered companies had established a foothold on the base of the crescent ridge, the rains set in, and overnight the whole battle front became a morass through which movement was impossible. Our battalion had then moved in to relieve the unit on Half Moon, and we were now under constant Japanese observation. We were shelled when anyone tried to move around.

"Off to our right and right front, there were at least ten or twelve knocked out Sherman tanks and amtracs. Most had apparently been hit by devastating Japanese artillery fire, particularly high velocity 47mm anti-tank guns."

Japanese dead were everywhere, and so was every imaginable item of infantry equipment—all discarded in the fury of combat.

"The longer we stayed in that terrible place—and we stayed there over a week—in almost incessant cold rain, our environment congealed more and more into a ghastly nightmare of mud, murderous shelling, casualties, rotting bodies, and maggots.

"The place was enough to drive a strong man insane—and some did become emotionally shattered because of it. I never saw more pathetic wounded and killed than we lost each day here."

My father found the only way he could mentally deal with this horrific environment was to look up at the grey, overcast sky and watch the low clouds slide over.

"My escapes from reality into cloud watching were never for long—shelling, orders to fire, orders to go up to the ridge through the shelling to the OP and observe, casualties, ammo carrying parties—it went on and on night and day until I was dazed with fear and fatigue.

"In the fighting to break the Naha-Shuri-Yonabaru line, the US Tenth Army had five combat divisions on the line. On the left flank, or eastern edge of the advance, the 7th Infantry Division faced Yonabaru, the 96th Division was next coming west along the line, then the 77th Division facing part of the wide Shuri front in our sector.

"Next in line, tied in with the 77th Division, was the 1st Marine Division. We also shared part of the Shuri front in our sector. On the American right (west) flank was the 6th Marine Division facing Naha.

"Many events my buddies and I experienced during that week to ten days in that stinking, shell torn morass in front of Shuri were strikingly similar to World War I trench warfare in the mud of Flanders and France. Our armor's inability to move because of the mud had created a stalemate situation.

"So when the rain made southern Okinawa impassable to tanks and other vehicles, our commanders had the choice of attacking through the mud without tanks, or waiting until the rain stopped and tanks could support us.

"The Japanese hoped for the first option so [that] they could bleed us dry, but fortunately our high command had enough sense to choose the second option. Thus, with our tanks immobilized, a stalemate commenced on Okinawa—bloody and miserable enough

as it was. It cost us fewer casualties than bludgeoning ourselves with no armor support against fortified Japanese positions.

"Civilians back home would have been shocked by realistic reports of life and death in the miserable conditions of the Shuri stalemate. Stories of filthy, wet infantrymen shaking with terror and being pounded for days on end by shelling and living in flooded fox holes did not make for stirring news."

How fitting that my father's memoir has been compared to *All Quiet on the Western Front.*

"When people want to hear 'war stories,' they are revolted by accounts of the true reality of infantry life. They want to hear stirring tales of dash and excitement, not of filth, shock, blood, and maggots. Possibly if they knew more of such things war would end."

It is for these reasons that my father never understood the appeal of war movies.

It was late May, not long after 3/5 had taken over the Half Moon Hill area. The K Company CO, 1st Lt. Stumpy Stanley, had to be evacuated because of another severe bout of malaria. He was the last of the old Peleliu officers.

"We had gotten in new replacements, officers, NCOs, and enlisted men during May to replenish the losses the company had suffered. There were fewer and fewer old familiar faces now."

The position of company commander was assumed by Shadow Loveday—and no one was happy about it.

"During this period, I was ordered to do the first unsupervised observing I had done for the mortar section. Because of the constant casualties among veteran mortarmen and new replacements coming in, George Sarrett and I were ordered to begin getting some experience in this role.

"On occasions he and I went up to the company front line to observe as a team, and sometimes we were rotated singularly. George, a Gloucester veteran, was in squad #2 with me, and whenever Snafu was observing, or otherwise occupied, George and I worked

#2 gun together. Sometimes we switched gunner and assistant gunner positions.

"We had been through a lot together on Peleliu and already on Okinawa. I admired George, or Danny George as Snafu always called him. He seemed to get just as scared as I did in 'hot spots,' but he had a habit of laughing and yelling 'San Antone!' at the most unlikely times under heavy fire, and it helped my morale. Like Snafu, he was without any swagger, but tough as hell.

"The mortar section OP on Half Moon Hill was situated toward the western end of the ridge. It was little more than a muddy, two-man foxhole in the K Company front line which ran along the crest of the ridge. The sound-power phone and the one or two mortarmen calling back fire orders were the only things different from the OP and all the other foxholes along the front line. Here on Half Moon, there was a .30 cal heavy water-cooled Browning machine gun in the hole on our left, and two riflemen on our right."

Half Moon Hill was shaped like a crescent, with two arms pointing south. The Marines were placed on the ridge that formed the base of the crescent, so the arms extended beyond their front lines. The area was a hot spot for 3rd Battalion because the Japanese still occupied caves on the reverse slopes of the arms of Half Moon, especially the one to their left, or east.

There was a road embankment about three hundred yards out, running east to west and parallel to their front. Through the embankment there was a large culvert opening toward them. It looked like a yawning black hole. The terrain was utterly bare, and a pair of ditches about fifty yards apart ran across the area between the southward tips of the crescent.

"Within the arms of the crescent and the road about 300 yards away you could have seen a mouse move. There were some Japanese corpses scattered over the area but no Marine dead here."

They were warned by Marines of 2/4 that the Japanese had been coming out of the caves on the reverse slopes at night. Because of this, ships offshore fired star shells, and the 60mm mortars kept flare shells up in the rainy, leaden skies all night.

"What amazed me at Half Moon was the extreme rashness of the attacks by small groups of Japanese across that completely open terrain directly to our front in broad daylight without any possible hope of success. This was contrary to most Japanese action on Okinawa.

"At Peleliu, the Japanese rarely emerged from their caves except at night, and on Okinawa most of their attacks, day or night thus far, were preceded by heavy mortar and artillery fire. But several times while I observed for my mortar section at Half Moon, ten or fifteen Japanese soldiers would come running out of the culvert or around the end of a ridge to our left front, fan out, and head silently toward us."

The day after arriving at Half Moon, my father and George Sarrett were sent to the OP at daybreak. It was drizzling and foggy. They registered the mortar section's three guns on key points—the reverse slope of the road embankment, the entrance to the culvert, and the reverse slope of the left southern extension of Half Moon.

"To register on these targets, we followed the usual procedure of having each mortar fire one, two, or three HE shells as we called corrections to the gun crews via the phone until the shells struck right on target. When they were zeroed in, we ordered cease firing."

Almost immediately the Japanese responded with their own mortar fire. It was a terrible bombardment that threw stinking mud everywhere with each shell hit and caused numerous casualties.

"The Japanese observers up on the shell scarred slopes of Shuri heights to our left front out and beyond the road could blast us at will, and we knew it."

The wounded were moved out down the ridge through the mud and tended to by a corpsman. Things became quiet as the men tried to recover their senses after the bombardment, much of which was by Japanese 90mm mortar fire. Suddenly someone shouted a warning, and a lone Japanese soldier darted out from the blackness of the culvert.

"He carried his bayonetted rifle at high port, wore full pack and other combat gear and had his helmet tilted over his forehead."

This man was trying to reach the shelter of the southern tip of the crescent arm to their left front. He was cut down in a hail of rifle and BAR fire, and the wet, miserable Marines cheered when he fell.

"During the day, the rain swept across the dismal scene in torrents, followed by a drizzle until the next deluge. Japanese mortars threw a few shells at us on the line as well as back where our K Company 60mm mortars were dug in causing some casualties. I called in our own 60s to fire a few HE shells over behind the end of the crescent arm to our left front, and across the road embankment for harassing fire.

"Whenever the Japanese mortars hit us hard, our artillery observer from the 11th Marines, who had his OP in a hole down the line from us, would radio back for fire support from a Marine battery of 75mm howitzers. Their shells would soon come swishing low over our line and burst out on the high ground toward Shuri, and they did cause the Japanese to lift their fire against us for a while. That gave us welcome relief."

The Japanese continued sending men out of the culvert in twos and threes to dash toward that left ridge extension and consolidate manpower for a counterattack or infiltration attacks on the American front line. They continued to be cut down by rifle and BAR fire.

"I yelled over the phone to my buddies on the mortars constantly giving them directions."

As my father's buddies around him fired away at the enemy infantry who came into view, he was sorely tempted to join in, but his job was to observe and call down mortar fire. He had his Tommy gun with him, but that would have been useless at the two hundred-to-three hundred-yard range between the ridge and the culvert.

"However, we had an M1 rifle and ammo belt in our OP left by a casualty."

His fire direction was effective because he could see their 60mm shells crashing away in the target area and Japanese being killed by them. Soon this activity abated, and he called for a ceasefire to the mortars.

"There was a period of relative quiet on our front—our artillery kept sending shells far out front on Shuri heights."

At this point my father moved over to the hole that contained the machine gun. The gunner had come into K Company on Pavuvu as a replacement after Peleliu, and he and my father had become good friends.

"He was in his middle to late twenties and had apparently gotten involved with a chorus girl in a California night club. He told me her name was Kathy. So, I nicknamed him 'Kathy.'"

Suddenly a Marine yelled that another Japanese soldier was running out of the culvert. Kathy spun around to man his machine gun. My father started back to the mortar OP hole but saw that Sarrett had the phone in hand and that the guns were still secured. Seeing this, he grabbed an M1 rifle that was in Kathy's machine gun pit.

Down below toward the culvert, about ten Japanese had emerged and were running toward them with rifles and fixed bayonets. My father and the other Marines began firing, and within seconds eight of the ten were down. The last two stopped and turned to rush back to the shelter of the culvert. One was shot and fell, leaving one remaining Japanese soldier. It looked as though he might get away when the order came down the line to cease firing—just as Kathy got his sights zeroed in on him.

The machine gun was hammering away, so no one heard the order. Kathy had just let loose a burst of about eight rounds, dropping the Japanese. My father saw a tracer round that must have hit him either in the vertebrae or some other bone deflect up from his right shoulder, and another tracer round arc up from the left shoulder as the Japanese soldier pitched forward face down and did not move. Kathy was ecstatic over his kill shot.

"'Kathy' had come into his gun squad as one of the newest ammo carriers. Casualties had eliminated everybody senior to him and he had now become gunner on his machine gun—he had just proven his ability to himself and was rightly exuberant."

The other Japanese who had fallen right before Kathy's victim was wounded and trying to crawl into one of the shallow ditches. Some of the men resumed firing, kicking up mud all around him and sending red arrows of tracer rounds up into the air. There was a brief unusual exchange as one of the men yelled at everyone to stop firing, since the Japanese was already hit. He was shouted down by another Marine who reminded him who their enemy was, and the firing continued until the Japanese soldier stopped moving in the shallow ditch.

My father was duly impressed by the incredible bravery of these enemy soldiers, futile though it was. It was another reminder to him of the horrible waste of human life that they had to witness every day.

As the firing subsided, the muddy Marines were feeling pleased that they had eliminated the threat of a later counterattack or infiltration by these Japanese soldiers. But as the smoke from their weapons dissipated, Shadow came along the line, yelling and cursing each man because they had not ceased firing when he ordered.

"After he passed I could see each man mumbling to his foxhole mate, and could well imagine what they were saying about Shadow's tantrum."

This unpopular officer got to the machine gun position and quickly silenced Kathy's exuberance. He then cursed my father for firing an M1 when he was supposed to be observing. My father fought the urge to club Shadow with the rifle.

"Insulting or striking an officer carried a severe penalty—an effective deterrent to my acting on impulse."

He may have weighed the consequences of hitting his superior officer and thought better of it, but Shadow's pathetic lack of self-control caused my father to rashly tell him that they were "sent there to kill Japs, and what difference did it make what weapon they used in the process."

He lacked any semblance of respect for a leader who would lose his temper and yell at or berate his men—men who had to trust his leadership and follow his orders.

Growing up, I encountered teachers, coaches, or bosses who would act in a similar manner. My father always brought up this example to show how a good leader should *not* act. One occasion that I remember well was when I was in the seventh-grade marching band. One afternoon at practice our band director berated us for not performing to his expectations. He completely lost his temper and began yelling at us as we stood in formation in the hot afternoon sun.

Our drum major stood silently and glumly by the director's side. The director took his clipboard and threw it on the ground in a paroxysm of rage. He then looked at the drum major and yelled, "Pick it up, Mark!" Mark quickly bent down, gathered the clipboard and the scattered papers, and obediently handed them back to the director. That night I told my father about this. When I got to the part about the director throwing his clipboard down and then ordering the drum major to pick it up, he had heard enough.

"If he ever does that to you, by God, you better not pick it up and hand it back to him! That's ridiculous. If he can't control himself any better than that he's got no business being in charge of a bunch of students!" He then proceeded to tell me about that muddy day on southern Okinawa at a place called Half Moon Hill and an officer they called Shadow whom no one respected.

"Our fire discipline in that moment might not have been the best, but we certainly didn't deserve to be cursed and berated for it. All the men around me, except the new replacements, were cursing Shadow between their teeth.

"This was abruptly interrupted by another brisk shelling from Japanese heavy mortars. The big shells came fluttering in as the gunner traversed right along our ridge crest again. We huddled in our muddy holes in terror while the big shells crashed and exploded along the company line. Our artillery fired in support of us and the 75s went rushing overhead. The Japanese secured their guns. There were surprisingly few casualties though, in this brief barrage."

My father and George Sarrett soon got orders to return to their mortar gun pits. Getting back to their positions was not easy.

"George and I carefully made our way to the bottom of the ridge without mishap and headed for the mortar section. The farther back from the ridge we got, the deeper the mud got. Every step was an effort. He passed me as I stopped to rest a couple of times. Hearing

the familiar approach of Japanese 150mm shells, I crouched low. Luckily, they were headed further to the rear.

"After they went roaring over, I hurried along and kept an eye open for likely shelter if needed. I found two craters which, though flooded, looked like a possibility. Then I saw that each crater was occupied by a dead Marine. I decided it would be better to die on my feet. But in the coming days I saw more than one of my buddies jump into them when a shell came over, only to come out with desperation written on their faces at the hideous sight of maggots tumbling off their equipment and dungarees.

"George and I related the day's events to our buddies back in the mortar section. I finished a can of cold C ration beans just in time to serve the gun. Our observer called for a few rounds of HE onto the reverse side of the road embankment. He told us over the phone that the Japanese were moving again, and we needed to make sure they could not pull off a night attack. We fired as ordered, and he said we were right on target.

"In response to our fire, the Japanese unleashed a barrage of their 81mm mortar and 75mm artillery fire that came storming in on us almost immediately, the shells flashing and thundering in the murky twilight. This was our regular punishment every time we fired our mortars during the coming days and nights in this place before Shuri. It was a miracle that they didn't knock out our whole mortar section."

At times the rain was so heavy that they could barely see their comrades in nearby foxholes. Snafu and my father modified their hole with pieces of wood from ammo crates—effectively designing a sump, but it had to be bailed out continuously. It was their special hole.

"One ameliorating circumstance I noted was that for the first time since early April I was free of fleas. This could have been because of the mud and my condition of general filth. Ernie Pyle said, according to the troops, that if you went long enough without a bath even the fleas would leave you alone. By late May I had reached that state. But it was a relief to be free of them, and I will always feel compassion for flea-bitten dogs."

One gloomy morning while they were still trying to crack the Shuri line, a pair of Japanese infiltrators made it into their area and were moving along a strip of firm ground about twenty yards away from the position occupied by my father and Snafu. It was difficult to discern much about the shadowy figures, but Snafu called out a challenge and got ready to fire at them with his .45. My father had grabbed up his Tommy gun and raised it to his shoulder. Despite the driving rain my father could see that it appeared they were wearing US helmets.

"They might be two Marines on patrol, or comm guys checking along the ground to repair a break in the signal wires cut by shelling. Then again, Japanese infiltrators frequently picked up US equipment and wore it to confuse us."

But the two men sped up instead of halting and identifying themselves. They headed toward the railroad bed where the K Company CP was located. Snafu fired several shots with his .45 but missed.

"The Marine in the next fox hole was a flamethrower gunner. He fired at them with an M1 rifle, but it jammed after the first shot. The ghost-like figures began running and disappeared into the murky gloom before I could fire at them with the Tommy. The flamethrower gunner had picked up a discarded M1 and it was muddy and rusty. He put the rifle butt on the ground and tried to eject the empty shell casing by kicking the operating handle."

They heard a couple of grenades explode a short distance away in the vicinity of the railroad bed. Someone yelled that the two Japanese had been killed.

"On Okinawa we had two men in K Company who were snipers. Each was armed with a 1903 Springfield bolt action rifle equipped with a scope. They always dug in together and had orders to stay near the company CP until called up on the line when they were needed. One was from Texas and the other was from Tennessee as I recall.

"In the company CP life seemed, at least to outsiders like us, safer, and the rations a little bit better than in the platoons. The snipers were considered part of the brotherhood of the common troops;

they had a special skill comparable to a machine gunner, mortarman, bazooka gunner or flamethrower gunner.

"There was some disdain for the enlisted men in the CP, because they carried themselves with an air of self-importance. They got the word before we did on everything, and in combat they ate with the company executive officer, skipper, and senior NCOs.

"When Snafu and I arrived at the fox hole on the edge of the railroad embankment where the two snipers were dug in, they were both grinning and laughing quietly. They looked first at the two Japanese killed down on the railroad track and then back a little way toward the company CP, which was under the tarpaulin stretched across from one bank to the other.

"They said that Snafu's shouts and the shots alerted them, so when the two Japanese ran by near their hole and then down into the sunken railroad bed, they threw a couple of grenades at them. Our buddies said, with much suppressed guffawing, they saw the infiltrators get hit by the grenade fragments, and then heard a great commotion in the CP as all the personnel scattered out from under the dry tarpaulin into the rain. The Texan compared it to a cattle stampede.

"Several other Marines dug in nearby came over to find out all about it, and we all grinned amongst ourselves as we stared back at the CP But we had to disperse so as not to invite Japanese shells. The hasty, although temporary, evacuation of the CP tent as told by the two snipers who saw it from their fox hole was a sea story that warmed the hearts of us all.

"Our planes were grounded by the inclement weather most of the last ten days of May, so we had not received airdrops of supplies or fire support from them while we were in the area of Half Moon. However, one day while I was on the OP up on the ridge, and the weather was so bad that most planes were grounded, a TBM torpedo bomber flew over, banked around and then flew from west to east straight along our line on the crest of the ridge.

"He was low and flying at a slow speed. I saw the gunner seated behind the pilot and facing aft—he slid his canopy open a little and dropped an object out to us. He and the pilot then gave us a thumbs-up for good luck and waved. Just then a Japanese machine gun out to our left front fired a burst at the airplane but missed as the pilot increased his speed. The object from the plane fell just to my left and in front of a foxhole. A buddy jumped out and retrieved what turned out to be a note written in pencil. It was wrapped around a small wrench and held in place by a rubber band. The note of course, was smeared with mud, but it was short, and we could read it. It warned us of the Japanese concentrating on the reverse slope and said something like, "You guys are doing a terrific job, God bless you."

"We passed the note along and when the TBM banked and flew slowly along in front of our line again we all cheered and gave the thumbs-up sign to the smiling aviators. I had tears in my eyes, because those two men in that plane risked their lives to drop us a warning note and tell us they appreciated what we were doing. That episode really boosted our morale.

"As they had flown by, I could clearly see both of them, and I couldn't help but notice how clean and neat they both appeared. I did not begrudge this—we admired aviators greatly because of the dangers they faced every time they took off, especially in such stormy weather.

"I tried my best to get the note to keep it as a souvenir but someone else kept it as his prize. I hope, if he survived Okinawa, he appreciated it in later years.

"I lost a close friend around this time—while dug in on Half Moon, a Japanese 75mm shell exploded near his foxhole. As the stretcher team brought him by on the way to the rear, several of us went over to wish him good luck. He was tall, but lying on that stretcher he was a muddy, limp form covered with several bloody battle dressings. One leg was completely severed at the ankle. The stump of the lower leg was also covered with bloody bandages. A

mud-caked boondocker, with the mangled remains of his ankle, was resting on the stretcher at a crazy angle beside his uninjured foot.

"'Do you think I'll lose my leg Sledgehammer?' he asked in a low, dazed voice. I swallowed hard, and managed to tell him he would surely recover before long and be back in those sweet smelling spruce forests that he was so fond of back home in the Pacific Northwest. The morphine injected by the corpsman was having its merciful effects in easing his pain.

"But as we watched the stretcher team struggling through the deep mud toward the rear, he died before they even got out of sight through the rain and mist. His death was a great loss to us all. The memory of our last meeting on that awful battlefield has been one of the most difficult death scenes I have not been able to forget."

I heard my father tell this story in a recorded interview. To this day it is hard for me to listen to it because, right about the part where the man asked him if he would lose his leg, my father's voice broke, and it was only with great difficulty that he was able to finish describing how his friend died right there in the rain and mist.

"Close behind this stretcher team was that of his mortally wounded foxhole mate. This boy had joined K Company recently, so I did not know him very well. The Japanese shell had sent steel fragments into his abdominal region. The corpsman had injected morphine, but it wasn't taking effect.

"As they carried him by us he was crying and moaning in agony.

"We all watched in helpless frustration. 'Jeez, Doc, can't you do nothin' for the poor kid? For Chrissakes!' exclaimed a buddy of mine from Chicago.

"The distraught corpsman explained that because of internal wounds and falling blood pressure they couldn't stop the pain. The anguished young man's prayers were answered soon enough however, because he died in a few minutes. We were all depressed and unnerved by this."

The wet conditions also caused sores—known as jungle rot—to develop on the knuckles and backs of my father's and many others' hands. Several of these can be seen in the iconic photograph of my father sitting on his bunk with the "thousand-yard stare"—the photograph that can be seen in *With the Old Breed.*

Around 1980, when the book was being prepared for publication, I remember my parents discussing this photograph and how my father's facial expression was mute testament to the horrors of war. He pointed out the sores to me and explained the wet, miserable living conditions that caused them.

"One day while I was up on the ridge observing, I was alone in the fourth foxhole from the right flank of the company. Things seemed fairly quiet, and then suddenly we were violently jolted by a shrieking shell passing along the ridge to our rear. There was a terrific crash as it exploded near the end foxhole on the right. Both occupants were seriously wounded.

"'Jesus, what the hell was that?!' someone yelled.

"'That's a Nip 70mm mountain gun, he's firing across our rear from over on our left flank,' answered a veteran NCO. An officer got on the radio in the artillery OP to check on it. Then another shrieking shell rushed over across our rear. It exploded near the next foxhole from the end.

"No one was hit fortunately, but we were terror stricken. A Japanese gun crew behind us was actually sniping at us individually with a 70mm field piece. He was sighting in and aiming on our foxholes, one right after another—not just the typical general shelling of an area.

"In response our artillery fired phosphorous in that direction. A patrol was ordered to go out and destroy the gun. It fired again before our artillery smoke screened us, and another man was wounded. I knew that my foxhole was next.

"'Sledgehammer, get back there on the mortar!' yelled one of our NCOs. 'Standby to fire support for that patrol!' I was never so glad to be ordered to leave a position during the entire war! I grabbed up the Tommy gun, sprang out of the hole, [and] raced down the

slippery, muddy ridge and across the intervening distance to the mortar gun pit.

"The Japanese 70mm did not fire again, and we stood by to support the patrol, but our help wasn't needed.

"In a couple of hours I was ordered back up on the OP on the ridge. Not long after arriving someone said, 'Hey you guys, looka there. Them guys on that patrol got that Nip gun.'

"Four or five bearded Marines were coming along the foot of the ridge behind us carrying the barrel of the Japanese 70mm mountain gun. Some of us went down and looked it over.

"'Thought we'd bring it over and show it to you guys before takin' it to G-2 cause it gave you so much hell,' said the NCO who was in charge of the patrol. He told us they attacked the Japanese gun crew, killed them all, and suffered no losses to the patrol."

"The barrel was about three feet long, and there were several nicks and scars on it from bullets fired by the Marine patrol. We thanked them for saving us from further grief from the 70mm and shared some rations with them before they left.

"We all agreed it was the worst 'sniper fire' we were ever exposed to.

"The ridge was littered with discarded American and Japanese combat packs and equipment. During some of the quiet periods we looked through the contents of the packs. Both U.S. and Japanese contained essentially comparable items. Pictures and letters were, of course, of most interest to us. We found the Japanese pictures interesting but naturally could not read the letters. All the Marine's letters carried the same cheerful and hopeful messages from home praying for their loved ones' quick and safe return.

"There were many photographs of Marines with family and girlfriends—the Marine always snappily attired in his dress blues with highly polished brass buttons and shined shoes. Something about the rain-soaked photos told you somehow, they had been taken on that last furlough before shipping overseas.

"It may seem improper that we read letters of dead or wounded Marines, but we meant no disrespect. It was not to pry into the private lives of others. We were living moment to moment, expecting violent death or injury at any time. We were simply seeking some escape from present reality by reading somebody's—anybody's—letters expressing love and concern and telling of home—any home.

"If reading discarded letters gave some vicarious comfort to the living, I doubt if the dead would have begrudged us our brief escape. I found a pocket-size Catholic Testament, but a bullet had passed through the center—the delicate little pages frayed and torn around the hole. I read fragments of verse around the tear and compared it to my Protestant pocket testament. Then I put it back in the discarded Marine pack. It seemed the proper thing to do.

"I replaced all the Marine letters or photos in their packs as best I could. However, these packs were now the mere flotsam of war that would probably never be picked up but would simply rot where they were.

"Another group of replacements came up to K Company during late May. Most of them were privates or PFCs straight from the States and had been in the Marine Corps only a few months.

"These poor fellows who struggled through the mud up to our positions on and around Half Moon Hill must have thought they had slipped over a precipice into Hell's own garbage dump. I saw their faces when they came up, and they all expressed disbelief and revulsion as they looked around at the battlefield.

"Some new men got hit and were evacuated so quickly that they never really belonged to the company. One man came up with a group and reported to an NCO who took his name. Just as the replacement stepped toward a foxhole a Japanese rifle shot rang out; we ducked instinctively, he spun around and fell to the deck—a flesh wound in the upper arm. A corpsman tended the wound and tagged the man. He left his rifle and cartridge belt and went straight back to the aid station. He wasn't even in K Company for more than five minutes.

"On another occasion a replacement reported for duty. A sniper fired, the replacement's helmet flew off his head and he collapsed on the deck like a man felled by a hammer blow. We thought he had been killed, but the bullet had penetrated his helmet and only grazed his skull. He went to the rear with a bandage around his head and carrying his helmet with the bullet hole for a souvenir.

"So ironic, I thought, when new men came into K Company, got hit within minutes, and their war was over. A few of us old hands had survived weeks and months of combat without injury, but the strange arithmetic of chance took its daily toll of old and new alike.

"At night in the Half Moon Hill/ridge area we fired 60mm mortar flares over the immediate company area every few minutes continuously. Navy ships kept the whole area well illuminated with star shells. The big shell would come whistling in out front, burst with a 'pow,' the parachute would blossom out and the bright flare would ignite and swing beneath.

"The empty nose cap would fall to the ground with a soft whistle, like someone blowing into the neck of a bottle, and hit the mud with a splattering sound. At Peleliu they had always hit the hard coral with a 'clank,' and sometimes I heard them bounce. The several minutes of illumination provided by the star shell was bright and very adequate.

"Our smaller 60mm illuminating shells functioned in a similar manner but burned for only about a minute. During stormy or windy nights, the star shells and our flares would be blown away with disturbing rapidity."

My father vividly described nighttime hallucinations and nightmares—often of dead Marines getting up and walking around.

"When I was awake and on watch and my buddy was sleeping, I never had any of these visions or hallucinations. When star shells and flares lit up the area my mind was more at ease—but I dreaded that unbearable sensation of being unable to help those pathetic phantoms in my nightmares.

"What psychological significance these dreams and visions had I do not know. Although I had many and varied nightmares about the war, I never had any dreams about reanimated Japanese dead, or ghosts.

"One night, the last thing I noticed before dozing off was a green G.I. five-gallon water can about three feet from the edge of our hole. I awoke after a period of time, and instead of the intact can, I saw a flat piece of metal with the silvery galvanized inner surface where the can had been.

"'Boy, Sledgehammer, did you sleep through it! They shelled the hell out of us, and you never even woke up!'

"A shell had blown the thick metal can wide open and flattened it out. I was elated over the fact that I had slept through a barrage and felt as though I had cheated the Japanese out of scaring me that time. It was unusual to sleep through something like that; the benumbing effect of fatigue was a blessing in this instance.

"The American artillery and naval bombardment of Shuri was an awesome spectacle to behold at night. The varied voices of the different caliber shells sounded over us as they sped on their way to the target area. Brilliant flashes close to us and then distant flickering behind the hills followed as the shells exploded on target with a crashing or thudding sound.

"A desultory harassing fire went on most of the time, but then there were the big barrages as mentioned before.

"White phosphorous shells were particularly spectacular at night. We dreaded being shelled by these when the Japanese were putting up a smoke screen in our area. Burning phosphorous caused terribly painful wounds, and I dreaded it. But when our big guns were shelling the enemy with phosphorous we enjoyed watching the brilliant flashes and billowing white smoke of the shells exploding in the darkness out to our front.

"Our battleships joined the artillery and shelled Shuri Castle for a prolonged period before we finally broke out to the south. We shivered in the rain in our filthy holes at night and watched the salvos

of three big 16-inch shells. From off the coast to our right we would see the big shells like three huge tracer bullets moving abreast across the black sky.

"Then we would hear the muffled 'kaboom' as the reports of the three turret guns fired simultaneously reached our ears. The huge shells gave the illusion of moving slowly and were clearly visible throughout their entire trajectory because each one glowed like a dull red light. They made a roaring, rumbling sound as they tore through the sky, like a freight train rushing along.

"This was a good comparison, but the sound was also like the sound of a jet aircraft moving along some distance away. When each salvo of three 16 inchers struck the target, we could see brilliant flashes followed by a deep 'boom, boom, boom.' Several times we saw one of these monsters ricochet off the target and go rumbling away up into the black sky out of sight."

In actuality, the old battleships on bombardment duty in this situation that mounted sixteen-inch guns carried them in four twin turrets. They usually fired half salvos, so three shells traveling together were possibly from one of the ships guns not being ready to fire at that moment. (From Rich Frank email.)[17]

"One day while George Sarrett and I were in the OP on Half Moon Hill, the Japanese were more active than they had been in trying to get from the road culvert to the reverse slope on the left flank, southern end of the crescent arm. We heard from someone on K Company's left that a large number of Japanese had been spotted moving around near some caves on that reverse slope.

"George and I had all three mortars firing on the target areas we had zeroed in on previously. The riflemen and machine gunners were firing away too. After several were killed this way, they began rushing out of the opening in twos and threes.

"Our firing line really heated up and some of the men began shouting, yelling, and joking—an unlikely combination of emotions

---

[17] Frank, email message to author.

in such circumstances. Some of the Japanese came out of the culvert and headed toward us, others darted in behind the ridge, and still others ran along the crest of it a short distance before jumping down on the reverse side. This kept everybody busy firing away at groups of six to eight enemy soldiers running in three different directions.

"Many of the Japanese got hit by small arms fire, and our mortars got most of the others. I watched the culvert with a pair of binoculars and saw an enemy soldier emerge who had a bandaged hand. With the binoculars I could see every detail about him. He had his helmet tilted over his forehead and held his rifle at high port. He ran right out of the culvert even though one of our mortars was dropping shells on the area as fast as the gun crew could fire.

"This man only took a few steps when one of our shells hit him on his left shoulder. He was enveloped in the flash and smoke of the shell burst. The blast knocked him a good distance and he flopped onto the muddy deck in a mangled heap. All the Japanese were either killed or out of sight at that point, and the men ceased firing.

"Shadow came slipping and sliding along the ridge cursing and berating everyone. 'You people are firing too much!" he screamed. 'The General says we are burning out our weapons too fast! Knock off that firing!'

"We all looked amazed as he went on past us raving. A man near me said, 'How the hell are we supposed to kill Nips if we can't fire at 'em? We can't help it if the damn machine gun barrels burn out. The artillery's been firing as much as we have.'

"After he had moved on down the line out of sight, a group of ten or twelve Japanese soldiers came bursting out of the protection of the culvert and ran right up on the crest of the southward extending ridge instead of running in behind its reverse slope. They were no more than 200 yards from us and running along single file, in plain view. They were approaching our front line to the left at about a 45-degree angle.

"'Look at them bastards, right on the crest!' yelled a Marine near me.

"'Rack 'em up!' another man shouted.

"There was a burst of rifle fire, and two of them toppled over and fell on the other side of the ridge. I threw down the phone (the guns were on a fire mission and needed no immediate fire orders) and grabbed up an M1 rifle. Kathy swung his machine gun around to the left and some riflemen opened fire.

"I sighted in on an enemy soldier, about third from the front, took up the trigger slack and controlled my breathing before I squeezed off the shot—I couldn't miss.

"'Cease firing, those are Marines!' ordered a lieutenant in the foxhole next to me.

"'Oh Christ,' I groaned as I relaxed my trigger finger.

"'Marines?! For Chrissakes, them's Nips!' someone yelled.

"'Cease firing,' the officer ordered sternly. 'Can't you see they're Marines? They're wearing helmet covers!'

"We all lowered our weapons, we had no choice, but everybody started yelling and cursing and insisting those men were enemy troops. Beginning with the lead Japanese in the file they peeled off and jumped safely from the crest down out of sight on the reverse slope. Some of our veteran officers and NCOs heard our yelling and came along to investigate. The lieutenant who ordered us to cease fire got out of his hole and went along our line to confer with them.

"We were infuriated that a combat officer didn't know a Marine from a Japanese in broad daylight; and because we knew that several Japanese had been able to escape behind that slope and would inevitably counterattack us later.

"This lieutenant had come into the company recently, and this was probably the first time he had seen live enemy troops. To us veterans, and even many new men, it was obvious they were Japanese. This officer's stupidity was to cause us several casualties, and a good bit of trouble.

"We secured the mortars. About seven men, with a sergeant in charge, were quickly detailed off for the task of clearing those Japanese off the reverse slope. They were issued extra grenades, both fragmentation and white phosphorous, and extra ammunition. We were to provide small arms covering fire.

"As the detail prepared to move out, I heard the lieutenant who had ordered us to cease fire quietly say to the sergeant who was standing near me, 'If you bring me back a saber I'll recommend you for a Silver Star.'

"The reason for the sortie was his own fault—failing to recognize the enemy in broad daylight and refusing to listen to experienced veterans. The sergeant looked at the officer in disbelief. 'I don't want a Silver Star, sir, I just want to get back home.' The lieutenant at least had enough sensitivity to look uncomfortable at that.

"They moved to the left down the slope in front of our line and then on up the side of the crescent arm. Just as they got to the area below the crest of the ridge, the sergeant gave an order, and all the men pulled the pins of their grenades and tossed them over the ridge.

"After the grenades exploded with a series of muffled bangs, they quickly but cautiously looked over the crest and fired their rifles and BARs as rapidly as possible at the enemy troops below who fired back up at them. A bullet grazed a man named Wells above the eye and knocked him down.

"We were afraid he had been killed, but he jumped up and ran back to our line holding his hand over his eye, blood streaming down his face. A corpsman bandaged Wells, and he proudly showed us his souvenir—a sliver of bone that had been chipped from his skull by the enemy bullet. He went back to the battalion aid station in high spirits.

"The Japanese kept up a brisk fire to prevent our men from looking over the crest of the ridge again. A young BAR man named Gomez held his BAR over the crest with his left hand and squeezed the trigger with his right forefinger. The big, heavy rifle jumped around from its own recoil, but Gomez kept pumping bullets down at the Japanese. Firing a BAR like that would have been difficult for a big man, and Gomez was small. We all shouted encouragement to him and the others. Shadow ordered the men of the sortie back to our lines because it was obvious the enemy troops were there to stay.

"The men returned to their foxholes by us. Someone yelled, 'Mortars!' Every man crouched in his hole as the big Japanese 90mm shells started crashing along the ridge.

"I was in the machine gun pit with Kathy but machine gun emplacements usually drew special attention from the enemy, so I scrambled out and jumped into a vacant foxhole nearby. Just as I settled in this hole, I saw the big shells begin to come down the line toward me.

"Those 90s exploded, and shrapnel was growling through the air. It reminded me of an angry giant stomping along the ridge, and each shell threw stinking mud all around the area where it went off.

"Suddenly, there was a flash, a deafening crash, and I felt as though a tremendous wave of painful pressure had engulfed me. Then, I experienced the visual sensation of glaring, white flashing light. There was no sound, only a loud ringing in my ears. This must have lasted only a few moments, because, as my vision began to clear, I could hear someone speaking to me.

"Looking up, I saw George anxiously peering down into the hole and asking me if I was alright. He told me later, after my head had cleared, that I had looked at him with a stupid grin, like a drunk recovering from an alcoholic stupor. I felt dazed—the shell must have landed right on the edge of my foxhole. Mortar shells did not typically leave a crater like an artillery shell but exploded upon striking the deck without penetrating. It was a close enough scrape to be unforgettable.

"We heard someone yelling for a corpsman over on our left. Our artillery observer called in the 75s to answer the Japanese mortars. They burst out over the enemy positions, and their mortars got quiet. George told me we had some casualties, but he didn't know how many.

"My ears were still ringing and my head was spinning, but I stumbled along with George over to see if we could help with the casualties, farther back below the crest of the ridge.

"We went over to a little knot of men around another corpsman and a casualty—a pathetic young boy, about 18. He was hit all through his chest and abdominal region. He died on that muddy,

stinking ridge. All this suffering; what a waste of humanity. It made no sense to me. Utter madness.

"Okinawa, in the early stages, seemed worthwhile because we were capturing an island on Japan's doorstep. But the Shuri stalemate demonstrated the Japanese were just holding out as long as they could to spill as much American blood as possible before they were annihilated. From Shuri on down to the end they had only one motive, and that was killing for the sake of killing.

"When I looked out at the flat, muddy cratered landscape it was a true no-man's land all the way to the railroad and far beyond."

Shuri

At last, the rain began to slack off. Rumors were starting to make the rounds that they would attack soon. As it turned out, the main Japanese force that was emplaced at Shuri had pulled out, but they left behind a rear guard that would fight very aggressively. Despite a withdrawal, everyone knew there was still a lot of fighting to do before Shuri would be taken.

About this time, Lt. Duke Ellington came up through the mud to visit the mortar section one day. Although Duke was not popular with some of the men, my father was not unhappy to see him. It was Duke who had held out a flask to him in the amtrac on the way into the beach at Peleliu, and it was Duke who had shown him compassion and a few words of encouragement and understanding that day on Ngesebus when my father's morale was at such a low.

"We asked Duke how things were going for him in the battalion 81mm mortar platoon. He said pretty well, and although they got shelled off and on they were better off than we were up here. Just then we heard Japanese 150mm artillery shells coming over. We hit the deck, but our experienced ears told us that they were high and going to the rear.

"We looked back toward Battalion CP. We saw smoke and heard three distinct 'kabooms.' One looked as though it had exploded on top of the hill in front of Battalion.

"A veteran said, 'Maybe you'd better stay up here with us Duke, looks like they got the range on Battalion.' Duke said it did look like they were catching it back there.

"I was surprised at how tired and worn he looked. We were all bearded and muddy, but Duke's face looked as though the strain of his third campaign was wearing him down. He told us what he knew of the impending push against Shuri, and then left us to return to his 81mm platoon."

Even when the men had a reprieve from being under fire and were distracted by something that generated a spirited discussion, or argument, there was always a grim reminder of the battle they were fighting near Shuri.

"During a quiet period, a brisk argument broke out between Snafu and Redifer about the number of cleats on each tread of an amtrac. Naturally they vehemently disagreed, so Redifer said he would settle it by slipping out quickly and counting the cleats on one of the burned out amtracs near us.

"Snafu told him he was crazy to go out there in that no-man's land, but to go ahead if he was that stupid.

"Redifer ran out across the area and then ducked in behind one of the vehicles. We saw him climbing in and out of amtracs and tank turrets, but he drew no Japanese fire. He returned and reported that he had been correct as to the number of cleats on an amtrac tread. Snafu, never one to give up on an argument or anything else, was obviously skeptical.

"Redifer then told us he had checked the machine guns on the amtracs and tanks and that he had removed the trigger mechanism to prevent a Japanese soldier from slipping into one of the vehicles and firing on us. He also told us, grimacing as he did so, that one of the amtracs had several stretchers aboard—each with a poncho-covered Marine corpse on it."

On the morning of May 28, the skies were clear. An attack was planned for later that morning.

Against surprisingly light opposition, the 3rd Battalion attacked around 1015. They progressed several hundred yards south closer to the village of Asato. At last they had escaped the half-flooded garbage pit around Half Moon. As Duke told them, the 5th Marines would move against Shuri ridge.

"Several battalions from both the 5th Marines and the 1st Marines moved in and around Shuri Castle after its capture, setting up a perimeter around its battered walls."

In fact, 1/5 and 3/5 had attacked eastward and crossed over into the zone of the Army's 77th Infantry Division to surround Shuri Castle. There were entrenched Japanese troops blocking the advance of the 77th Division, who were north of Shuri Castle. The Japanese were positioned between them and the area the Marines captured.

"The Marine units pulled off a surprise flank attack on the Japanese and captured the place with few casualties."

Interservice rivalry notwithstanding, taking Shuri Castle was a crucial moment for American forces. It was the very heart of the Japanese defense system on southern Okinawa. Even though the place was in ruins by the time 3/5 dug in around it, the men felt a sense of accomplishment—they knew its strategic relevance.

"Although it was not built on the grand scale of some European castles, ancient Okinawan kings had resided there in olden times because of its natural defensive position."

Among the artifacts my father brought home from Okinawa were a Japanese sake cup and a samurai sword. In later years as I began to take a deeper interest in his WWII experience, I asked him about them. Of the little porcelain sake cup he said, "I picked it up amid the ruins of Shuri Castle on Okinawa."

The saber, he said, was "an NCO's sword—not an officer's sword, because it doesn't have a jewel in the hilt—so I don't think it's worth anything really, but it was just lying there in the rubble and I picked it up. You know pilots and rear echelon guys would go nuts over samurai sabers. A lot of guys would trade things for them."

Regardless of that saber's collectible value, it has been and will always be one of my most prized possessions.

CHAPTER NINETEEN

Beyond Shuri

Although the Americans were finally making progress in the Shuri area, the Japanese were still holding out in the center of their line.

"The mud and natural defensive lay of the land were more to the advantage of the Japanese in the center of the line."

The 6th Marine Division on the western flank—the Naha area—and the Army divisions on the eastern flank were making rapid progress in the south. This forced the Japanese to withdraw to the south so that their main defenses would not be encircled. This was the situation by May 30, 1945. The battle had so far lasted sixty-one days. Japanese casualties were 62,458 killed and 465 captured. The Americans had lost 5,309 dead, and 23,909 wounded.

Once past Shuri, the Americans were able to move quickly through the muddy hills in areas where there was light opposition, if any at all. Mud was still an issue, but it rained less frequently. At one point they came to an excellent coral-surfaced road.

"We were ordered up the rock-covered bank onto the best road I had seen thus far on Okinawa. This may have been the east-west Naha- Yonabaru highway, a segment of which our regiment captured about this time."

They filed up onto the road and then over to a field on the other side, where they flopped down to rest.

"The area around was open country and the field was covered with grass instead of mud. We didn't dig in because we were moving

out soon. We were deployed behind a long, semi-circular grass-covered earthen mound about two feet high. The men all removed their packs and equipment for a real relaxing respite. I took my pipe and tobacco pouch out of my pack and started to light up.

"The calm was shattered by three 47mm high velocity shells that exploded all within the company area. They were zeroed in on us with perfect range. There were no casualties—but if the guns had been of larger caliber we would certainly have lost a number of men.

"'Back down the bank on the double!' yelled an officer waving his hand toward the place where we had come up on the road. We scooped up our gear and went running across the road and tumbling down the embankment. We couldn't remain in that field. Those 47s would later give us a good pounding.

"We had been suffering casualties steadily since 3/5 attacked out of the Half-Moon area on May 28."

On June 1, the battalion captured a portion of a large, grassy, tree-covered ridge. Okinawan burial vaults and enemy emplacements were scattered all along the slope of the ridge. It had been lightly but tenaciously defended before being cleared out. A Japanese 75mm dual-purpose gun was abandoned in this area, in perfect condition. As the sun was going down that evening, my father and his buddies were examining it, turning the cranks and wheels and watching the barrel move up and down.

"Next to the gun emplacement was a burial vault so packed with 75mm ammunition that one could barely squeeze around the neat stacks of shells. I thought what a blessing it was to see them stacked, knowing they would never be fired at us."

Suddenly several enemy artillery rounds bracketed the area.

"There was the desperate cry of 'Corpsman!' My buddies and I who had been playing on the Japanese gun like boys around a park cannon raced up onto the ridge."

They could see smoke from the shell hits and Marines scrambling around to help the wounded.

As twilight began to cloak the rock-strewn ridge, they saw a small group of Marines gathered around a casualty. My father ran up to them.

He saw that it was Joe Lambert, the big, good-natured, cigar-chewing demolitions expert with whom he had been friends since Peleliu.

My father knelt down beside him, immediately recognizing that Lambert was hit badly and was going to die.

"No one had been able to locate a stretcher because [within] the company, having had a number of casualties moving up on the ridge so rapidly, all stretchers were in use."

Lambert had an unlit cigar clenched between his teeth as he lay there wincing in pain. My father lamented that he couldn't light it for him because the smoking lamp was out. He did his best to comfort Lambert, joking with him about flirting with the nurses on the hospital ship, being able to drink a beer, but it was obvious the man was mortally wounded.

"The jokes made to a buddy with the million-dollar wound were much more light-hearted and ribald."

As Lambert was carried off down the slope of the ridge on a poncho, my father reflected on the big, beautiful pine trees silhouetted against the darkening sky; the wind blew their scent into his face, and the contrast between it and the stinking quagmire around Shuri struck him. He was thankful that Lambert at least had that for his last moments on earth.

One day in 2003, or around that time—I don't remember exactly—I got a phone call from a man who said he was Lambert's son. He asked if I was related to the Eugene Sledge who wrote *With the Old Breed.* I told him I was his son. The gentleman, who described himself as "a fifty-eight-year-old retired coalminer from West Virginia," went on to relate how he had never met his dad because his dad been killed on Okinawa toward the end of the war. His dad had had one last liberty, it seems, and had met his mother to spend that time with her before he had to go back out to the Pacific and rejoin K Company before they invaded Okinawa.

Lambert was then tragically killed, and he never got to know that he had a son who was born nine months after that liberty in 1945.

Lambert's son was very emotional on the phone, and he told me how those words my father wrote about being with Lambert when he died were the closest he had ever come to knowing his dad. He had always gotten some comfort from the knowledge that when his dad died, he was in a nice place, with the setting sun, a gentle breeze, and the fresh scent of pine trees—and surrounded by his buddies.

The Marines moved into a wide valley below the ridge the next day. The area was littered with discarded Japanese equipment and the dead from their evacuation of Shuri in the last days of May.

"Unfortunately, there were many dead Okinawan civilians, killed because they thought they would be safer retreating with the Japanese than surrendering to us. We also encountered numerous Japanese supply dumps, all covered with large tarpaulins. We found all kinds of uniforms, equipment, and food. The elaborate rubber protective coverings for horses against poisonous gas fascinated us all. The rubber face pieces for the horse had big goggle-eyed clear plastic lenses.

"Late one soggy afternoon, on the top of a steep ridge, an NCO called to me, 'Hey Sledgehammer, you want to see something pretty?'

"'Yeah,' I replied as he beckoned to me from where he lay looking over the ridge crest. I went over and he pointed across a wide valley to the next ridge beyond. We could see 30–40 Japanese running away up that ridge. They were far away, and so cease firing was ordered all along the company line.

"Our artillery shrieked overhead, and we could see the shells, as well as our 81mm mortars, bursting on the ridge slope among them. They looked like miniature soldiers dodging and darting about, their mushroom helmets bobbing up and down. We watched in silence as the shellfire took its toll and the survivors made it over the crest and out of sight. It was unbelievable to me, seeing enemy soldiers running away—even though it was to fight us another day."

"One day, it was just before dark, an enterprising Japanese knee mortar gunner, somewhere up among the rocks, opened fire—lobbing shells at our mortar gun pits.

"My gun was the only one with a full crew—the other mortarmen were carrying supplies—so we had a real duel on our hands. Our observer had a difficult time even locating the knee mortar

gunner who apparently fired a few rounds, then moved his position. This enemy soldier was an experienced gunner because he had those 50mm shells going off with their characteristic 'twang' all over and around us. We were firing frantically every time our observer gave us a new range and sight setting.

"Finally, after an agonizing period of this, we managed to drop a shell right in among the rocks where the Japanese was located and knocked him out. Our observer yelled over the phone, 'You got him, zeroed in, right on target! Good oh, boys!'

"Incredibly, we suffered no casualties during the duel, but even at that it had been more thrill and excitement than any of us wanted.

"That night the word was passed that sufficient supplies could not be brought up to us because of the muddy roads and our rapid advance. It was announced that each rifleman in K Company had one—and only one—extra clip of 8 rounds of ammo for his M1. We hoped it would be a quiet night with no counterattacks.

"During the periods I was on watch I had to actually hold my eyelids open with the thumb and forefinger of each hand. If I did not do this, my eyes would close involuntarily.

"'By God, Sledgehammer, this is the kinda' night you gotta prop your eyes open with matchsticks,' said a weary buddy in the next fox hole. I wondered how long we could keep going like this without dropping from exhaustion—many men had already passed out and been left behind earlier. Star shells and our flares kept the ridge and the valley brightly illuminated all night. Fortunately, the Japanese were surprisingly quiet, but I was almost too tired to care anymore.

"One of the many enemy supply dumps we came [upon] had a large assortment of medical supplies packed under canvas. I took a thermometer with a leather case as a souvenir for my father. Red, with his sixth sense for anything alcoholic, found a bottle of ethyl alcohol among the surgical supplies. With creative ingenuity he and George Sarrett soon developed a cocktail.

"It consisted of Japanese medical alcohol, water, and a lump of K ration sugar, and a pieced of K ration hard candy all dissolved in a dry C ration can. George and Red got roaring drunk.

"While the rest of us were pawing through enemy supplies, George sat on a box and grinned with the bulkhead stare at empty space. Red started waving his loaded carbine around, threatening to shoot any officer or NCO who might hove into view. A corporal in the mortar section walked over and said, 'Put that weapon down, Red, or I'll run you up.'

"The combination of Red's mountaineer blood, alcohol, and a loaded weapon was a potentially dangerous mixture. Red glared at the NCO, brought the carbine up to fire from the hip, and said, 'I ain't gonna take another order from you or nobody else by God. I'll blow your ass off if you come any closer!'

"I was standing about ten feet away and could do nothing but try to speak calmly to Red and distract him. He paid no attention to me and kept his eyes fixed on the NCO—a veteran of three campaigns. He walked right up to Red. Red waved the carbine menacingly. The NCO grabbed the barrel, jerked the weapon from Red's hands and flipped on the safety.

"That ain't nothing but liquor talkin', Red. Next time you pull somethin' like this I'll whip your ass before I run you up.' Red promptly sat on the deck, held his head in his hands and complained of a severe headache.

"When he sobered up, the Corporal returned his carbine to him along with a tongue lashing embellished with Marine Corps slang and profanity. Red was sincerely apologetic. He still complained of a violent headache, but he knew full well some other NCO might have broken the carbine stock over his head for his indiscretion.

"During the push out of Shuri we were able to examine deserted Japanese emplacements from which they had removed artillery pieces when they withdrew. One large revetment was particularly interesting because it had been the site where a formidable 150mm

howitzer was emplaced. They had moved the big gun with tow ropes and muscle power across muddy ground to a coral surfaced road. We marveled at their physical strength, and their security-consciousness.

"The only trace they left behind around that revetment was tracks in the mud. It was an eerie sensation to stand atop the big emplacement and see nothing but thousands of tracks in the mud, yet not a single artillery shell case, rifle cartridge, matchstick, cigarette butt, or ration can."

They continued moving south through open country. On June 4, it rained heavily. Opposition was sporadic after they got past Shuri, but they still had to check all huts and houses. One such dwelling was a small grass-thatched hut. My father walked cautiously through the door, his trusted Tommy gun at the ready. An elderly Okinawan woman was sitting on the floor just inside the doorway, wearing a blue kimono and in great pain. She had been wounded in the abdomen, and she wanted my father to put her out of her misery. When she took the muzzle of his Tommy gun, put it to her forehead, and motioned with her other hand for him to pull the trigger, he quickly withdrew it, indicating to her that he would not kill her. He slung the Tommy over his shoulder and went out to shout for a corpsman.

When he described this episode to me, I was an adolescent. In my mind's eye I could picture him, at that point a battle-hardened survivor, earnestly promising her that he would try to help her, his Tommy gun back on his shoulder, hurrying out of the hut and back up the road to find a corpsman. Then, just as he found one and started back to the little hut, a shot rang out, and my father and the corpsman instinctively crouched down until they realized it was an M1.

As he told me, the man who obliged her was lighting a cigarette as he walked nonchalantly out of the hut and checked the safety on his rifle. My father knew him and recognized him as the company skipper's orderly—a man who stayed in the CP most of the time—and definitely not someone who would kill a helpless old woman in cold blood.

"He seemed more suited for serving joe [coffee] to officers in the CP or for carrying messages back to battalion than for shooting at

anything; he always appeared to be rather neat and clean under the most trying field conditions when the rest of us were typical muddy, raggedy-ass Marines. Regardless, he had taken it upon himself to function as executioner."

When my father saw what he had done, he began yelling at the man, and so did the corpsman. An NCO came up and took the situation in hand after my father and the corpsman had to rejoin the mortar section who were moving out. They never knew if the executioner was disciplined or not.

The word came down that the 5th Marines would be relieved on June 4 by the 1st Marines. The 5th Marines went into reserve near Gisushi. Their main task became aggressive patrolling and mopping up. Although this meant that the 5th Marines would be in a better situation than previously, even mopping up could be hazardous.

"A man could easily get hit or killed during 'aggressive patrolling and mopping up.'"

Some ruins of Okinawan houses stood behind them as they dug in along a low ridge. They were now a secondary line, and there was a broad valley stretching away to their front looking south.

"The 1st Marines and 7th Marines continued to push south against varying opposition. The rain kept us in a muddy, miserable state. While my buddy and I were completing our foxhole, a couple of K Company men began firing their M1 rifles at something in the ruins of a large house about 20 yards behind us. An NCO went over to them grumbling and cursing about 'trigger-happy yard birds.' I trotted over with several others to see what was up. It was actually funny to see the chagrin on the sergeant's face when he arrived at the ruined house and discovered that the men had just killed two fully equipped Japanese riflemen and an Okinawan woman with a haversack full of grenades. All three had been hiding out under the floor of the house when discovered. They would have caused casualties among us as soon as it got dark."

The rain ended on the night of June 5 to 6. My father and George Sarrett had a two-man hole on the low ridge, next to a roadcut that came through at right angles to the ridge. They fired flares over the area at night periodically to discourage Japanese activity.

"This was necessary because Japanese we had bypassed always started roaming around raising hell as soon as darkness fell. In addition, increasing numbers of Okinawan civilians were now surrendering and seeking shelter from all this. These pitiful refugees usually came directly along the road, and frequently at night.

"One night a group of about 15 kimono-clad men and women, with a few children, approached along the road. They stopped just short of the road cut when challenged. By the light of a flare, an officer peered out at them and signaled for them to pass on through to the rear. I looked at them casually, and noticed they were all stooped and huddled together. The flare burned out when the group was scarcely twenty to thirty yards behind us.

"Someone from the group shouted a command, and we heard low, frantic murmuring from the women and children. A mortarman quickly fired another flare which illuminated the area just as I saw two fully uniformed Japanese standing fully erect facing us. Each was holding his rifle in one hand and throwing aside his kimono disguise with the other—the Okinawans were down and scrambling for safety. A Marine yelled 'Nambu!' just as several of us grabbed our weapons. The thought of a Nambu behind us at that close range was not a pleasant one.

"A burst of firing from us dropped both Japanese soldiers before either could fire a shot. The Okinawans began screaming and the children crying. There were several frantic shouts from Marines to cease firing. Flares were kept aloft, and several men were ordered to check out the group. The Japanese were both dead; they each had rifles, but we did not see a Nambu."

"Unfortunately, several civilians had been hit. We put a cute, bright-eyed little girl, four or five years of age, in the foxhole with us. She had a bullet wound through the calf muscle of one leg. It was

surprising how quickly she stopped crying when we gave her some C ration candy. The corpsman tended her wound and she seemed quite calm. She remained in our foxhole until dawn, eating all the candy we had. At daylight she rejoined the group of Okinawans and was helped to the rear by some of the adults.

"As our troops moved further south, the problem of Japanese soldiers trying to infiltrate disguised as surrendering Okinawan civilians became worse. The Japanese realized that we encouraged the civilians to come through and pass to safety, so they used this as an opportunity to slip in behind us when they could. I heard from buddies in other units of numerous instances like this.

"During one of the patrols consisting of four or five mortarmen, in early June, we came across a large cave entrance which opened into a Japanese underground hospital. We had one flashlight, so we cautiously checked out the area just inside the entrance. There were wooden racks built against the wall and extending all the way to the ceiling.

"These served as hospital beds and in one of the lower ones we found an emaciated Japanese soldier clad only in baggy shorts. He seemed docile and utterly helpless as we carried him outside and placed him on the ground. We spoke to him with the few Japanese phrases we had been taught to assure him that we would not harm him. Some authorities believed that the fierceness of the fighting on Peleliu was because of the reluctance of Marines to take prisoners, so before Okinawa we were schooled on the advantages of capturing the enemy rather than fighting him.

"It made sense, but it was hard for us to accept the idea of offering chocolate bars and cigarettes to an enemy who always shot our stretcher bearers and wounded. An American was risking his life anytime he attempted to take a Japanese prisoner. But, we had been ordered to capture any and all prisoners possible.

"One mortarman stood by to keep an eye on the prostrate enemy soldier while the rest of us walked a short way off, sat on our helmets

and had a smoke. We were waiting for a corpsman to come and check him before he was carried to the rear. The man guarding the prisoner was an experienced Gloucester veteran, and as compassionate as any of us could still be at this point. In fact, he had carefully lifted the prisoner out of his bunk and gently laid him on the ground.

"While we waited, I glanced toward the prisoner and my buddy who was looking our way and talking to us. The prisoner saw his chance and he reached into his baggy shorts, pulled out a grenade and jerked out the pin. Before any of us could even shout a warning, our comrade saw the movement. The prisoner was holding his grenade in one hand and hitting the detonator cover with his other fist to try to pop the fuse cap."

My father described this incident to me: "The Marine said, 'You sonuvabitch,' and he drew his .45 and shot him right between the eyes. You just had to really watch it in those situations."

"We were never questioned about the incident, but if we had been, the simple answer would be that we took a prisoner, he attempted to explode a grenade, and a Marine shot him. The hospital was a wet, foul place and the occupants must have suffered greatly in there before they were removed and sent south, given an overdose of drugs, or committed hari-kari. We did not go past the area of the entrance. Engineers would later probably dynamite the entrance to seal it up.

"We found even more supply dumps covered with camouflage and tarpaulins. We attempted to use some of the dry Japanese Army socks we found, but they gave us trouble because there was no extension for the heel. The socks were made like a straight cloth tube. We tried on some of the hob nail field shoes which squeaked when one walked in them. The strangest sensation was to wear a pair of split-toed tabi."

My father and another mortarman were chosen to carry a message to the west coast regarding supplies. Gunnery Sgt. Hank Boyes briefed them on the mission.

"'OK you guys, stay on the east–west road all the way to the beach. The 7th Marines have pushed through to the west coast and

cleared the road all the way. They'll be pushing south on your left, and on your right, north of the road, the 6th Division is still fighting the Nips bottled up there south of Naha. Contact the people on the beach where supplies are being brought in and casualties are being evacuated. Tell them exactly where we are located and explain the route you took so they can supply us by the same route. Got it?'

"'Sure Sarge,' we answered.

"'OK then, remember to stay on the road. It's been cleared, but if you get off it and start screwing around souvenir hunting you might run into trouble. Some Nips have been bypassed. Get back here as soon as you make contact. Now get going.'"

They set off down the road on what they thought would be an adventure. The weather had improved, their dungarees and leggings were the closest they had been to clean in weeks, and they were in high spirits. My father had his Tommy gun and .45 pistol, and his buddy had a carbine. Their boots crunched on the gravel road as they walked. They saw almost no one.

"The 7th Marines had fought through this area to the coast and then moved south, and we could hear the sounds of their continuing battle to our left further away."

The telltale signs of heavy fighting were everywhere, including numerous corpses of dead Japanese.

They came to a deserted town with heavily damaged but still standing buildings. Their attention was drawn to a shop whose front window was smashed.

"The window glass was smashed and littered the neat displays, and the roof had a huge, jagged skylight made by a shell."

They kept going and saw a burned-out bus station with a ticket booth.

"'Keep on the look-out for Nips, Sledgehammer,' said my buddy. We had left open country and it was quite possible that Japanese might be lurking among the ruins of buildings. Without incident we continued through the ruins toward the site where a beach supply and evacuation point had been established."

In a few minutes an amtrac came clanking toward them. They hailed each other—he was from the supply area and was expecting them. They relayed the information to him as ordered.

"He said, 'I guess you guys can head on back. There's no need for you to go all the way to the beach now that I know how to find your outfit.'

"We agreed and turned back the way we had come. Supplies could now be brought in and casualties evacuated from the western beach without having to hand-carry them through miles of mud north of the area we had just fought through to break the Shuri line."

The amtrac had headed back to the beach, so they were alone as they came back through the ruined town. It could have been a scene from an old Western movie—the only sound they could hear was a piece of loose tin on the roof of the burned-out bus station clanking in the breeze. They decided to stop for a break and explore the ruins of the bus station. Just as they got to the front of the ruined structure, a burst of machine gun fire sent tracers zipping by right in front of them. It was a Japanese Nambu. They dove for cover behind the ticket booth of the station. The gunner fired a few more short bursts at the ticket booth, narrowly missing my father. They could hear the slugs ricocheting around hitting metal and glass back in the building among the derelict, burned-out buses.

"To have made a dash for safety in any direction (like they always do in the movies) would have been foolishly risking certain death."

Every time they even thought about moving, the Nambu loosed a burst in their direction. He had them pinned down tightly. The minutes dragged by and turned into hours.

"The Japanese gunner had apparently established himself in a fine vantage point to fire on all movement along the road. It was obvious that this road would soon have vehicles, troops, and casualties moving back and forth in large numbers, and this Nambu gunner intended to take his toll. We were evidently to be the first of his kills."

It was getting into late afternoon, and they heard the welcome sound of M1 rifle fire. It seemed to come from the general direction where they thought the enemy gunner was. They looked out cautiously and were relieved to see several fellow K Company Marines walking toward them from the road. One of them yelled out and asked if they were OK.

"'Yeah, boy are we glad to see you guys!' I said."

The gunny sergeant, apparently, had gotten worried about them and sent help.

"'When we heard that Nambu firing, we figured he was after you guys,' said a corporal.

"'Did you have any trouble with him?' I asked.

"'Naw, that son of bitch was so busy keeping you people pinned down we just slipped behind him and racked him up,' answered another man.

"'You sure pulled our ass out of a crack,' said my buddy. The others grinned.

"'Did you guys make contact with the supply people before you got pinned down?' asked the corporal. We told him we had.

"'OK, let's move out back to the company before dark.'

"As we returned along the road I thought how wonderful it was to be back with old comrades after those lonely hours my buddy and I had spent pinned down behind that ticket booth.

"All of our companies had lost heavily in the desperate fighting around Shuri. There was no doubt that K Company was vastly understrength—all one had to do was look around and see we didn't have anything like 235 men present [the normal strength of a Marine rifle company]. I never kept notes on our strength and number of losses. If we were forbidden from keeping diaries because they could be useful if they fell into enemy hands, I knew that keeping notes on casualty figures would really get me into trouble."

Kunishi Ridge

The weather got drier and warmer as they moved south. The sounds of battle grew louder and brought back the familiar fear and dread. All the Japanese who had bugged out of Shuri had established themselves along a line of ridges near the southern end of Okinawa. Kunishi Ridge, a coral escarpment about 1,500 yards long and riddled with the usual caves and protected strongpoints on both forward and reverse slopes, was the western anchor. To the east of Kunishi was Yuza-Dake, and further eastward was Yaeju-Dake. The 7th Marines had made a predawn attack on June 12 and gotten up onto a section of Kunishi.

"It was so unusual for Americans to attack at night that it caught the Japanese by surprise."

In a tactical scenario reminiscent of Iwo Jima, the Americans were on the ridge and the Japanese were in it.

"For four days after the 7th Marines got up on Kunishi they were relatively isolated, with the 800-yard fire-swept approaches to their rear called 'No Man's Valley,' being completely covered by enemy fire. Casualties had to be strapped to tanks and sandbagged for protection against Japanese fire during evacuation."

The 1st Marines attacked parts of Kunishi on June 14. Yuza-Dake fell to Lt. Col. Austin Shofner's 1/1 but took heavy casualties.

"An Army attack against Yaeju Dake had not kept pace with the attack of the Marine battalion's attack on Yuza Dake and consequently men of 1/1 received heavy fire from their left flank. (Personal letter from Austin Shofner.)"

They had been assured that the 5th Marines would not be committed again. This was the main thought in their minds as they trudged along a road watching ambulance jeeps drive past with wounded from Kunishi Ridge. In the afternoon the mortar section dug in. They could hear heavy firing ahead, to the south. They were deployed to fire flares over an intact bridge. This bridge spanned a high stream bank, and the water below gurgled peacefully.

"We were warned that Japanese infiltrators might try to blow it up, so flares must be kept aloft. Next to a sheer bank and almost under the bridge was a large battalion aid station tent. The medical personnel were getting their gear set up and squared away to handle the inevitable casualties.

"My buddies and I walked around the outside of the large tent peering under the opened flaps to see what we could. A friendly

corpsman, a pharmacist's mate 1st class, came over to us. The other medical personnel went about their duties but eyed us with mixed expressions of respect, pity, and suspicion. Even though we had been able to clean up while we were in corps reserve for nine or ten days, were still recognizable as infantrymen. It seemed that infantrymen always had a weather-beaten hungry look about them.

"'You guys from a line company?' he asked. We responded that we were, and our unit was K/3/5. 'Want a cup of joe?' he asked. No Marine I knew ever refused a cup of coffee when in the field.

"'Sure thing,' we said. So, the corpsman invited us into the tent and served us each a canteen cup of very good coffee—not what we got in our rations. He asked us questions about the fighting we had been in thus far and seemed genuinely interested in our replies, and particularly delighted over our high opinion of Navy Corpsmen. He told us he had come in with the most recent group of replacements.

"'I've been stationed Stateside on a Navy base and been trying to get overseas for two years. I finally had to pull all kinds of strings before I got shipped out,' he said. We must have looked somewhat amazed over his tremendous enthusiasm at finally getting into the war.

"He added, 'I didn't train to be a corpsman to sit on my can Stateside. I want to help Marine casualties and do the combat troops some good.' He was very sincere and enthusiastic. [With great pride he showed us the various instruments and equipment being set out to tend casualties. As I viewed the impressive array of shiny instruments, I hoped none of them would have to be used on me.]

"Finally, with dusk approaching, we ended our visit and thanked him for the coffee. My buddies and I walked the short distance back to the company to get squared away for the night.

"We kept the area well illuminated with flares during the night. The guns were set to throw the flares almost straight up above the bridge area. During my watch on my gun, the skipper's orderly came over and asked me to let him fire a flare shell. I told him he didn't know how to operate the mortar and I couldn't let him do it. He kept

begging and made a pest of himself. I had disliked him since the day he had shot the poor old Okinawan woman.

"I told him if he got permission from our mortar section senior NCO it was all right with me. He asked the sergeant, who said he could fire one shell, and then get back to the company CP where he belonged. So, I explained very carefully to him how to pull the safety wire to arm the flare shell so it would open and release the parachute and flare after it was fired.

"I fixed the increments to be sure the number was correct and handed him the shell. It was too dark to see him clearly, so I double checked with him about pulling the safety wire, and he said everything was squared away. He dropped the shell into the tube, it fired normally, and we looked up and waited for the shell to pop, the parachute to open, and the flare to ignite—at which point the empty light metal casing should fall harmlessly to the deck. But the flare didn't pop open. Then we heard a shout from the aid station tent.

"'You stupid son of a bitch!" I hissed. 'I bet you didn't pull the safety wire—that's why the damn shell didn't open. I'll bet a month's pay it fell on somebody over by the sick bay!'

"The orderly started whining and admitted he was so excited about firing the mortar that he did forget to pull the safety wire. The four-pound shell went up and didn't open the parachute but came down right through the aid station tent. It fell on the corpsman I had met the previous afternoon, and he had to be evacuated at dawn with a badly broken arm.

"I gave the orderly a thorough chewing out—he was more fit for heating up the officers' coffee in the CP than firing weapons. We never let anyone but trained mortarmen near the gun after that.

"We relieved the survivors of 1/1 on Yuza Dake, and they were glad to leave the place."

They could see Kunishi Ridge on their right and Yaeju-Dake on their left. My father was reminded of the hellish coral ridges on Peleliu when he saw the appearance of the terrain. It was the middle of June, and even though they were at the southern tip of the island, it wasn't over yet.

"Casualties were evacuated by tanks. The stretcher cases that could not be taken up into the tank through the escape hatch were tied to the rear decks—some of them were wounded a second or third time on the way to the aid station. The Japanese shot our helpless wounded on stretchers as strongly at Kunishi Ridge as any place we had fought."

There was a Japanese counterattack, and K/3/5 played a crucial role in eliminating the enemy troops who broke through the lines.

"From my own observations in the area, the worst was yet to come for K Company; the killing of a few Japanese who broke through the lines of 2/5 was minor compared to what we experienced on June 18, when K/3/5 attacked and captured the eastern portion of Kunishi Ridge."

This attack occurred a little after four in the morning—well before daylight. My father and the other veterans of the company were not at all happy about deploying for an attack while it was still dark. It went against everything they had learned so far in the war in the Pacific. Despite that, the experienced men also knew that it was the only way to approach a position like Kunishi Ridge, since they had to cross an expanse of open ground before they got to the ridge itself. He felt physically sick when he saw the jagged outline of this ridge silhouetted against the skyline and realized it was just like Bloody Nose on Peleliu. He wondered how much luck he could possibly have left.

"We moved out in the darkness with strict orders to keep contact but remain absolutely silent. Word was passed quietly that we would soon move up to the base of the ridge behind Marines already in position, and then attack to the left up along the ridge to its end.

"I couldn't tell much about our new position in the darkness. We were ordered in among some rocks right at the base of the ridge and told not to move back from them at daylight because Japanese snipers on the crest of Kunishi would fire down and pick us off."

In the weak, gray light of dawn, K Company began moving east along the ridge. In the jagged terrain it would be a rifleman's fight, so the mortarmen stood by to act as stretcher bearers, or riflemen if the situation required it. It didn't take long for men to get hurt, and the stretcher teams were hustling. The main concern was to get the wounded to cover where enemy snipers could not hit them again. Tanks were again used to strap casualties onto the rear decks.

"The weather was clear and hot as the day wore on. (By Peleliu standards it was only warm.) One of the wounded brought off by a stretcher team I was on was 2nd Lt. Sidney Wasserburg who had been shot in the head and was still conscious. Sid (his code name) hadn't been in the company long. He managed to thank us with a kind smile as we lifted him off the rocks onto the stretcher.

"Our men finally killed enough Japanese on the ridge that our wounded could be carried by stretcher teams out to the road a good distance to our rear and there picked up by ambulance jeeps. Thus, they no longer had to be evacuated by tanks."

At this point K Company was close to the east end of Kunishi Ridge.

I once asked my father if he had ever been decorated for bravery. He said that he had not. I asked him if he had ever done anything that perhaps would have justified such a medal. He then told me the story of how, on Okinawa, toward the end of the battle, he and some other Marines had to go up into a rocky area and bring down a casualty. The Marine had been wounded by a Japanese sniper in both feet and was lying helpless on a rocky ledge. My father explained how the casualty was in direct line of sight of the sniper, who was waiting on the man to be rescued. The four stretcher bearers, my father being one of them, huddled just under the ledge where the wounded man lay. As the rescuers looked at each other with searching glances, my father realized that their comrade was depending on them to help him. Even though he knew he would be exposed to the fire of the sniper, my father made the only decision he could make.

"I just figured to hell with it," he told me. "I jumped up on the ledge beside him, grabbed him under the shoulders, and helped lower him down to the other guys. Somebody had to do it."

The man's name was Leonard Vargo, and they carried him down Kunishi Ridge without further incident.

"On the way I remember vividly that he asked us to hand him his combat pack, which we had removed and placed on the stretcher beside him. He took out a large photograph of his bride in her wedding dress and proudly showed it to us. He also said that he had done some amateur boxing and had been in the Golden Gloves before entering the Marine Corps. Vargo was quite concerned as to whether his feet would heal to the point that he would have the agility for the footwork required of a boxer.

"As I looked at his feet, I could not help but wince; the leather of each boondocker was torn by a Japanese bullet and blood was seeping out through the torn leather. We assured him he would be as good as new when the Docs finished treating him.

"A 105mm shell exploded short just as we started along the road. A larger piece of shell about the size of the palm of one's hand came whirring close, hit the road, and skidded across into a shallow ditch. Another stretcher team came up from the rear to take our casualty, so I ran over and scooped up the piece of hot metal in my hand. There were US markings clearly visible on it. So, I put it on the stretcher and told the men to give it to the first officer they saw because it might give a clue to the identity of the gun that was firing short. That gun had still not been identified after hours of effort and frantic radio phone calls.

"When I returned to where my fellow mortarmen were located I saw that Tex was not there. My buddies told me that while I was up on the ridge a sniper along the crest had shot Tex. He was seriously wounded in the side, but he recovered. He retained his usual gusto for guitar picking and singing ballads after he returned from the hospital.

"One of our NCOs was squatting nearby holding a walkie talkie and shouting and cursing into it and making fierce faces at the same time. Curious, I went over to him. He was yelling, 'You son of a bitch I'd like to get my hands on you! I'd tear your ass up!'

"'What's up Sarge?' I said. He handed me the walkie talkie and said, 'Listen to that! Some goddamn Nips got hold of a walkie talkie. Jeez, I'd like to find that bastard!'

"I put the walkie talkie to my ear and heard a shrill voice repeating over and over like a broken record, 'Banzai, banzai, Nipponese kill! Marine you die!' He repeated the same thing over and over. Yelling into the radio only encouraged him to speak louder. The sergeant took it back and he continued yelling curses."

Sometime during the afternoon of June 18, K Company was relieved on Kunishi Ridge after reaching the eastern end. They were able to make contact with army units that had taken Yaeju-Dake and Yuza-Dake.

"Some companies had fought longer and lost more men on Kunishi ridge than K Company, but we had had as much of Kunishi Ridge as any of us wanted. While attached to 2/5, our K Company had captured the eastern flank of the ridge from the Japanese."

End Game

The 1st Division's fight at Kunishi Ridge lasted from June 11 to June 18 and cost them 1,150 casualties. But it was the end of organized Japanese resistance on Okinawa. The enemy made it hellishly difficult right up to the end. It was a difficult objective, and the night attacks had played a crucial role in getting the job done.

"A couple of hours before K Company completed the capture of its sector of Kunishi Ridge, a Japanese machine gun was firing furiously across the flat ground just to the extreme left of the ridge. This meant that our K Company Marines could not establish contact with army troops further to our left.

"'OK you guys, stand by, we've got to charge that machine gun and knock it out,' said a new replacement NCO to his already depleted rifle squad. Confidence and grim determination were glowing on his

face. I was resting with some of my buddies in his squad after carrying out a casualty and saw their reactions of disbelief.

"'Ain't he ever heard of calling in artillery or mortars?' someone else said. Some of the veterans in the squad tactfully convinced the new squad leader of the infeasibility of his plan. The machine gun was silenced by a heavy concentration of artillery fire.

"On one occasion while we were trying to evacuate a casualty, a replacement NCO said to me on Kunishi Ridge, 'You know what to do. I've been on guard duty on the main gate at Boston Navy Yard for the last two years. I've never been in anything like this before.' I appreciated his good sense and we all squeezed out of the hot spot without mishap.

"A small landing strip for Piper Cub spotter planes was constructed along a section of a coral road near the village of Itoman. I was on a stretcher team that carried one of our last casualties to this evacuation point. We carried the wounded man over rough terrain and down to the coral road. The casualty was lifted from our canvas stretcher and strapped into a wire basket litter which was lashed to the wing struts of the plane, next to the fuselage.

"Another casualty was put on the other side. We got out of the way as the pilot revved up his engine and the little plane took off, headed to a rear area hospital. As we watched the airplane take off, one of my buddies said, 'You know boys, I just don't know whether I'd want to go back to the hospital like that.'"

Even though the Japanese were effectively finished by now, there still groups of diehard holdouts causing trouble for the Americans in caves, pillboxes, and burned-out villages. Despite this, they continued moving to the southern end of the island rapidly.

My father's 3rd Battalion was one of the first American units to reach the end of the island overlooking the sea. He described it as a beautiful sight.

"Even during the last desperate stand of the Japanese defenders, accidents took their toll. Corporal Farmer in the G-2 section of 3/5

was examining an enemy Arisaka rifle and fatally wounded himself. I was standing nearby and had seen Farmer looking it over. He was a Peleliu veteran and certainly familiar with this common enemy weapon. When the rifle discharged, we hit the deck. Someone yelled for a corpsman.

"We quickly realized Farmer had shot himself. The Doc did what he could, but the wound was fatal. Farmer was a good, decent fellow and well-liked. We stood around him there on that ruggedly picturesque hill overlooking the brilliant blue sea -as he quietly died, from an accidental wound while the battle of Okinawa was also dying around us. His death was such a tragedy because the madness was all but over."

On the night of June 20, they dug in on this high ground overlooking the sea in a defensive perimeter. Japanese were moving around in small groups, and there was a lot of shooting as they were eliminated. My father and the other Marines emplaced near him could hear groups of Japanese running past them on the road, gravel crunching under their hobnail boots. The Japanese began firing in their direction.

A rifle bullet zipped right by my father and hit the small hydrogen cylinder of a flamethrower that was sitting on the side of a foxhole next to him.

He described what happened in a conversation we had once about flamethrowers. I guess I expressed an interest in the weapon or some aspect of it, and I think I asked him if he ever saw one blow up from being punctured by a bullet or shrapnel.

"There was this one time on Okinawa. It was dark or close to it, and we were sitting in our holes. A buddy of mine who was a flamethrower gunner had taken the thing off his back and set it on the side of his foxhole. A Jap bullet whizzed by me and hit it. Well, it started making a sharp hissing sound and I asked my buddy if it was gonna blow, and he said, 'Naw, it just hit the hydrogen tank. It won't ignite.' Sure scared the hell outa me though."

The Japanese who had been running along the road in the darkness were toppled by Marine rifle fire. But others were swimming or walking along in the water just offshore. They were dimly visible in flare light.

"The Japanese were apparently trying to concentrate over on the beach in the 8th Marines sector and kept slipping along offshore through the shallow water.

"There was a line of Marines standing behind a stone wall on the beach firing at them. Jim came running back up from the wall [to where we were dug in] to get more carbine ammo. "Come on Sledgehammer, it's just like Lexington and Concord.'

"'No thanks,' I said, 'I'm too comfortable in my hole.' He went on back down to the wall and they continued firing through the night. The truth is that even as much as I hated our enemy, I was disgusted with killing."

In the corner of my father's study was the Japanese samurai saber that he had picked up amid the rubble of Shuri Castle. One day I had it out of the scabbard and was testing its weight and balance. He described an incident that did not involve this particular saber—mind you, my father, being a stickler for the truth, made sure I was aware of that—but still that conversation has stayed in my memory over the years.

As the action on Okinawa was winding down, a Marine 37mm gun crew was attacked just before daylight. This gun position was not far from where my father was dug in. A corpsman, a new kid who hadn't really seen any action, heard the call for help after the enemy grenades went off. My father grabbed his Tommy gun and went after the young corpsman in case he ran into trouble.

Apparently two Japanese officers had charged into the 37mm position, throwing grenades and swinging their samurai sabers. As my father described to me, as one of the Japanese officers swung his saber down at a Marine, the Marine parried it with his carbine.

"That saber was so sharp it sliced the stock of the carbine all the way to the metal barrel. It also sliced off one of the Marine's fingers. Well, another Marine shot that Jap and he fell over backwards down the slope they had just charged up. The other Japanese officer with him had already been killed and was lying on his back near the wheel of the 37. I'll never forget—there was a Marine standing over him with his M1 rifle in both hands, and he was just driving it up and down into the head of that corpse. It was just horrible. And this poor Marine—he was just at the end of his rope. He just kept plunging that M1 up and down. I mean, it just made me sick. We gently grabbed him by the arms and tried to restrain him. We got the rifle away from him and his buddy got him outta there."

I didn't say much, and he concluded by saying, "Anybody who thinks there's glory in warfare—they should've seen that."

Later in the day on June 21, 1945, after the High Command issued the word that the island was secure, my father took out his pipe, lit it, and looked out over the blue sea with the sunlight dancing on the water. He had survived eighty-two days and nights on Okinawa.

After performing some menial cleanup tasks, my father and some of his buddies were ordered to board some trucks one day and go up north to the Motobu Peninsula, to a division tent camp, to guard some K Company gear. It turned out to be good duty. They had plenty of fresh water and decent rations, and the weather was warm and dry.

Although the Marines experienced immense relief at having survived the meat grinder of combat, yet again, there were still days of uncertainty. The long process of mental convalescence would begin at that tent camp on northern Okinawa. The photo of my father sitting on his bunk, shirtless, showing the strain of a long battle as he stares blankly into space with "the thousand-yard stare," underweight from the stress of combat—that photo was taken one day at the tent camp. The photographer is unknown. It was always my mother's favorite picture of him—the haunting look in his eyes, I think.

They heard on August 8, 1945, that the first atomic bomb had been dropped a couple of days earlier. They knew that Japan itself would have to be invaded, and they would be the ones to have to do it. We had many conversations about his feelings on the atomic bombs. I won't weigh the morality of that issue here, only his experience. As he told me, "After what I had been through to that point, I knew there was no way I could survive another battle in the Japanese home islands. We knew we would have to kill them all to win."

Many of his buddies, such as George Sarrett, Hank Boyes, Snafu Shelton, and Jim Anderson, were Gloucester veterans and would rotate home. But for the men like my father who had come out to the Pacific in early 1944, they were in until the war was over. He and I talked of how many American casualties were expected; he always said it was around one million.

"We had no idea what an atomic bomb was. When we saw the news on the bulletin board after the second one, that the Japanese had surrendered, we just didn't believe it. You hear these stories that everybody was running around shouting for joy and shooting fireworks…it was the rear echelon guys who did that. Those of us who had been on the front lines, we just sat around in disbelief. We weren't running around celebrating—we just didn't believe that it was over. We felt relief, of course, but it was just so hard to believe.

"I remember the day that the Japs sent peace envoys into Ie Shima. We saw them come in; they were in a Betty bomber that was specially painted with big green crosses to identify them. I think they were escorted by American P-38 fighters."

My father went to northern China for occupation duty after Okinawa. He remembered his time there fondly, and it was there that he began his own healing process after the fighting was over. He finally returned to Mobile in early 1946. He had made it out of the abyss of war.

CHAPTER TWENTY

Coming Home

My father and I spoke often about what it was like for him to finally come home. When he walked through the front door of Georgia Cottage, he told me that Captain, one of the family dogs, literally jumped straight into his arms and began joyfully licking his face. He was struck by how much his parents had aged. It was little wonder that the emotional strain of having both their sons in heavy combat, one in Europe and one in the Pacific, had taken its toll. "Gran and Pop both looked so old," he told me.

The war had changed him too. My mother (who did not come into the picture until 1952) remembered how my grandparents noticed that their youngest son, so well-mannered and genteel before the war, was a different man now. He seemed rougher around the edges, he used poor grammar and appeared to have forgotten the finer points of social etiquette when at the dinner table.

He said he spent a lot of time sitting around and staring at the wall. My grandmother, never shy about imposing herself upon others or expressing her opinions, would often come into the room and begin exhorting him to do something with his life. At that point, all he wanted was to be left alone.

"Pop would hear her getting on to me and bothering me," he once told me. "And then he would come in and say, 'Mary Frank, leave that boy alone! You have no idea what he's been through! You have no idea what those men have been through! Now go on and leave him alone.'" I could imagine my grandmother grumbling and walking out of the room in a huff.

The differences showed themselves in other, more insidious ways too. His mother and her sister, his aunt Octavia, were sometimes nervous around him because he had changed so much. One afternoon, not long after he got home, my father went into the back bedroom to lie down and take a nap. At some point Octavia went in and shook him on the shoulder to wake him. He came up with his hands around her throat. She recoiled in horror, and he, of course, felt terrible when he realized what he had done. The nightmares began, too, waking him up in the middle of the night in a cold sweat and with a pounding heart.

Pop was always there for him, though, and his calm, intelligent advice kept my father grounded. He began trying to figure out what he would do for the rest of his life. Always interested in biology, he wanted to pursue a degree in science. His mother, however, sniffed at the idea, declaring that such a career field would not be prestigious enough.

He went to Auburn, which at the time was Alabama Polytechnic Institute. He told the story of his conversation with the young woman in the registrar's office many times, but I remember him telling it to me in his own words.

"The room was full of people; I walked in and went up to a table with a young woman sitting behind it, and when it was my turn, I walked up to the table and was standing in front of her. She was shuffling some papers around and had some form in front of her and started to ask me some questions. She asked me what branch of the service I had been in, and I told her the Marine Corps. She asked me if had been taught anything about repairing electrical things, I said, 'No, ma'am.' She asked me if they had taught me anything about mechanical things, I said no. She asked me something else, I said no, they didn't teach me that. And I could see she was starting to get flustered, and the girl sitting there with her started to smirk, and I could hear some people behind me starting to snicker at me. Well, I was starting to feel pretty embarrassed, and then she looked at me and said, 'Did the Marine Corps teach you anything?'

"And I just stared down at her and said in voice as loud as thunder, 'Lady, they taught me how to kill Japs! There was a killing war going on and I had to do some of the killing, and if that don't fit into an academic course, I'm sorry! Some of us had to do it and most of my buddies got killed or wounded!'

"Well, the room was dead silent—you could've heard a pin drop—and she just looked shocked and mumbled something about being sorry, and I said, 'It's OK, you couldn't have known.'"

He earned a bachelor of science degree in business in 1949 and went back to Mobile to work in an insurance office. As he told me many times, he detested it. "I should've never listened to Mary Frank," he said. And he would usually end such conversations with me by saying, "Big Shot, you have to do what you want to do. Follow your own path. Don't let someone else make that decision for you."

Later Life

My father took his own advice and, after marrying my mother in 1952, returned to Auburn for a master's degree in botany, which he earned in 1955. After that he went to the University of Florida and earned a PhD in zoology and biochemistry in 1960. He and my mother ended up in Montevallo in 1962, where he began teaching biology at Alabama College (later the University of Montevallo). He became a full professor in 1970 and specialized in zoology and ornithology. It was his dream. In his own words, "Science was my salvation."

Despite his horrific experiences as a combat veteran, I never felt as though I was living in a house with a disturbed individual. As I have stated publicly many times, he was an all-American dad. He was, in my own view, a paragon of self-control. He drank moderately, but never to excess. He swore frequently but never needlessly, and he absolutely eschewed the so-called four-letter words. Like any man, he appreciated beautiful women, but there was only one who mattered—my mother. He treated her with absolute respect and devotion and demanded the same of my brother and me, not that that was a hard thing to do. He always called her Shug, Chief, and sometimes simply Mrs. Sledge.

In 2004, I was interviewed in Los Angeles by James Moll, the documentary director and producer. He asked me, "Was your dad a hero?" This was a predictable question under the circumstances, but I had to think for a second. I answered that, perhaps to some, he could be considered a hero because of his service in World War II, and because he was a member of the greatest generation. I continued by saying that millions of men and women served in World War II, and to them, the heroes were the ones who never made it home. He was a hero to me, because he was my dad and provided a wonderful home for my mother, brother, and me. As expected of any father, he was a model of stability, strength, and leadership, and we had a traditional and close relationship.

When I was four or five years old, I remember him coming home from work and joining me in the living room to watch *I Love Lucy*. He would have a beer or two and would always sit with our family dachshund, Holley, in his lap. The memory of his guffawing at the antics of Ricky and Lucy makes me smile even today, all these years later. If I was sitting near him, he would slap me on the back as he laughed, but always gently, since I was still a little fellow at the time. My mother would bring in Planters peanuts or some other snack, and the mood in the room would be wonderfully cheerful. My father was an absolute believer in the idea that even if you had a horrible day at work, under no circumstances did you bring that home and "kick the dog" or inflict it on your family.

The mood became perceptibly darker and less cheerful, however, when the evening news came on after *I Love Lucy*. The year would have been 1970 or 1971, and the war in Vietnam was in full swing. I won't attempt to recreate dialogue of such evenings, because I honestly don't remember, but I do have a vivid mental image of the grainy news footage flickering across our little black and white RCA television set, Marines and soldiers running and fighting through Southeast Asian jungles, and the ubiquitous Huey choppers, their rotors thumping and the air stream flailing the palm trees as they landed to take on torn and bloody young men for evacuation.

My father, Sledgehammer, would sit there with Holley still in his lap, watching tensely, his jaw clenched and a grim expression on his face.

Now there was no laughing and uproarious guffawing like during *I Love Lucy*—he would just mutter "goddamn" under his breath as the voices of Walter Cronkite and John Chancellor droned on solemnly over those flickering images of choppers, palm trees, and wounded young men.

My mother and I talked about this not long before she passed away. She said, "He was so discouraged and profoundly disturbed at things like the Vietnam War—it made him feel as though what they did in World War II was for nothing. He thought that they had made the world better—that all the suffering and dying on places like Peleliu and Okinawa was so that we would never have to see these things again."

In the early years of his career as a biology professor, he had many close friends among his students. In those days they called him Uncle Eugene. It was the early 1970s, and young men were coming home from Vietnam. One of my favorites was Jim Kitson, an excellent biology student who had been a Marine and suffered four combat wounds. He had a sense of humor and zest for life that had to be experienced—something he had in common with my father—and he, like my father, had seen the most bitter side of humanity while still retaining his own. He made it out of the abyss, and perhaps that shared experience was why he and my father got on so well.

Although I have spoken here of my father's war experience looming large in my own childhood, he was, in essence, a scientist—and that is how I saw him.

One day I walked into his study while he was at his desk writing. I don't remember exactly how old I was—at least a teenager, I think—but I sat down in the rocking chair near the desk and asked him how many Japanese soldiers he killed during the war. He stopped writing, looked out the window thoughtfully, took a sip from the ever-present glass of iced tea, and answered the question like the scientist that he was—giving an articulate and analytically worded exposition on the effectiveness of the 60mm mortar when properly employed.

Like the NCO had said back on Pavuvu all those years ago, "It'll tear their asses up."

When he finished, I didn't say anything, just sat looking at him expectantly. A slight pause—he knew what I was looking for. Then he looked me in the eye and simply said, "__________, maybe __________."

It wasn't a large number, but some things must remain between father and son.

When I think of this, I cannot help but contrast it with the day we sat in the same room, him gently cupping his hands around a tiny bird that had been brought to him by a neighbor who found it in her yard. The bird had flown into a window and was mortally injured. He knew there was nothing to be done for it; he simply held it, keeping it warm until it died. There were no false tears, no histrionics, just his quiet humanity. The juxtaposition of his pragmatic, matter-of fact honesty and his benevolence and compassion was astonishing.

Although he bore strong feelings toward the Japanese soldiers of WWII, he did not hate modern-day Japan. I know he struggled with it, as I saw one day in the mid-1970s when we were walking through the terminal at Birmingham Airport. We had dropped off my mother, who was flying out on a trip. As we walked back through the building to the parking deck, a group of Japanese tourists passed us going the other direction. They were laughing and talking loudly. I could see my father tense up and grit his teeth as he hurried me along. I asked him if he was OK, and he just shook his head and muttered something about the sound of the language. I knew what he was thinking.

And yet, many times in later years I heard him express admiration and respect for Japanese self-discipline and work ethic. My parents drove a Nissan Maxima at one point, and the first car I bought when I graduated from college was a Honda CRX. I asked if it bothered him to drive a Japanese car. "Hell, no," he answered. "It's a consumer product and they build a better one than we do. American cars are garbage." Always the pragmatist.

My mother told me of a day when, not long after they were married and he was a young professor, he brought home a Japanese biology graduate student for lunch. Their love of science transcended everything and forged a bond of commonality.

I have many recollections of our walks over to the University of Montevallo's campus when I was still in elementary school. He would frequently need to check on a project in his lab on a Saturday, and usually I accompanied him. Being a weekend, the science building, Harman Hall, was almost always deserted. I can still remember the way his keys jangled as he pulled them out of his pocket, that Japanese dog tag from Cape Gloucester—the one from Sid Phillips—visible on the key ring, and the smell of the building when he unlocked the door and we walked in. I can still hear our footsteps echoing down the dark, empty halls, my father softly humming to himself as we walked, the only light coming from the red glow of the exit signs above the doors.

When we would walk into his lab, the distinct odor of crystallized paradichlorobenzene filled my nostrils. This chemical compound, the same used in mothballs, was used at the time to preserve specimens that were used in his anatomy classes. Exposure to it can be harmful to humans, but we didn't know that in the early '70s. I breathed it in—it was part of my childhood. I remember he gave me a small dissecting kit, the same kind purchased by his biology students, and I spent many hours using its implements on dead bugs or leaves I found in the yard, just as he did when he was a kid.

Other memories of my father fill my mind, almost like a collage of sorts: the smell of his aftershave when he would come into my room to tell me goodbye in the mornings before he went to work—he wore British Sterling for a while, I remember, and when he came home in the afternoons, he would kneel down in the front hall and joyously greet the dogs as they happily barked and wagged their tails. My mother would lament the noise as she walked out of the room, complaining about the dog hair getting on his suit, but she didn't really mind it. We were lucky to have a father so determined to bring cheer into the home whenever he could, and she knew it.

I remember the long trips we took as a family, my brother with a science fiction paperback and me with my Etch A Sketch in the back seat of our green 1971 Ford LTD, my father driving and my mother beside him in the passenger seat. I can still see the butt of that .45 pistol, snug in its holster under the front seat, the same .45 he carried through Okinawa.

I was fascinated by that pistol—especially knowing that it had been my grandfather's and that he had sent it to my father after Peleliu. My father kept it in his study in later years, and often I would pull it down off the shelf—always under his supervision, of course—and admire it, feeling its cold steel against my hand and smelling its oiled sheen in the light. Knowing that he had carried that thing in combat captivated me. I begged him to teach me to shoot it, but he made me wait until I was sixteen. A pistol is like a snake, he would say; it can turn around and bite you. But I remember the cold, blustery winter afternoon when we finally took it out in the woods behind the house. I reveled in the buck and recoil, the smell of the smoke, the sharp report from each shot echoing through the woods.

My mother frequently hosted evening bridge parties. The doorbell rang out as each lady arrived, and soon the driveway was full of Lincolns, Oldsmobiles, Buicks, and Chevrolets, and the living room would be full of card tables, raucous laughter, ice cubes tinkling in glasses, and beehive hairdos as she and her friends played their card games and caught up on the latest Montevallo gossip. The air hung heavy with the smell of coffee, perfume, and cigarette smoke, and my father and I would retreat downstairs or to his study to wait it out until all the ladies had gone home and it was quiet again. I would do my homework, and he would grade test papers or answer letters from old friends. I could almost feel him gritting his teeth with each gust of laughter from the living room.

He may have begged for a smoke on Peleliu after they landed that day in 1944, but he was never a cigarette smoker. After the ladies had gone home, we would open the sliding glass doors to the living room to let in fresh air while he growled, "I tell you, Big Shot, that goddamn cigarette smoke, it's got to be the most disgusting thing in the world!"

Though he was sociable and lively and loved nothing more than a good laugh, he cherished his private time. In the evenings, either during supper or after, whenever he got a phone call, his reaction would always be the same—looking down, shaking his head, and muttering "goddamn" as he did so. But he would haul himself out of his chair, march off to the bedroom, and close the door. If it was an old buddy from his Marine Corps days, like Bill Leyden, Stumpy Stanley, Jay De L'Eau, or Snafu, the uproariously joyful conversations went on for hours, reminiscing and guffawing far into the night.

His legendary sense of humor stands out so well in my memory. In later years, when I was a student at the University of Montevallo (before I went to Auburn, where I graduated), I heard from so many other students who had been in his classes that "Henry, your dad is absolutely hilarious." I would only smile and nod, because invariably this would be followed by a comment about how tough he was as a professor. Never one to simply hand out grades, my father demanded academic integrity. My friend Jimmy Desmond from Fairhope, Alabama, said it best: "Your dad was a hard-ass. People either loved him or hated him, but they all respected him." That was Sledgehammer.

We took a trip to Panama City around the summer of 1975. While we were out walking on the beach, my father found an empty liquor bottle that had washed up on the sand. He snatched it up in between long looks at pelicans and other sea birds with his ever-present binoculars. I think my mother said in an exasperated tone, "What are you going to do with that?" He just grinned and said nothing.

After we got back to our condo, he sat down at the dining room table, pushed his straw hat back on his head, and adopted a pose like an old drunken beach bum, complete with an appropriately dazed, stupefied facial expression. "Quick, Shug," he exhorted my mother, "take a picture!" She took the picture with our Polaroid camera, and when it popped out and developed, he printed on the base of it in blue ink his own caption: "Ye old toper." It was comically ridiculous, and of course that was exactly the point. That picture is in an old shoebox somewhere.

My father was completely unselfconscious and literally had no fear of embarrassment. One warm, pleasant Sunday morning, when I was nine or ten, we were in church when a wasp suddenly appeared and started buzzing around. Everyone around us nervously kept an eye on it as the wonderful pastor, Rev. Paul Gaunt, preached on. This went on for a few minutes, and Reverend Gaunt became aware of it just as the wasp landed in the lovely, snowy white hair of a nice lady directly in front of us. The reverend said, "We've got a wasp flying around in here, folks; keep an eye out for it!" Just as he said that my father, in one quick motion, flicked the wasp out of the lady's hair with his handkerchief and crushed it. He then deftly held it up by one of its wings and proudly announced, "Reverend Gaunt, here he is!"

Everyone in the room stared at us, then laughed uproariously, and quite a few applauded. I, of course, in my own childish, self-obsessed way, was totally mortified and embarrassed. My mother just smiled and rolled her eyes, and my father seemed quite pleased with himself. I think my embarrassment just amused him even more.

When I was a little older and he left me notes in the kitchen, either reminding me of a chore or passing along a phone message, he always signed them "YHAOS, Dad." Which of course stood for "your humble and obedient servant."

Although he was intolerant of many things, he could also, in the words of my brother, "rise to great heights" in compassion and understanding. But one thing he could not tolerate was egocentrism; he had little time or patience with people who were self-aggrandizing and ostentatious. It was little wonder that any mention of Gen. Douglas MacArthur would elicit a snort of disgust.

One of my wife's fondest memories of him was when she came to my house after work one afternoon and saw my father sitting on the patio swing having a beer. She and I had just gotten engaged, and my father had driven up to be fitted for his tuxedo, since, naturally, he was to be my best man. His recently purchased late-model white Volkswagen bug was parked in the driveway. It was reminiscent of the 1967 yellow VW he bought when I was just a few years old that he drove for years. He called it his "field car," and it was well known around Montevallo in those days. Sadly, he would not get the chance to wear that tuxedo when she and I married a few months later.

Sledgehammer fought his battles against the empire of Japan with courage and honor. When the war ended, he made his peace, came home, and got on with his life as best he could. Perhaps it could be said that his war never completely ended—not that it did for any of them—because I know he never forgot his buddies who didn't get to have a life after the war. Even though he always grieved for them, that grief gave him an enhanced appreciation of his own life.

I heard him say once, "The experience was so incredibly intense, that after it was all over with, life was never the same, because the sunrise is always more beautiful to me now than it ever was before I started into Peleliu on that amtrac."

But his last battle would be one that he would not win. He was diagnosed with stomach cancer in October 2000. The prognosis was not good. It was a tumultuous time for me, getting ready for a wedding and at the same time trying to come to grips with his illness.

I found, at times, that it was almost as if my mind was playing tricks on me. Many nights I dreamed that we had just found out that he actually didn't have cancer, and I would feel a huge wave of relief and happiness. But then, inevitably, I would always wake up to the sad reality in the predawn gloom, grappling with it before I had to get up and get on with the day. These dreams continued for a while after he was gone, but such maudlin thoughts eventually stopped, and I was left with the memories of a life well lived and a proud, enduring legacy.

Watching my father endure his illness helped me understand the true meaning of inner courage and fortitude—as if reading of his war experiences were not enough. I sat with him many days and nights, and I honestly never heard him complain about the pain he was in. I came to understand the difference between being a tough guy and being a strong man. I never saw my father as a tough guy in the proverbial sense; he exuded gentlemanly forbearance and composure, but he was one hell of a strong man. That was Sledgehammer.

My brother has said I have a freakish ability to recall minute details about certain events. I won't necessarily agree with that, but I do remember the day we lost him. My memories of that time are something I have tried for twenty-two years to forget. I have shared a lot in these pages, but I will not share that. I'll only say that the first man I called was Bill Leyden, and later, at the family visitation, I remember walking into the softly lit room and sensing the heavy, respectful silence, with the flag-draped casket under the spotlights and the two Marines in dress blues standing guard over it. He would've liked that, I think.

He was laid to rest in Mobile, on a warm, sunny Alabama spring morning—the kind of morning when he would have been out with the dogs bird-watching—the smell of flowers in the air, the Spanish moss hanging from those majestic oak trees and swaying gently in the breeze. I can still see it more clearly than I would like, another collage of memories: the line of cars pulling into the cemetery, the awful sense of finality when I saw the hearse and the Marine pallbearers; my wife, dressed in black, her perfectly coiffed hair and her sunglasses, who never looked more beautiful; my mother's quiet resilience, her strength, her grace and composure as the Marine First Sergeant knelt at her side and read to her a personal letter from the Commandant of the United States Marine Corps; the starched precision of the Marines in their dress blues, their brass buttons shining in that morning sun; my eyes clouding with tears at the mournful sound of *Taps*, and how we all flinched when the riflemen's salute cracked in the morning air; the young Marines smartly folding the flag, the way one quickly inserted the brass shell casings from the salute in his white-gloved hand into the flag—that kid didn't look a day over seventeen, and he was crying as he did so; the First Sergeant kneeling in front of my mother and bowing his head as he presented the flag to her, and the way she smiled and quietly said thank you as he stood up and slowly saluted.

After my father was gone, my mother told me about a conversation she had with my brother. He had had a vision, it seems, and saw our dad in this vision. My brother and I talked about this recently, and he does not recall the details that my mother described to me years ago—only that dad seemed happy and in a wonderful place surrounded by bright light. But with his permission, I will relate this in the way my mother described it.

My brother saw him in a dream and said he looked wonderful—radiant, healthy, and happy. He was standing there smiling at my brother. My brother wanted to say something, and he started to speak to him, but dad just held up his hand and smiled at him. Then he reached out, tapped my brother on his knee, and said, "There's a future out there, boy, and I've got to get to it!"

EPILOGUE

On a hot, sunny afternoon in the summer of 2022, I went back to Montevallo. My English friend Leighton Hughes was with me. He had come for a visit and wanted me to show him around the wonderful town where I grew up, where Sledgehammer, a man he admired tremendously, spent most of his life.

We went by the old local swimming pool, on Overland Road, the one where my brother and I reenacted scenes from *Voyage to the Bottom of the Sea* when we were kids. It's forlorn and abandoned now—the concrete buildings crumbling and falling in, the pipes all rusted, and the paint chipped and faded, weeds and vines growing through the cracks and disused furniture lying in a few feet of rainwater in what's left of the pool. It's almost as if the field in which it was built back in 1970 is reclaiming it. If I closed my eyes I could almost imagine being five years old again, saying "Dad, watch this!" as I jumped into the water.

"That's great, Big Shot!" he would proudly call out.

We went by the old Bean's Barber Shop on Middle Street where my dad took me as a kid; the barber shop is long gone. It was a tattoo parlor on that day in 2022. We drove around the rest of the town and saw the beautiful university campus. We stopped and went into Harman Hall; it was dark and quiet on that day since the students were all away on break, but we walked down those familiar halls to see my dad's old office where I had gone to visit him so many times. Despite the inevitable cosmetic changes, Montevallo's well-kept streets were almost as familiar to me that day as they were when I played in them as a kid.

Naturally I wanted to take him to the house on Cardinal Crest Road where I grew up and where my dad wrote *With the Old Breed.* My mother sold the house in 2017, and I had not been back since.

The memories came flooding back as we walked into the house, standing in the front hall where my dad would greet the dogs every afternoon, making my way through the rooms where I had spent most of my formative years. We stood in the kitchen, and I told David and Leslie, the lovely couple who live there now, the story of when I hid in the pantry cupboard and jumped out to scare my dad with my little plastic Tommy gun. That tall cupboard is still there.

We walked down the back hallway to what had been my dad's study. So many of the conversations and memories I have described in these pages happened in that little room. It looked completely different on that afternoon from the way I remembered it, but in my mind's eye it was still the same. I could still see his desk against the wall, the same desk where he did much of his writing; the bookshelves under the windows overlooking the backyard and the lush, verdant woods beyond; and the spot on the floor where I spent so many hours looking through World War II books. I could still see his binoculars on the bookcase and his Ka-Bar and Japanese samurai saber in the corner. I could imagine him sitting in his chair, swirling his iced tea in its glass and staring thoughtfully out the window, and I could almost hear the familiar sound of his pencil scratching away on a yellow legal pad.

David, Leslie, Leighton, and I were having an animated conversation as we walked into the study, but then it got quiet. They could see that I was lost in my thoughts, thinking back, remembering, working it all out in my mind.

We went downstairs and out onto the patio where my brother and I had built our spaceship when we were kids. I remembered how my mother commented to my dad that we were making such a mess building that thing. Dad just told her, "Leave 'em alone, the day will come soon enough when they'll be gone, and you'll miss them."

I looked out at the backyard where he taught me to shoot that M1 carbine the Marine Corps way, and I could imagine my dad standing there, wearing his hat and peering intently through his binoculars at a bird up in the trees, with our dogs at his side. So many times, I'd see him like that as I was leaving to go somewhere. I'd call out to him, "Hey Dad, I love ya." He'd always turn around and grin and say, "I love you too, Big Shot," and then he'd turn back to his bird-watching.

I walked into what had been my room, and I showed them the cedar closet where my dad had kept his Marine dress blues. The door to the laundry room was closed, but I told them that was where my mom had typed a large portion of the manuscript for *With the Old Breed* and *China Marine*.

Eventually, it was time to go, and Leighton and I walked out to the car. David and Leslie expressed their happiness at having me visit, bidding a warm goodbye and imploring me to come back again. I probably won't—too many emotions there. We got into the car and left as they waved and walked back into the house. And that reminded me of when I would come back and visit my parents after I had moved out on my own.

It was a scene that had been played out so many times over the years: We'd have a pleasant visit, my mom would fix lunch, and we would talk for a while as I caught them up on what was happening in my life. We might even catch a rerun of *The Andy Griffith Show*, or *Deputy Fife* as my dad always called it. Then, as the afternoon wore on and the time came for me to go, we would walk out on the front steps. The late afternoon sun would be slanting through the trees, bathing everything in the front yard in golden light. Off in the woods behind the house we might hear the shrill cry of a hawk or a crow fading away in the breeze as I got into my car, my parents standing there arm in arm to see me off, Dad—Sledgehammer—in his L.L.Bean flannel shirt with his pipe and leather belt with the Marine emblem, and Mom, looking radiant and lovely, waving to me as I drove away.

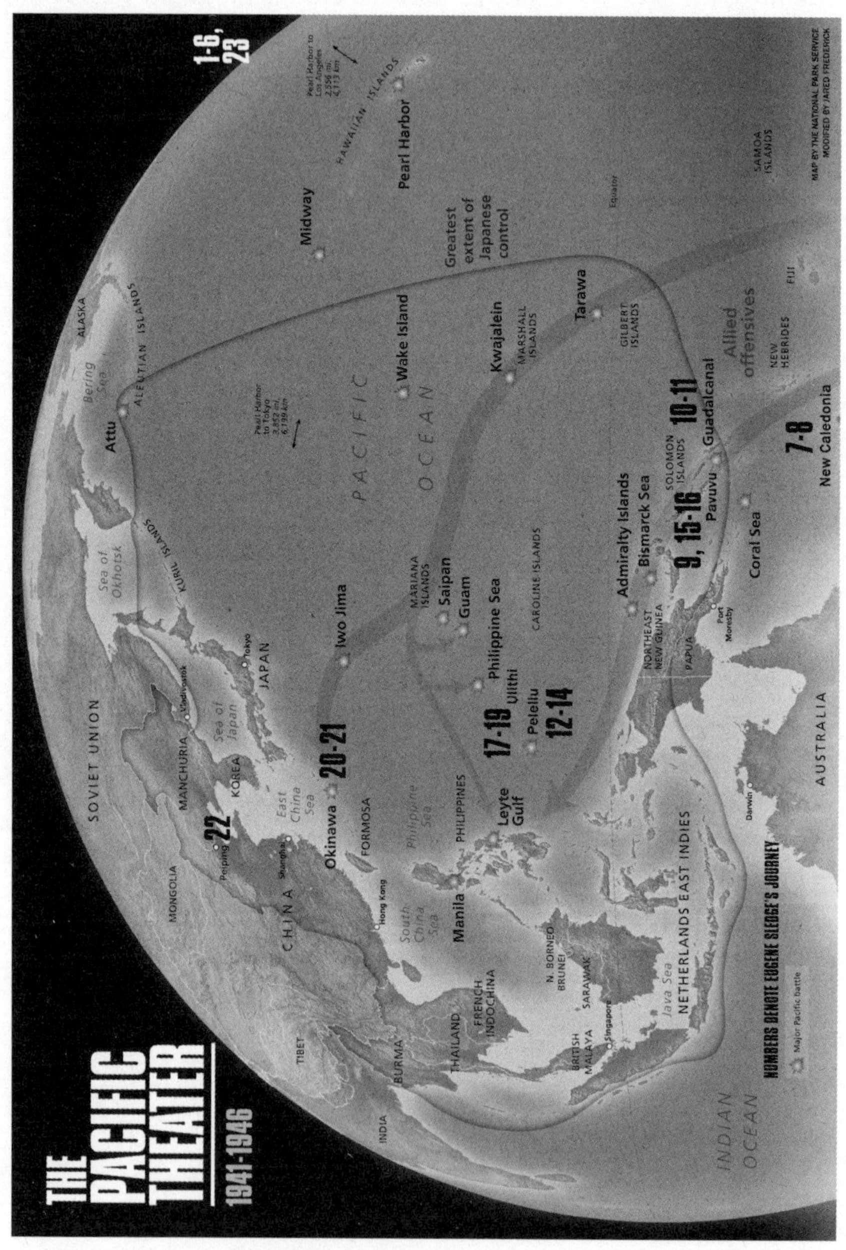
THE PACIFIC THEATER
1941-1946
1-6, 23
22
20-21
17-19
12-14
9, 15-16
10-11
7-8
NUMBERS DENOTE EUGENE SLEDGE'S JOURNEY
Major Pacific battle
MAP BY THE NATIONAL PARK SERVICE
MODIFIED BY JARED FREDERICK
SOVIET UNION
MONGOLIA
MANCHURIA
CHINA
TIBET
INDIA
BURMA
THAILAND
FRENCH INDOCHINA
BRITISH MALAYA
SARAWAK
BRUNEI
N. BORNEO
KOREA
JAPAN
FORMOSA
PHILIPPINES
NETHERLANDS EAST INDIES
PAPUA
NORTHEAST NEW GUINEA
AUSTRALIA
ALASKA
Peiping
Shanghai
Hong Kong
Vladivostok
Tokyo
Singapore
Darwin
Port Moresby
Sea of Okhotsk
Sea of Japan
East China Sea
South China Sea
Philippine Sea
Java Sea
Bering Sea
Bismarck Sea
Coral Sea
PACIFIC OCEAN
INDIAN OCEAN
KURIL ISLANDS
ALEUTIAN ISLANDS
HAWAIIAN ISLANDS
MARIANA ISLANDS
CAROLINE ISLANDS
MARSHALL ISLANDS
GILBERT ISLANDS
SOLOMON ISLANDS
NEW HEBRIDES
SAMOA ISLANDS
FIJI
Equator
Attu
Midway
Pearl Harbor
Wake Island
Kwajalein
Tarawa
Iwo Jima
Okinawa
Saipan
Guam
Philippine Sea
Ulithi
Peleliu
Leyte Gulf
Manila
Admiralty Islands
Pavuvu
Guadalcanal
New Caledonia
Greatest extent of Japanese control
Allied offensives

EUGENE SLEDGE TIMELINE AND MAP KEY

1. December 3, 1942—As a freshman at Marion Military Institute in Alabama, Sledge enlists in the Marine Corps.
2. July 1, 1943—Sledge reports to the Georgia Institute of Technology for the V-12 officer training program.
3. Fall 1943—Sledge heads to Marine Corps Boot Camp in San Diego, California, after intentionally flunking out of the V-12 program.
4. November 4, 1943—Sledge celebrates his twentieth birthday.
5. December 24, 1943—Sledge graduates from Marine Corps Boot-camp and heads to Camp Elliott for advanced infantry training.
6. February 28, 1944—Sledge boards the *President Polk* troopship to depart San Diego for the Pacific.
7. March 17, 1944—Sledge arrives on New Caledonia for more training.
8. May 28, 1944—Sledge boards the *General R. L. Howze* troopship to leave New Caledonia.
9. June 2, 1944—Sledge arrives on Pavuvu in the Russell Islands where he joins K/3/5, First Marine Division.
10. August 26, 1944—Sledge, along with the 1st Division, completes training on Pavuvu and heads to Guadalcanal for maneuvers.
11. September 4, 1944—Sledge completes training on Guadalcanal and embarks for Peleliu.
12. September 15, 1944—D Day, Peleliu.
13. October 30, 1944—Sledge and his fellow survivors of Peleliu board the *Sea Runner* troopship for the return to Pavuvu.

14. November 4, 1944—Sledge celebrates his twenty-first birthday.
15. November 7, 1944—The *Sea Runner* returns to Pavuvu.
16. Late January 1945—The 1st Division boards LCIs bound for maneuvers on Guadalcanal.
17. March 15, 1945—After returning to Pavuvu from the Guadalcanal training, Sledge and the 1st Division sail to Ulithi atoll, where the Okinawa invasion fleet will assemble.
18. March 21, 1945—Sledge arrives at Ulithi.
19. March 27, 1945—The invasion fleet weighs anchor and sails for Okinawa.
20. April 1, 1945—D Day, Okinawa.
21. June 21, 1945—Okinawa is declared secure; Sledge and his buddies go to a tent camp on northern Okinawa.
22. Late October 1945—Sledge boards a ship bound for Peiping, now Beijing, China.
23. February 1946—Eugene Sledge returns from China to Mobile, Alabama.

FURTHER READING

Alexander, Joseph H. *Storm Landings: Epic Amphibious Battles in the Central Pacific*. Naval Institute Press, 1997.

Appleman, Roy E., James M. Burns, Russell A. Gugeler, and John Stevens. *Okinawa: The Last Battle*. United States Army in World War II: The War in the Pacific. Center of Military History, United States Army, 1948.

David, Saul. *Crucible of Hell: The Heroism and Tragedy of Okinawa, 1945*. Hachette Books, 2020.

David, Saul. *Devil Dogs: King Company, Third Battalion, 5th Marines: From Guadalcanal to the Shores of Japan*. Pegasus Books, 2023.

Davis, Russell. *Marine at War*. Scholastic Book Services, 1961.

Falk, Stanley. *Bloodiest Victory: Palaus; America's Pacific Offensive 1944*. Ballantine Books, 1974.

Frank, Benis M. *Okinawa: Touchstone to Victory*. Ballantine Books, 1973.

Frank, Benis M., and Henry I. Shaw, Jr. *Victory and Occupation*. Vol. 5 of *History of U.S. Marine Corps Operations in World War II*. Historical Branch, G-3 Division, Headquarters, U.S. Marine Corps (HQMC), 1968.

Garand, George W., and Truman R. Strobridge. *Western Pacific Operations*. Vol. 4 of *History of U.S. Marine Corps Operations in World War II*. Historical Division, HQMC, 1971.

Hough, Frank O. *The Assault on Peleliu*. Historical Division, HQMC, 1950.

Isley, Jeter A., and Philip A. Crowl. *The U.S. Marines and Amphibious War: Its Theory, and Its Practice in the Pacific*. Princeton University Press, 1951.

Leckie, Robert. *Helmet for My Pillow: From Parris Island to the Pacific*. Bantam Books, 2010.

Leckie, Robert. *Strong Men Armed: The United States Marines Against Japan*. Random House, 1962.

Mayer, S. L., ed. *The Japanese War Machine*. Chartwell Books, 1976.

McMillan, George. *The Old Breed: A History of the First Marine Division in World War II*. Infantry Journal Press, 1949.

Morison, Samuel Eliot. *The Two-Ocean War: A Short History of the United States Navy in the Second World War*. Little, Brown and Company, 1963.

Moskin, J. Robert. *The U.S. Marine Corps Story*. McGraw-Hill Book Company, 1977.

Muster Roll of Officers and Enlisted Men of the U.S. Marine Corps: Third Battalion, Fifth Marines, First Marine Division, Fleet Marine Force. From September 1 to September 30, 1944, inclusive; from October 1 to October 13, 1944, inclusive; from April 1 to April 30, 1945, inclusive; from May 1 to May 31, 1945, inclusive; from June 1 to June 30, 1945, inclusive. History and Museums Division, HQMC.

Nichols, Chas. S., Jr., and Henry I. Shaw, Jr. *Okinawa: Victory in the Pacific*. Charles E. Tuttle Company, 1966. First published 1955 by Historical Branch, G-3 Division, HQMC.

Shaw, Henry I., Jr., Bernard C. Nalty, and Edwin T. Turnbladh. *Central Pacific Drive*. Vol. 3 of *History of U.S. Marine Corps Operations in World War II*. Historical Branch, G-3 Division, HQMC, 1966.

Sledge, E.B. *China Marine*. University of Alabama Press, 2002.

Sledge, E.B. *With the Old Breed: At Peleliu and Okinawa*. Classics of Naval Literature. Naval Institute Press, 1996.

Sledge, W. Henry. "When Things Get Tough." *World War II*, August 2022.

Smith, S. E., ed. and comp. *The United States Marines Corps in World War II*. Random House, 1969.

Steinberg, Rafael. *Island Fighting*. Time-Life Books, 1978.

Stockman, James R. *The First Marine Division on Okinawa, 1 April–30 June 1945*. Historical Division, HQMC, 1946.

Time. "World Battlefronts: Men at War: Compassionate Confusion." *Time* 44, no. 16 (October 16, 1944): 38.

Time. "World Battlefronts: To Save Men's Lives." *Time* 44, no. 15 (October 9, 1944): 29.

Toll, Ian W. *Twilight of the Gods: War in the Western Pacific, 1944–1945*. W. W. Norton, 2020.

United States 1st Marine Division. Operation Plan 1-44. Annex A, B Serial 0003 over 1990-5-80 over 458/332. August 15, 1944.

Palau Operation. Special Action Report. Serial 0775 over 1990-5-80 over 458/390. September 13, 1944.

Field Order No 1-44 through 9-44. Serial 1990-5-80 over 458/332. Dated September 20, September 21, September 22, September 25, October 2, October 5, October 8, October 10, and October 13, 1944.

ACKNOWLEDGMENTS

A book may be written by one person, but it is in fact a collective effort. As I have already mentioned, a chance conversation with my mother in the fall of 2021 was the source of my inspiration that began this process. I want to express my gratitude to her for her prescience. I only wish she were still here to see the results.

This project would not have been possible without the kind cooperation and assistance of Greg Schmidt and Tommy Brown from the Auburn University Special Collections and Archives. They were invaluable in assembling the unedited original manuscript of *With the Old Breed* and then getting it into my hands so that I could begin my research.

My friend John C. McManus, military historian and author of numerous books, was one of the first people I approached about my concept for this project, and he willingly provided superb guidance, advice, and encouragement along the way. He also read the manuscript and provided wonderful feedback. In the beginning, when I was filled with self-doubt because I had never written a book and thought I needed a coauthor, he simply said, "You can do this on your own, Henry. You don't need a coauthor."

Historian and friend Richard B. Frank was also one of the first individuals I went to for advice. Despite his incredibly busy schedule, he always took my calls and gave me advice and inspiration when needed. He also took the time to read the manuscript and offer comments on accuracy, and he generously agreed to write the foreword. Historian Saul David, also a great friend and an admirer of my father, took the time to read the manuscript, assist with providing maps, and graciously agreed to write the preface.

Many other friends took time to read the manuscript and provide valuable feedback or contribute their talents in other ways, and so I wish to thank John M. Curatola of the National WWII Museum, Brad Byerley, Jullie Chung, Rob Barrow, and Garret Shetrawski. Jared Frederick provided the Sledge timeline map, and my friend Eric Mailander provided insight and encouragement. Leighton Hughes encouraged me throughout the entire process.

Anthony Ziccardi of Post Hill Press, and Caitlin Burdette, my managing editor along with her expert team, including Lucy VanBerkum, deserve my gratitude for bringing this book to life. It would not have happened without them. I am also deeply grateful to my agent, Greg Johnson of WordServe Literary, for believing that this book needed to be published.

I must also express my deepest appreciation, posthumously, of course, to my father—not only for his service to this country as a US Marine in WWII but also for his contribution to American culture by writing *With the Old Breed* and *China Marine*.

And, finally, I am forever grateful to my family: my son Jack for his appreciation for what his grandfather did, and my wife Andrea, for not only reading the manuscript and providing valuable perspective throughout the process, but also for her steadfast encouragement and never failing to believe that this would happen.